Salome's Modernity

Salome's Modernity

Oscar Wilde and the Aesthetics of Transgression

Petra Dierkes-Thrun

THE UNIVERSITY OF MICHIGAN PRESS

Ann Arbor

Published in the United States of America by
The University of Michigan Press
Manufactured in the United States of America
⊛ Printed on acid-free paper

2014   2013   2012   2011   4   3   2   1

A CIP catalog record for this book is available from the British Library.

Library of Congress Cataloging-in-Publication Data

Dierkes-Thrun, Petra, 1968–
   Salome's modernity : Oscar Wilde and the aesthetics of
transgression / Petra Dierkes-Thrun.
      p.   cm.
   Includes bibliographical references and index.
   ISBN 978-0-472-11767-3 (cloth : alk. paper) — ISBN 978-0-472-
02754-5 (ebk.)
   1. Wilde, Oscar, 1854–1900. Salomé.   2. Wilde, Oscar, 1854–1900—
Influence.   3. Salome (Biblical figure)—In literature.   4. Deviant
behavior in literature.   5. Modernism (Aesthetics)   I. Title.
PR5820.S23D54   2011
822'.8—dc22   2011000474

For Sebastian and Jasper, with love

Methinks my life is a twice-written scroll
Scrawled over on some boyish holiday
With idle songs for pipe and virelay
Which do but mar the secret of the whole.
    —Oscar Wilde, "Hélas!"

[P]hilosophy has been, up to this point, as much as science, an expression
of human subordination, and when man seeks to represent himself, no
longer as a moment of a homogeneous process—of a necessary and pitiful
process—but as a new laceration within a lacerated nature, it is no longer
the leveling phraseology coming to him from the understanding that can
help him: he can no longer recognize himself in the degrading chains of
logic, but he recognizes himself, instead—not with rage but in an ecstatic
torment—in the virulence of his own phantasms.
    —Georges Bataille, "The Pineal Eye"

Acknowledgments

Salome's Modernity would not exist without the people who accompanied and nurtured it as mentors, colleagues, and friends over the years. It started as a dissertation in the English Department at the University of Pittsburgh, and to my teachers there, I owe my deepest intellectual debt. My heartfelt gratitude goes out to Paul A. Bové, who made the thinking and writing of this book possible through unfailing intellectual challenge and support. He has exemplified all the inspiration, trust, and skeptical rigor a true mentor and partner in critical dialogue can offer. Jonathan Arac, Lucy Fischer, and the late Eric O. Clarke served as committee members at the dissertation stage and spent much time talking and throwing around ideas about books, films, and feminist, queer, and critical theories with me in their offices and classrooms. They have been indispensable role models for me in countless ways throughout the years. Eric O. Clarke tragically passed away just a few months before this book was going to press, and I will miss him always. Philip E. Smith II supervised earlier stages of this project and published a pedagogical article of mine in his edition *Approaches to Teaching the Works of Oscar Wilde* (2008); I benefited greatly from his personal and professional support and deeply admire his scholarship on Wilde. Herbert S. Lindenberger (Stanford University) exhibited amazing energy, enthusiasm, and generosity in sharing his scholarly and pedagogical expertise and his love of opera with me, at the dissertation stage and ever since.

To Susan Teuteberg, Martina Gschell, Judy Suh, Eleni Anastasiou, Saeeda Hafiz, Beth Wightman, and Dorothy Clark, I say a special thank you for the best of friendship and shared love of people, books, and culture. David C. Rose, editor and founder of the *Oscholars* Web site and group of journals, gave me the opportunity to take charge of *The Latchkey: Journal of New Woman Studies,* and to expand my professional horizons in the realm of online publishing. As I was putting the finishing touches on *Salome's Modernity,* I was teaching a seminar at Stanford University entitled "Salome, Modernity, Transgression," and I sincerely thank the students in that class for making the last stages of writing this book not only bearable but fun. One of them, the artist Dorian Katz, contributed an illustration to this book, for which I am especially grateful.

An earlier version of chapter 2 appeared in *Modern Language Quarterly* 69.3 (September 2008): 367–89. For crucial institutional and financial support, I would like to acknowledge the Comparative Literature Department at Stanford University; the English Department and College of Humanities at California State University, Northridge; the English Department at Santa Clara University; the Andrew W. Mellon Foundation; the Faculty of Arts and Sciences at the University of Pittsburgh; and the German Catholic fellowship organization Cusanuswerk. For patient and helpful research support at various stages of the project, I am grateful to the staff at the William Andrews Clark Memorial Library (University of California, Los Angeles), the British Library, the Library of Congress, and the Theatermuseum Köln-Wahn, Germany. At the University of Michigan Press, my editor Tom Dwyer, editorial associate Alexa Ducsay, and managing editor Christina Milton were indispensable sources of support, and I thank them for their professionalism and enthusiasm in bringing this project to fruition.

Very special words of love and thanks go out to my family, especially to my husband, Sebastian Thrun, and our son, Jasper; my father, Rainer, and stepmother, Susanne Dierkes; and my brother, Sebastian, and his family. Without their unconditional love, unflagging support, and sense of humor, life could not be half as wonderful.

Contents

Introduction

Oscar Wilde's 1891 symbolist tragedy *Salomé* has had a rich afterlife in literature, opera, dance, film, and popular culture. Even though the literature and art of the European fin de siècle produced many treatments of the famous biblical story of Salome and Saint John the Baptist, virtually every major version in the twentieth and twenty-first centuries has been some creative adaptation of or critical reaction against Wilde's *Salomé,* with its infamous Dance of the Seven Veils and Salomé's shocking final love monologue and kiss to the bloody, severed head of John the Baptist. For a work banned from the English stage by the theater censor before it was even produced, a play whose author remained intensely controversial for several decades after his notorious 1895 trials, this is a curious legacy. Why was it specifically Wilde's play, among the many provocative literary and artistic versions of the story of Salome, that proved so popular and fascinating? Why would Wilde's conception of a sexually anarchic, aestheticized Salomé speak so importantly to artists and audiences of the twentieth and twenty-first centuries? What were the historical and cultural forces that established Wilde's *Salomé* as a canonical text that, in turn, inspired more than a century's worth of creative cultural reinscriptions, adaptations, and transformations in many different genres and media? Finally, what can Western culture's ongoing fascination with figures like Salomé and Wilde tell us about ourselves and about modernity? These are the some of the central questions *Salome's Modernity* sets out to answer.

In recent years, the bulk of Wilde's work has come into the purview of modernist studies, and Wilde is often discussed as a modernist as a matter of course,[1] yet *Salomé* is often still seen as an idiosyncratic stand-alone within the body of his work. Although Jean-Paul Riquelme's mid-1990s article "Shalom/Solomon/*Salomé*: Modernism and Wilde's Aesthetic Politics" opened up the subject of *Salomé's* general relation to modernism, Wilde's play continues to be examined almost exclusively through the lens of fin de siècle aesthetics, historical and biographical details of Wilde's contact with the French symbolists and decadents, and aspects of gender and sexuality related to this period (e.g., the femme fatale and the dandy).[2] In writing his version of the popular Salome myth as a French symbolist tragedy in 1891, Oscar Wilde was undoubtedly inspired by literary-philosophical themes, concepts, and stylistic ideas in previous versions, as well as by his vast knowledge of Salome in the visual arts from the Renaissance to his present.[3] But Wilde developed and exacerbated his literary and artistic influences to a point that also marks a radical departure from his predecessors. Wilde's *Salomé* defines a complex cultural tradition of ideas about aesthetics, eroticism, and transgression, a tradition that forms an important undercurrent in the development of twentieth-century modernism and modernist aesthetics.

Building on an innovative reading of *Salomé* as a forward-looking modernist text rather than a backward-looking compendium of fin de siècle themes and styles, *Salome's Modernity* argues that Wilde's play and the cultural reception of Wilde's homosexuality after his 1895 trials helped fuel and express the rise of a new type of modernist aesthetics in early twentieth-century literature and culture. I call this the "modernist aesthetics of transgression," by which I mean a replacement of traditional metaphysical, moral, and cultural belief systems with literary and artistic discourses that develop utopian erotic and aesthetic visions of individual transgression and agency. With roots in literary symbolism and decadence,[4] *Salomé* participates in the modernist field of radical thought and aesthetic practice symbolically marked by the work of Friedrich Nietzsche, on the one hand, and Georges Bataille's and Michel Foucault's literature and philosophy of transgression, on the other. In Wilde's play, we find a unique pairing of utopian and apocalyptic elements that embody both a sense of crisis and a rebellious commitment to human agency in response to the fundamental shattering of worldly as well as transcendental authority and truth that is modernity. It develops a fierce, shocking, and alluring vision of erotic and aesthetic transgression as an ecstatic new realm for modern individualism and transformed secular humanism. Wilde directs artistic violence against the traditional institutions of moral, religious, and philosophical authority with his seductive, spectacular staging of a perverse, larger-than-life, yet deeply human Salomé. Salomé finds a way out of the misery of pitiful modern humanity by fearlessly establishing her own rules and committing to the beauty of immanence and the violence of the human struggle, rather than seeking metaphysical transcendence. *Salomé's* modernist aesthetics of transgression bridges the nineteenth-century philosophical and artistic concerns of such writers as Mallarmé, Pater, Nietzsche, and Wilde; the modernist and postmodernist literature and philosophy of transgression (Bataille, Foucault); and late twentieth-century popular culture, which still contains many of these modernist elements. In describing these connections and developments, *Salome's Modernity* touches on the larger relationships between discourses of erotic transgression and modernist aesthetics that underlie and support these powerful fantasies and account for their proliferation: such themes as the death of God, the rise of modern individualism, debates about the theory and practice of avant-garde art in a consumer society, and the crisis of human agency and freedom in a radically changed, secular, modern world. As an iconic rebel who makes do without religion and instead devotes herself to a secular gospel of erotic and aesthetic ecstasy, Salomé prefigures modernism's central project of transforming metaphysical sublimity into physical and artistic sublimity. In her, Wilde created a complex utopian-dystopian image of the modernist struggles with secular individualism and agency—versions of the problematic of the postmetaphysical subject of consciousness that form a central concern of cultural and philosophical modernity and its respective modernism(s).

Salome's Modernity studies this phenomenon through a wide interdisciplinary and transnational range of Salome adaptations in literature, opera, dance, film, and popular culture from the 1860s to the 2000s and across the spectrum from high to popular culture. Accompanied by changing cultural attitudes toward Oscar Wilde's "perversity" and Salomé's paradoxical feminist-misogynist potential, these adaptations make up a rich archive of cultural fantasies of aesthetic and erotic transgression that have been negotiated and continuously reinvented via the Salome theme. In the wake of Wilde's 1895 trials, Salomé was often read as a mask for Wilde's own homosexual desires and as his aesthetic and erotic alter ego. Hence both Salomé and Wilde became fertile sites for artists' and audiences' fantasies of erotic and artistic nonconformity and icons of protest against repressive moral and social censorship in these adaptations. The play *Salomé* and its author amalgamated transgressive aesthetics, perverse sexuality, shocking blasphemy, and modern individualism, an explosive and potent mixture that fuels the creative imagination of artists and audiences to this day.

Wilde originally composed *Salomé* while staying in Paris in late 1891, and he did so in French, the language of Sarah Bernhardt, Stéphane Mallarmé, and the circle of symbolist writers with whom he fervently wished to align himself. The surviving manuscripts of early drafts, all in French (housed at the Bodmer Library, Geneva; at Texas University; and at the Rosenbach Museum, Philadelphia), show that Wilde enlisted the linguistic help of such friends as Pierre Louÿs, Stuart Merrill, and Adolphe Retté, who commented on various drafts and corrected Wilde's few obvious Anglicisms. Talking about ideas for *Salomé* and circulating drafts at literary soirees, Wilde was already establishing a place for himself among the most interesting, innovative, and trendsetting writers and artists of his time. (The Bodmer manuscript appears to be the earliest draft; the Rosenbach manuscript bears Louÿs' interlinear comments and corrections.) As an experiment in symbolist aesthetics—and, indeed, in the French language—*Salomé* was to have become Wilde's contribution to French literature. According to Wilfrid Blunt, at a breakfast in October 1891, Wilde conceived of the play as follows: "Oscar told us he was writing a play in French to be acted in the Français. He is ambitious of being a French Academician" (*Complete Letters of Oscar Wilde* 506n1). The play would have established Wilde as the first English-speaking writer to adopt and promote symbolist aesthetics for the London literary world, "demonstrating his true cosmopolitanism but also revealing to his countrymen that they had a writer of international stature in their midst" (Bird 57).

In late June 1892, however, while London rehearsals with Sarah Bernhardt as Salomé were already in full swing, *Salomé* was abruptly banned by the London examiner of plays, Edward F. Smyth Pigott, whom Shaw posthumously described as "a walking compendium of vulgar insular prejudice" (*Complete Letters of Oscar Wilde* 98n1). Pigott cited a sixteenth-century law prohibiting the representation of biblical characters on stage (which had never been enforced very strictly) as his official reason for the prohibition, but in a private letter to Spenser Posonby, he admitted his disapproval of the play's offensive mixture of female sexuality and religious blasphemy.

> It is a miracle of impudence; . . . [Salomé's] love turns to fury because John will not let her kiss him *in the mouth*—and in the last scene, where she brings in his head—if you please—on a "charger"—she *does* kiss his mouth, in a paroxysm of sexual despair. The piece is written in French—half Biblical, half pornographic—by Oscar Wilde himself. Imagine the average British public's reception of it. (Quoted in Stephens 112)

Pigott's criticism focuses on Wilde's finale, pathologized by the phrase "paroxysm of sexual despair" and cast as "pornographic," and affirms its anticipated shock effect for "the average British public." In its unsigned book review of the French edition, the *London Times* echoed the censor's outrage, focusing on *Salomé's* sexual perversity and blasphemy, its depiction of "situations the reverse of sacred" (February 23, 1893, 8). In interviews, Wilde acknowledged *Salomé's* likely shock effect but presented it as further evidence of the play's avant-garde qualities: different from the French, who loved his play, the barbaric English merely banned what they had not understood (*Oscar Wilde: Interviews and Recollections,* ed. Mikhail, 186–91). Wilde was then at the peak years of his career. A beloved *enfant terrible* of London society (satirized by Gilbert and Sullivan in *Patience* and in numerous *Punch* cartoons), he was a respected author. In 1890, *The Picture of Dorian Gray* had been published, and *Lady Windermere's Fan* had opened to rave reviews. The censor's decision came as a surprise not only to Wilde himself, who famously declared in interviews with English and French journalists (*Oscar Wilde: Interviews and Recollections,* ed. Mikhail, 188) that he would give up his citizenship and would become a citizen of France (leading to a famous *Punch* cartoon of Wilde as a French soldier carrying the *Salomé* script as his enlistment papers), but to most of the theatrical world as well. The unsympathetic *New York Times* reported on July 3, 1892, "All London is laughing at Oscar Wilde's threat to become a Frenchman" (quoted in Ellmann, *Oscar Wilde* 373). Wilde never did leave England, however, and it is a cruel irony of fate that Wilde could have avoided his 1895 trials and imprisonment had he only done so.

Sarah Bernhardt never played Salomé, even though the financially desperate Wilde offered her the script from prison in 1895. "She wept (the right response) and then . . . —for whatever reason—she refused," so the censor's decision thus "marks . . . the collaboration that was never completed, the dream-team that never played, the supergroup that never appeared" (Stokes 150, 149). *Salomé* was finally published in two editions, French (1893, by Library de l'Art Indépendent, Paris) and English (1894, by the Bodley Head [i.e., John Lane and Elkin Mathews] of London) with Aubrey Beardsley's famous illustrations, which Wilde disliked but tolerated, as Joan Navarre and others have shown. Although Lord Alfred Douglas's name is given as the official translator for the 1894 book in the dedication ("To Lord Alfred Bruce Douglas the translator of my play"), we know that Wilde was so dissatisfied with Douglas's translation that he revised and completed it himself. Hence the English text of *Salomé* is both Wilde's own and, chronologically speaking, Wilde's final version. For this reason, I have decided to quote from the English edition in *Salome's Modernity,* while consulting the French original where appropriate.

The play saw its world premiere in Paris on February 11, 1896, under the direction of avant-garde director Aurélien Lugné-Poë and featuring Lina Munte in the title role. Wilde was still in prison, and the legal status of *Salomé*'s production rights was unresolved. Beset by "various backstage disasters" and masking the homoerotic relationship between the Page and Narraboth by assigning an actress to play the page (a decision that reportedly upset Wilde, who was otherwise very grateful to Lugné-Poë), the production nevertheless received warm reviews and continued the French esteem for Wilde (Tydeman and Price 25–31). In Germany, where Max Reinhardt had launched a splendid production that moved Strauss to compose his opera, Wilde's play was equally admired; shortly thereafter, *Salomé* also became popular in Russia, Japan, and China. In England, however, *Salomé* was only accessible via the book editions and private performances of the play, until the ban from the public stage was finally lifted in 1931. The first private performances in England—hence the British premiere of the play—were undertaken in 1905 by the New Stage Players at the Bijou Theatre and shortly thereafter by Charles Ricketts (who had consulted Wilde on stage design for a previous aborted French production, of which significant sketches by both Wilde and Ricketts survive) at King's Hall, Covent Garden (Tydeman and Price 40–57). Unfortunately, Wilde never saw the play performed during his lifetime.

Any Wilde scholar can attest that the most profound pleasures of working on Wilde—his antimimetic stance, his anticipation of much of contemporary critical and cultural theory, his personal and professional paradoxes, the impossibility of pinning him down completely, conclusively, forever—are also somewhat vexing reminders of the limitations of literary and cultural criticism. Despite more than a century's worth of inquiry, Oscar Wilde, as man and writer, remains "a chameleon, forever defying authentic, transhistorical definition, forever donning new masks, forever being reinvented" (Böker, Corballis, and Hibbard 9). As Peter Dickinson, tongue in cheek, puts Wilde's slipperiness,

> The proliferation of Oscar's posthumous personae . . . continues unabated: Oscar the literary modernist, the sexual liberationist, the Irish nationalist, is joined by Oscar the anarchist, Oscar the socialist, Oscar the individualist, Oscar the feminist, Oscar the iconoclast, Oscar the pop star. The list expands exponentially until the frustrated scholar/reader wants to scream "Will the real Oscar Wilde please stand up?" To which the inevitable reply must necessarily be: "No, not that one, the other one." (430–31)[5]

Yet Joseph Bristow writes in his introduction to the recent volume *Oscar Wilde and Modern Culture,* "At present, there seems to be no end in sight to Wilde's enduring attractiveness to our contemporary world" (xiii).

My object in *Salome's Modernity* is not to add another set of inalienable "truths" about Oscar Wilde or about *Salomé* to the critical canon. Rather, my project is more modest than that; it is oriented toward the performative mechanisms and functions of these two floating signifiers in twentieth- and twenty-first-century modernity and investigates the various ways in which Salomé and Wilde have become ideal placeholders for larger cultural and philosophical concerns of modernity. I agree with Dickinson that "one of the central contradictions about the process of 'interpreting Oscar' . . . is that it always reveals more about us readers than it does about him as a writer" (431). In *Salome's Modernity,* I wish to examine the specific reasons why and the ways in which Salomé and Wilde have come to acquire important meaning in our own modern culture and what that reveals about us as readers.

My own approach to Oscar Wilde, *Salomé,* and their cultural afterlives has been influenced by feminist and queer literary and cultural criticism, critical theory, and my Foucauldian understanding of transgression as an integral part of the very society and culture against which it is ostensibly trying to rebel. But while these theories function as lenses that direct and help sharpen my gaze at certain issues and phenomena, I do not feel beholden to any particular theoretical approach. By inquiring into the Salome theme across different periods, media, and genres and across the spectrum from high- to middle- to lowbrow culture and by keeping its theoretical commitments flexible, *Salome's Modernity* also affiliates itself with the new modernist studies that has forcefully arisen in the last decade or so. As Douglas Mao and Rebecca Walkowitz write in the introduction to *Bad Modernisms,* "the new modernist studies has moved toward a pluralism or a fusion of theoretical commitments, as well as a heightened attention to continuities and intersections across the boundaries of artistic media, to collaborations and influences across national and linguistic borders, and (especially) to the relationship between individual works of art and the larger cultures in which they emerged" (2). This comparative and flexible, yet always historically grounded, approach in *Salome's Modernity* is dictated by the nature of my project, which has followed Salome wherever she danced, making use of many original archival materials that required close attention to context and intertextual relations. More generally, though, I believe that the new modernist studies is uniquely suited to bringing to the forefront those pervasive modernist ideas and concepts that are spread across many different areas of culture and that have influenced or continue to live on in Western culture even "after" literary and artistic modernism proper. Among these are the aesthetics of transgression and its continuation of modernist investments in the ecstatic, subversive, individual body that have made the Salome theme so popular in the twentieth century.

The two concepts that define my title and focus, modernity and transgression, are notoriously difficult to define, yet it is necessary to give at least working definitions at the outset. Some of the most useful general definitions of modernity—such as Theodor Adorno's declaration (in *Minima Moralia*) that modernity is a qualitative, not a chronological, quality—are necessarily open and vague. Modernism, modernity's literary-cultural twin, has proved impossible to pin down in terms of historical period and spatial reach (modernity and modernism are phenomena that have occurred and are occurring nonsimultaneously in different parts of the world, with critical favor or bias leaning toward the West and the North). I generally concur with Rita Felski's views in *The Gender of Modernity* that what we define as modern is a heterogeneous phenomenon related, at least in the West, to Enlightenment discourses and is subject to historical interpretation and conflict: "modernity is not a homogeneous Zeitgeist which was born at a particular moment in history, but rather . . . it comprises a collection of interlocking institutional, cultural, and philosophical strands which emerge and develop at different times and which are often only defined as 'modern' retrospectively" (12, 15). Literary and artistic modernism can usefully be understood as "a set of responses to problems posed by the conditions of modernity" in the late nineteenth and twentieth centuries. In the case of the Salome theme, such problems include the crisis of faith, the aesthetics-ethics controversy, stereotypes of femininity, the fascination with sexual perversity, and the rise of modern individualism, to name just a few (Whitworth 3). "To be modern is to be part of a universe in which, as Marx said, 'all that is solid melts into air'" (Berman 15), but it is also to be part of a universe in which forceful aesthetic responses to problems of modernity actively establish new forms of utopia and action. The modernist aesthetics of transgression we find in the Salome theme after Wilde, with its often scandalous secular and physical commitment to rebellious individualism, is one of those forms.

My understanding of *transgression* as a critical term derives from a Foucauldian understanding of transgression as interdependent and interacting with the very limits and boundaries it supposedly violates. One might say that transgression is always a part of the system and power structures it is ostensibly directed against, a point Foucault himself made in "A Preface to Transgression" and one that has been picked up for feminist and queer studies of gender and sexuality by critics like Biddy Martin, Jana Sawicki, and Eve K. Sedgwick. According to this understanding, transgression is not a stepping outside of power or overthrowing it but, rather, the testing and engaging of moral, aesthetic, sexual, and other cultural discourses, paradoxically affirming while also clearly challenging and expanding them. Understood this way, the concept takes us back to its etymology (English *transgression* from Latin *transgredi,* "going over" or "stepping across"), which denotes a deliberate and intentional overstepping of an established boundary, norm, or habitual state; the transgressive act intentionally passes over and thus violates a prescribed limit.[6] As Chris Jenks writes, transgression is "not merely the breaking of a code, a rebellion against normative social or cultural constraints; rather, it is the very pulse that constitutes our identities" (1); it is "the traversal of a boundary, and with that motion or passage, the deformation of the limits of form, identity or institution momentarily or provisionally" (10). In applying the concept to Wilde's *Salomé* and to Wilde himself in this book, I also borrow from Georges Bataille's interpretation of excess as a redefined physical (erotic and obscene) version of metaphysical ecstasy, a definition on which Foucault also builds (see chap. 1). I find Bataille's definition useful to describe the larger modernist, cultural-discursive movement toward sensation, transgressive eroticism, and physical ecstasy at work in Wilde's *Salomé* and some of its twentieth- and twenty-first-century heirs, which employed these as secular replacements for the religious sublime.

The modernist aesthetics of transgression has an interesting relationship with the humanist tradition, in that it disregards or negates the idea of individual transformation (*Bildung*) for the good of society yet paradoxically continues, through utopian artistic images of the triumphant transgressive body, the very idea of individual fulfillment and self-actualization. The post-Enlightenment investment in art as a moral and social agency of individual and social transformation was intrinsically intertwined with the history of humanism itself, associated, within the German tradition, with such figures as Goethe, Schiller, Lessing, and Schelling (and in the background of this tradition, Aristotle) and, in the English-speaking world, especially with the names of Matthew Arnold, John Ruskin, and Walter Pater, with the latter acting as a complex transitional figure. For the high humanist tradition presented by these writers, art was an effective tool of not only individual but also, via the individual, often social, political, moral, and religious transformation, but it was not transgressive in the sense of an individual rebellion against those traditional authorities.

Interestingly, Wilde's *Salomé* dramatizes the *fantasy* of violent transgression more than it constitutes so much of a transgression itself, even though it was banned and, together with Strauss's opera, censored in many countries. However shocking they seemed to contemporaries, the play and, indirectly, the opera built on various elements of nineteenth-century tradition, taking these elements yet further and innovating their purpose, to be sure, but not really intending to insult and alienate their audiences. Rather, both Wilde and Strauss wanted their work to appeal to contemporaries and thereby to consolidate their own fame; as I argue in chapter 2, theirs was a popular avant-gardist intent, not an entirely subversive one. We must make a distinction, then, between the contents of the Wildean vision of Salomé as a transgressive individual and twentieth-century fantasies of Wilde, on the one hand, and the form and style of the play and the opera as historically situated texts that mixed innovative avant-garde elements with well-known, accepted, popular features and strategies, on the other. A similar relationship between avant-garde and popular aspects can be found in many of the twentieth- and twenty-first-century adaptations and transformations of *Salomé* as well, indicating and exemplifying again the entanglement and interdependency of discourses of transgression with their opposing, normative ideologemes and with material conditions.

In the images of Salomé and Wilde in Western culture, transgressions of the female body—both the straight one and, in the case of the two women discussed in chapters 3 and 4, the lesbian or bisexual one—intersect with those of the male homosexual body. Salomé and Oscar Wilde have been read with and through one another as icons of modernity for more than a century now, and there are reasons both for their longevity and fecundity as cultural images and for their special appeal, the utopian-dystopian signification of their transgressive bodies. In analyzing a variety of *Salomé* adaptations and related texts in literature, opera, dance, and film from the 1890s to the 1990s, I am interested in identifying and illuminating the central epistemological underpinnings and functions of these two images of Salomé and Wilde, which have told the cultural stories of individual erotic-aesthetic transgression and sensational excess differently at different times. In analyzing individual versions, I ask: What are the specific aesthetic figurations and mechanisms of the Salome and Wilde figures in each version, and what functions and effects do they produce—both specific and general, within a comparative analysis that ranges from the 1850s to the present?

More generally, what can a cultural epistemology of the Salome theme tell us about the state of the modern cultural imagination itself, its continuing enlistment of aesthetic and sexual ideologemes as utopias of modern individualism, human agency, and freedom? How did Salomé and Wilde become "us" or "them"?

In paying attention to the separate circumstances as well as the intersections between these two differently gendered figures of transgression—female and male; straight, gender-ambigous, and gay—my study continues and expands the critique of gendered notions of modernity begun by feminist modernist scholar Rita Felski. *Salome's Modernity* draws attention to the larger fields of discourse—literary, cultural, philosophical, political, social—that surrounded and suffused fantasies and fears of the transgressive erotic body and transgressive aesthetic agency that attached themselves to *both* of these two icons of modernity, Salomé and Wilde. As Felski writes, "many of the myths of modernity that pervade the last fin de siècle can be detected again in our own, suggesting that we may yet have to free ourselves from the seductive power of grand narratives" (10). Looking at the grand narrative of transgression surrounding Salomé and Wilde in the twentieth and twenty-first centuries suggests that Felski was right.

Chapter 1 provides the textual and historical grounding for *Salome's Modernity* by offering an innovative reading of Oscar Wilde's *Salomé* as a modernist text that built on thematic elements in nineteenth-century predecessor texts while promoting a genuinely modernist aesthetics of transgressive erotic and aesthetic agency. My purpose in revisiting texts like Mallarmé's "Hérodiade," Flaubert's "Hérodias" and *Salammbô,* and Huysmans's ekphrastic Moreau passages in *À rebours* is not to repeat previous scholarship on their relationship to Wilde but to read these texts together with and through *Salomé* in such a way that each text's specific importance to Wilde's modernist refashioning of certain themes and styles comes into sharp focus. Chapter 2 then offers a reinterpretation of *Salomé's* first and most famous adaptation, Richard Strauss's opera *Salome* (1905), the first modernist music drama. Contrary to most scholars, I argue that Strauss's revolutionary score presents an aesthetically attuned, creative programmatic development of Wilde's play rather than an idiosyncratic overhaul of its libretto source. It emphasized, rather than obscured, the ecstatic, sensationalist, and transgressive elements of Wilde's *Salomé* and shared with it the stylistic goal to manufacture overwhelming sensation and secular sublimity by aesthetic means.

The next two chapters are dedicated to two modernist female artists, the Canadian American dancer Maud Allan and the Russian American actress and producer Alla Nazimova, who found in Wilde's play a fertile ground for their feminist creativity as pioneers of modern dance and modernist art cinema, respectively. Chapter 3 introduces Maud Allan's famous and popular dance piece *The Vision of Salomé* (1908) and goes on to analyze Allan's painful involvement in the so-called Pemberton-Billing Trial in England (1918), which illustrates a problematic cultural conflation in late Victorian and Edwardian culture between female aesthetic and erotic independence, homosexuality, feminism, and aesthetic transgression. In chapter 4, my reading of Alla Nazimova's *Salomé: An Historical Phantasy by Oscar Wilde* (1922), the first surviving feature film adaptation of Wilde's play, connects Nazimova's previous Broadway stage career—particularly her rise to fame with Henrik Ibsen's complex New Woman characters—with her work as an independent Hollywood producer. Nazimova put forward a daring gay-affirmative and avant-garde interpretation of Wilde's play that must be understood not only in the context of the film's queer aesthetic and its homage to Oscar Wilde, Nazimova's own bisexuality, and her creative popular avant-gardism but also in the context of her previous theater career and her interest in feminist themes: a direct line leads from Nazimova's interest in promoting modern drama and its complex female heroines to her take on Wilde's *Salomé*.

Finally, chapter 5 turns to recent adaptations of Wilde's Salome figure in film and popular literature and culture since the 1980s and shows how the modernist aesthetics of transgression lives on as a powerful myth in postmodern Western culture. In recent decades, Wilde and Salomé have been claimed for our own times and contexts as predecessors of a supposedly more enlightened era of sexual and artistic freedom: artists and audiences alike have interpreted Wilde's *Salomé* as a flagship text of coded gay desire and have seen Salomé either as Wilde's transgendered alter ego or as an aggressively sexual New Woman, reflecting a changed cultural climate comparatively more accepting of male homosexuality and feminist rebellion, but also problematically reducing *Salomé*'s original transgressive impact.

Salome's Modernity can neither hope to give a comprehensive survey of almost one hundred years of Wildean *Salomé* adaptations, transformations, and theatrical productions nor do justice to all the different contexts in which they so richly appear. Hence I have focused on a few selected renditions judged best to show the broad spectrum opened by any inquiry into Wilde's take on the Salome figure in the twentieth and twenty-first centuries, leaving out others whose connections to Wilde's *Salomé* are looser or less pronounced than those that feature prominently. Among the earlier nineteenth-century versions, I concentrate on those that had a direct bearing on the modernist, transgressive elements in Wilde's play and only mention in passing Heinrich Heine's ironic Herodias episode in "Atta Troll" and Jules Laforgue's masterful spoof of Mallarmé's and Flaubert's fin de siècle Salomé obsession in *Moralités Légendaires*. I also set aside Arthur Symons's transformation of the Irish Sidhe myth in "The Daughters of Herodias" (along with Yeats's corresponding poem "The Hosting of the Sidhe") and other dance poems, which I have dealt with elsewhere in relation to Mallarmé's dancer trope and symbolist theory (Dierkes-Thrun, "Symons' Decadent Aesthetics") and to which Wilde's play is not directly relevant. For the same reason, I decided not to discuss Michael Field's Salome-themed poem "A Dance of Death" from *Poems of Adoration* (1912) and scattered references to Salome in their later work (*Queen Mariamne* [1908], *The Accuser* [1911]). Yeats's play *A Full Moon in March* (1935) and the symbolic role the Salome figure plays in his climactic fifteenth phase of *A Vision* would have been a better candidate for inclusion in *Salome's Modernity*, but again these materials bear little direct relation on Wilde's *Salomé* and have already been treated by Frank Kermode (*Romantic Image;* "Poet and Dancer Before Diaghilev"), Sylvia Ellis, Amy Koritz ("Women Dancing"), and others.

Among the better-known twentieth-century Salome versions I decided not to discuss in detail are Rita Hayworth's biblical-orientalist Technicolor spectacle *Salome* and Billy Wilder's wonderful film *Sunset Boulevard* (with Andrew Lloyd Webber's corresponding musical), which either are not based on Wilde's *Salomé* at all or incorporate it only as a minor, if integral and crucial, element of a different plot. The twentieth-century versions of the Wildean Salomé in popular culture are endless, and some are rather obscure, so that I had to make choices here as well. Among the versions I looked at but ultimately did not pick up for *Salome's Modernity* are Viereck and Eldridge's pulp fiction novel *Salome: The Wandering Jewess* (1930) and the 1986 Canadian graphic novel *Salome* by P. Craig Russell.

I also decided to leave out the reception of Wilde's *Salomé* in China and Japan (dealt with by Xiaoyi Zhou, Linda Pui-ling Wong, and Ayako Kano), which exceeds my current focus on Wilde's and *Salomé's* interpretation in Europe and North America. I left out as well the actual stage production and performance history of Wilde's play and Strauss's opera, except where it is directly relevant to my argument. William Tydeman and Steven Price already provide an invaluable survey of this stage history of *Salomé* in *Wilde—Salome* (1996). One theoretical question that could not be fully addressed in this book is *Salomé's* possible relationship to Wilde's reception of Hegel's idealism and Kant's theories of the beautiful and the sublime. As

Philip E. Smith and Michael S. Helfand have shown in their introduction to Wilde's *Oxford Notebooks,* Wilde was deeply immersed in the intellectual debates of his time, especially in Hegelian idealism. Hegel's and Kant's earlier influences on Wilde's aesthetics of transgression and modern individualism in *Salomé* and across other works would need further study than this volume can hope to provide.[7]

Finally, in my use of the French, English, or German spellings *Salomé/ Salome* in this book, I follow the original spelling in the specific text I am discussing. I use *Salomé* for Wilde's French play and character, as well as for renditions by Flaubert, Huysmans, Allan, and Nazimova that originally use the accented spelling. For German and English usage (e.g., Strauss's, Russell's, or Krishnamma's versions), I use *Salome.* In passages that address the Salome figure in a more general semiotic, rhetorical, or historical sense tied to more than one text, I also use the regular English spelling.

1
Dancing on the Threshold:
Wilde's *Salomé* between Symbolist,
Decadent, and Modernist Aesthetics

By the time Oscar Wilde got to the story of Salome, such writers as Heine, Flaubert, Mallarmé, Laforgue, and Huysmans (together with Moreau, Regnault, and other visual artists) had already fundamentally transformed the sparse biblical account of John the Baptist's martyrdom in the gospels of Mark (6:14–29) and Matthew (14:1–12). From the tale of a nameless, innocent daughter who obediently helps her power-hungry mother get rid of her dangerous personal and political opponent John the Baptist, who had denounced Herodias's incestuous marriage to Herod, the story had morphed into a lurid tale of dangerous female sexuality and cunning, physical passion, and pathological perversity. It focused on the daughter herself, who had by now regained the name first given to her by the first-century Jewish historian Flavius Josephus in *Antiquities of the Jews* (the first written historical record of John the Baptist's imprisonment and death at Herod's court, c. 93).[1] As far as the gospel writers' accounts were concerned, Wilde "complained of the docility of the Biblical Salome, who simply obeys Herodias, and, once she receives the head, conveys it to her mother. The inadequacy of this account, Wilde said, 'has made it necessary for the centuries to heap up dreams and visions at her feet so as to convert her into the cardinal flower of the perverse garden'" (Ellmann, *Oscar Wilde* 344). Such scholars as Françoise Meltzer (*Salome and the Dance of Writing*) and Megan Becker-Leckrone have analyzed the intertextual and "fetishistic" obsessions with the fin de siècle Salome figure, which have much to do with the mystery and "secret-effect" of her irreducible narrative, which produced "a two-thousand-year-old game of textual telephone" (Becker-Leckrone 242, 251). Yet "[t]he dancing daughter we envision in the twenty-first century is a product of the mythic figure created by Wilde and Strauss" (Skaggs 125), not the biblical one or any of the other Salomes created during the European fin de siècle, when the Salome theme was "so prevalent in painting, literature, and music of the French-oriented Decadence, 1870–1914, that it has to be considered a significant cultural phenomenon, a symptom" (Rose, "Synchronic Salome" 146).[2]

This chapter starts with the premise that simply looking at Wilde's *Salomé* in the nineteenth-century context disregards the truly innovative, subversive, forward-looking features of his play.[3] Salomé's and Wilde's erotic and aesthetic transgressions embody central fantasies and fears of Western cultural and philosophical modernity far beyond the fin de siècle. Hence my analysis does not merely reconstruct the obvious historical chain of influence on Wilde's play and weigh his debts to predecessors, as other scholars have done, but offers a critical assessment of some of the major intellectual and aesthetic figurations that broadly prepared and influenced Wilde's conception and helped Wilde create a seminal text for the modernist aesthetics of transgression.[4]

Mallarmé's "Hérodiade" and *Salomé's* Modern Aesthetic Idealism

Wilde's Salomé is a peculiar dramatic character. Profoundly isolated and alienated from others in her vaguely biblical yet timeless world, ruthless to the point of murder, obstinate and self-determined, touchingly vulnerable and soaring to lyrical heights of both hatred and love in her obsessive pursuit of pure beauty, Wilde's princess inspires horror and fascination in equal measures. For Salomé's configuration as an existentially lonely, misunderstood lover of ideal beauty, her contradictory character traits, and her symbolic scenic counterpart in the play, the moon, Wilde is particularly indebted to Stéphane Mallarmé's "Hérodiade." First conceived as a verse drama to be performed at the Théâtre Français but reconfigured as a dramatic poem after its rejection, "Hérodiade" was Mallarmé's self-declared masterpiece and obsession for over three decades. Despite multiple revisions, the piece remained unfinished at the time of Mallarmé's death in 1898. Fragments were circulated among the symbolist *maître's* adoring friends and associates in Paris, however.[5] Of these, "La Scène: La Nourrice—Hérodiade" is the most relevant for Wilde's version, since it contains the most extensive characterization of Hérodiade and most closely expresses the symbolist aesthetic that attracted Wilde. It was also the only one published during Mallarmé's and

Wilde's lifetimes. Wilde attended many of Mallarmé's famous *mardis* gatherings while writing *Salomé* in Paris (1890–91) and was well acquainted with the work (Shewan, *Oscar Wilde,* 106–13).

"Hérodiade" was important as a model of the avant-garde French symbolist poetics and style that Wilde sought to emulate for the English stage. Even though Hérodiade does not dance in this text, it is the crown jewel of a larger body of work on dancers and dance by Mallarmé, in which he used female ballet dancers and the famous Loïe Fuller as ideal models for the fraught poetic quest for truth and beauty, encapsulated in these well-known lines from his essay "Ballets": "the dancer is not a woman who dances . . . she is not a woman, but a metaphor . . . she does not dance, suggesting, through the miracle of shortcuts and bounds, with a corporal writing what it would take paragraphs of prose, in dialogue and description, to express: she is a poem set free of any scribe's apparatus" (*Mallarmé in Prose* 109).[6] Mallarmé lets his Hérodiade speak in beautiful, evocative poetic riddles to transport the reader into a symbolist universe of synesthesia, ennui, and reverie; the style of the poem embodies the corporalization of affect on which both Wilde and Strauss build in their versions. Chapter 2 discusses Mallarmé's style in more detail; here I wish to focus on his second major area of influence on *Salomé:* the protomodernist character of the Salome figure, whom Mallarmé calls "Hérodiade" to set her apart from previous Salomes. Mallarmé breaks with the gospels' presentation of the nameless, innocent dancing daughter used as a tool by her power-hungry mother (Mark 6:17–28; Matthew 14:3–11) and also with the theme's indirect association with incest and prostitution in Josephus's *Antiquities of the Jews* (the historical first-century AD account on which the biblical story is based). Instead, he made Salome/Hérodiade the central figure and put her inner struggles as well as her search for ideal beauty at the center of the legend. This creative interpretation of Hérodiade prepared the ground for Wilde's focus on Salomé's aesthetic individualism. Along with the iconic embodiment of symbolist aesthetics in "Hérodiade," Wilde also picked up Mallarmé's protomodernist conception of Hérodiade as a postreligious, rebellious, and split self in search of wholeness. "Hérodiade" anticipates such intrinsically modernist human concerns as existential isolation, human alienation, and rebellious modern individualism (the individual's attempt to argue and wrestle with fate in order to establish agency in the face of likely meaninglessness and defeat), and so does Wilde's Salomé. Hérodiade's suffering, pride, and impetuous rebellion already connect her to the crisis of the modern subject that we identify with early modernist culture, so aptly described by Nietzsche and the literary modernists as a challenging and confusing world after the death of God, in which human beings have to fight with existential loneliness and meaninglessness.

A strong sense of isolation, enclosure, and lack of human interaction permeates "Hérodiade." Mallarmé's heroine lives in a walled-in, hermetic "tour cinéraire et sacrificatrice, / Lourde tombe qu'a fuie un bel oiseau" ("cinerary tower of sacrifice, / Heavy tomb that a songbird has fled"), a tomblike place of stasis, decay, and disillusion (*Collected Poems,* trans. Henry Weinfield, 29).[7] This was later splendidly parodied by Jules Laforgue, who placed his own ironic modernist Salomé in a hyperbolic place of solitary confinement, as a lonely princess in an isolated fortress in the remote Esoteric White Islands in his *Moralités Légendaires* (1887). With a kind nurse as her only caretaker and companion, Hérodiade is "exilée en son coeur précieux / Comme un cygne cachant en sa plume les yeux" ("exiled in her proud heart / Like a swan that hides its eyes in its plumage" [trans. Weinfield, 29]). In an 1865 letter to Eugène Lefébure, Mallarmé expressed his wish to isolate Hérodiade like a "solitary tableau," drawing her purely as "a creature of dream, with absolutely no link with history" (*Selected Letters* 47). Although she interacts with the Nurse, Hérodiade rejects the latter's fond kisses and touch. She is unable to feel any human kinship or fond connection even with her earliest caretaker, and she experiences her virginal beauty as a deadly, frozen state that not even the Nurse's kisses are able to penetrate: "Reculez. / . . . O femme, un baiser me tûrait / Si la beauté n'était la mort" ("Stand back. / . . . O woman, a kiss would kill me / If beauty was not death" [trans. Weinfield, 29]).

As Mallarmé's mouthpiece of the new symbolist aesthetic, Hérodiade turns away from the organic and celebrates the artificial. Hérodiade exists in isolated splendor and self-sufficiency, pure and perfect, highly stylized and artificial, virginal and sterile. She is "a creature self-purified of humanity" (Rose, "Daughters of Herodias" 174), signified by the metaphor of the "blond torrent" of Hérodiade's metallic, immaculate hair, which Hérodiade keeps stripped of all signs not only of femininity (flowers, perfumes) but of humanity (human pain).

> Je veux que mes cheveux qui ne sont pas des fleurs
> A répandre l'oubli des humaines douleurs,
> Mais de l'or, à jamais vierge des aromates,
> Dans leurs éclairs cruels et dans leurs pâleurs mates,
> Observent la froideur stérile du métal,
> Vous ayant reflétés, joyaux du mur natal,
> Armes, vases depuis ma solitaire enfance.
>
> (30)[8]

Hérodiade pursues this ideal of cold, hard, sterile stasis even though it separates her entirely from other human beings. Utterly solitary, she has
learned to delight in the autoerotic touch of her pure hair on a virginal and
gloriously "useless" flesh.

> J'aime l'horreur d'être vierge et je veux
> Vivre parmi l'effroi que me font mes cheveux
> Pour, le soir, retirée en ma couche, reptile
> Inviolé sentir en la chair inutile . . .
>
> (34)[9]

Mallarmé brings Hérodiade's extreme self-centeredness to the fore when
the Nurse asks for whom Hérodiade saves herself. Hérodiade replies un-
equivocally, "Pour moi." Hérodiade seeks nothing human; she sees herself
like a deserted flower that blooms only for herself, in isolated splendor ("je
ne veux rien d'humain . . . / Oui, c'est pour moi, pour moi, que je fleuris,
déserte!" [33]). Such unapologetic narcissism prefigures the insistence of
Oscar Wilde's Salomé on her own idiosyncratic pleasure when she proudly
asserts, "I do not heed my mother. It is for mine own pleasure that I ask the
head of Jokanaan in a silver charger" (*Collins Complete Works of Oscar Wilde*
[henceforth cited as *CCW*] 600).

Salomé's concept of beauty is abstract and pure, similar to Hérodiade's.
In Salomé's invocations of the moon, she professes an inhuman ideal of
beauty; similarly, it is not Jokanaan's human aspect but, rather, his abstract
qualities as an earthly embodiment of the pure ideal that attract Salomé.
Jokanaan the person is beside the point; Salomé's descriptions of his beauty
suggest the same preference for coldness, chastity, inhumanity, and precious
metals or materials (silver, ivory) that she associates with the moon. When
she first lays eyes on Jokanaan, she calls his body a thin ivory statue, an image, and a shaft of silver. She also admires Jokanaan's "terrible" eyes, black
and lifeless like black holes, caverns, or lakes. Emphasizing the uniqueness
and otherworldliness of Jokanaan's beauty, she points out repeatedly that
"nothing in the world" can compare to him. She cannot forget or overcome
her desire: "I loved thee yet, Jokanaan, I love thee only. . . . I am athirst for
thy beauty; I am hungry for thy body; and neither wine nor fruits can appease my desire. What shall I do now, Jokanaan? Neither the floods nor the
great waters can quench my passion" (*CCW* 604). In Mallarmé's "Scène," by
contrast, Hérodiade's love for John the Baptist and the story of his death are
strangely absent (if perhaps unintentionally so, since the text remains a
fragment).[10]

Like Salomé, Hérodiade finds no solace among human beings. In fact, it is an especially ironic feature of Mallarmé's text that others, who admire the beautiful Hérodiade with radiant, diamond-like eyes, only increase her loneliness: they do not see Hérodiade's incompletion and unhappiness even though they are looking right at her. Ironically, others' adoration of supposed perfection only further cements Hérodiade's utter loneliness, and she is aware of it: "Je me crois seule en ma monotone patrie / Et tout, autour de moi, vit dans l'idolâtrie/ . . . [d'] Hérodiade au clair regard de diamant . . . / Ô charme dernier, oui! Je le sens, je suis seule" ("I am alone in my monotonous country, / While all those around me live in the idolatry / Of . . . Hérodiade, whose gaze is diamond keen . . . / O final enchantment! Yes, I sense it, I am alone" [trans. Weinfield, 34]).

The isolating look or gaze is a major theme in Wilde's text as well. Like Hérodiade, Salomé is constantly pursued and haunted by adoring eyes and minds attracted to her outward beauty. The other characters approach Salomé as a looking glass for their own narcissistic desires and needs, and yet they do not truly see her: Salomé is simultaneously the center of attention and completely alone. Wilde's play unfolds as a circle of frustrated looking with desire, awe, or doubt, introduced via two characters who look at Herod looking at someone.

> First Soldier: The Tetrarch has a sombre look.
> Second Soldier: Yes, he has a sombre look.
> First Soldier: He is looking at something.
> Second Soldier: He is looking at some one.
> First Soldier: At whom is he looking?
> Second Soldier: I cannot tell.
>
> (*CCW* 584)

Herod's looks at Salomé are initially open to interpretation, but it quickly becomes clear that they are inappropriately sexual. Salomé is repelled by Herod's looks; she asks herself why the Tetrarch "look[s] at me all the while with his mole's eyes under his shaking eyelids? It is strange that the husband of my mother looks at me like that" (586). She initially pretends ignorance, but she quickly admits to herself that she intuits his meaning: "I know not what it means. In truth, yes I know it" (ibid.).

Others are also looking at Salomé or look at others who look at Salomé. Narraboth constantly follows Salomé with his gaze; the Page of Herodias looks at Narraboth and warns his beloved that he should not look at the princess: "You are always looking at her. You look at her too much. It is dangerous to look at people in such a fashion" (584). Salomé promises Narraboth to look and smile at him through her muslin veil when she passes by in her litter the next day, yet she only uses Narraboth, who kills himself in despair. The soldiers look at Herod looking at Salomé; Herodias also looks at Herod and tries to avert his gaze from her daughter. She echoes the page's earlier warnings: "You must not look at her! You are always looking at her!" (592). Salomé, of course, looks at Jokanaan, who refuses to look at her and pays the ultimate price. Looking too much implies danger in Wilde's play; it is precarious and fatal. The circle of desire, like an eddy, will draw one in closer and closer, until all willpower and agency are lost: "Something terrible may happen," the page ominously intones (584). Not only are three characters dead by the end of the play (Narraboth, Jokanaan, and Salomé), but no one truly commands the object of his or her passionate fantasies. All lose what they most desire.

A similar gloom of failed connections, unfulfilled desire, and fatality hangs over "Hérodiade" as well. In Mallarmé's poem, Hérodiade sits in front of a mirror as she contemplates her beauty and laments her fate. The mirror was a major trope in symbolist art and literature, where it was frequently "used to explore a sense of the disoriented or fragmented subject. . . . The symbolist imagination consistently employs the mirror as an icon for the ambivalence of existence, because of its mysterious betrayal of uncertainty in what is perceived and the strangeness of its shadowed world. A sense of ontological anxiety underlies many uses of the motif" (Stoljar 363, 364). Hérodiade seeks to grasp a sense of selfhood in the cool surface of her own reflection, but the mirror interposes itself like a physical barrier or a sheet of ice.

> Ô miroir!
> Eau froide par l'ennui dans ton cadre gelée
> Que de fois et pendant des heures, désolée
> Des songes et cherchant mes souvenirs qui sont
> Comme des feuilles sous ta glace au trou profound,
> Je m'apparus en toi comme une ombre lointaine,
> Mais, horreur! Des soirs, dans ta sévère fontaine,
> J'ai de mon rêve épars connu la nudité!
>
> (30–31)[11]

The mirror interposes itself like a hymen between Hérodiade's inside and outside, marking her inescapable subjection to time and her inability to overcome the barrier and be whole. She can only glimpse her other half, like a shadow in fleeting moments or, in memories, like fallen leaves underneath the ice: markers of past life, decaying fragments of the past enshrined in the ice in maddening timelessness. The mirror thus acts as an artificial interface that separates, distances, and alienates the two Hérodiades. Hérodiade's recognition of her own distant shadow in the mirror shows her the other half as if through a dark pane of glass, so that she can recognize but not reach and reconcile herself with it. In contrast to the cultural tradition that elevates mirrors as inalienable keys to truth and symbols of mimesis, Hérodiade's mirror allows access only to the surface of her beautiful body but not to the depths of her soul. It introduces a fundamental instability and uncertainty: who is this Hérodiade? What truth is hidden behind her smile, the beautiful face reflected in the mirror?

The mirror motif is connected centrally to Mallarmé's symbolist-modernist poetics through the figure of the hymen, the seemingly permeable but ultimately insuperable screen. As Jacques Derrida and Paul de Man pointed out, the hymen is a dominant and pervasive theme in Mallarmé's work from early on (e.g., in poems like "Les Fenêtres" and "L'azur" [1864], in which metaphors of a windowpane and a thick fog indicate the limits of poetry and aesthetic representation themselves, and also in "Mimique," which Derrida discusses in *Dissemination*).[12] Referring both to the vaginal membrane, the physical equivalent of a virgin's bridal veil, and the marriage ceremony, traditionally associated with defloration, the term *hymen* marks a liminal moment in which original unity and intactness is forever destroyed. The mirror and Mallarmé's hymenic figures in general are symbols of modernity's destruction of innocence and naïveté—of language, of agency, of faith. Until his death, Mallarmé himself struggled with his own goal to realize a new language of poetry in "Hérodiade"—never fully satisfied with it and never finished.[13]

Adored yet isolated (like an immortal), gazing at her own "dreadfully beautiful" image in terror, Hérodiade remains locked up with her unresponsive other in the mirror, living through lonely moments of mourning, awe, and terror. Hérodiade's hymenically divided self suspends her between the artificial perfection she craves and the maddening temporality and organicity of her body, which she knows she will not be able to conquer. Opaque and evanescent, Hérodiade's mirror frames a self that is fluid in time and thus elusive, listless, and unable to move. It imprisons her in the circle of time, condemned to endlessly reenact the failure of the self to reach its object of desire. At the end of "Scène," Hérodiade, unable to gain a sense of selfhood, admits not only to her loneliness but also to a certain sense of drifting in time, of undetermined waiting for an unknown thing or purpose: "J'attends une chose inconnue" (35).

Following Mallarmé's symbolic use of the mirror motif, Wilde uses the moon in *Salomé* to create a similarly complex mirror effect and a reading foil for his protagonist. A strong sense of ontological ambiguity and foreboding attaches itself to the moon, which reflects Salomé's unfathomable femininity and mystery. The moon conjures up Salomé's inaccessible double nature, which cannot be truly understood or mastered by anyone, including Salomé herself. From the very opening of the play, the princess and the moon are symbolically intertwined, and both are split into two opposite halves, consisting of a seemingly ideal, beautiful half that radiates purity and perfection, on the one hand, and a much darker half comprised of cruelty, selfishness, and extreme ruthlessness, on the other. Wilde's opening scene sets up this symbolic mirror relationship between the princess and the moon by conflating them while introducing the main themes connected with Salomé in the play: beauty, danger, predatory behavior, dance, veiling, innocence, and death.

> The Young Syrian: How beautiful is the Princess Salome to-night!
> The Page of Herodias: Look at the moon! How strange the moon seems! She is like a woman rising from a tomb. She is like a dead woman. You would fancy she was looking for dead things.
> The Young Syrian: She has a strange look. She is like a little princess who wears a yellow veil, and whose feet are of silver. She is like a princess who has little white doves for feet. You would fancy she was dancing.
> The Page of Herodias: She is like a woman who is dead. She moves very slowly.
>
> (*CCW* 583)

Moon and princess are figuratively and linguistically intertwined in this passage and elsewhere. The skilled conflation of these referents (the "moon," like the "princess," is gendered female in both the English and French versions) puts both on shifting, ambiguous hermeneutic ground—virginal and precious, morbid and fatal. The moon is personified as a dead woman with amber eyes and as a princess with dovelike white feet, for example, so the field of similes could equally apply to both referents. The association sometimes functions allegorically, too, as in the following passage, in which Salomé first speaks of smiling at the Young Syrian from her litter through a muslin veil and then the moon is described as a princess smiling through the muslin clouds.

Salomé (*smiling*): You will do this thing for me, Narraboth, and to-mor-
row when I pass in my litter beneath the gateway of the idol-sellers I
will let fall for you a little flower, a little green flower. . . . I will look at
you through the muslin veils, I will smile at you. . . . I know that you
will do this thing. . . .

The Page of Herodias: Oh! How strange the moon looks. You would
think it was the hand of a dead woman who is seeking to cover herself with a shroud.

The Young Syrian: She has a strange look! She is like a little princess,
whose eyes are of amber. Through the clouds of muslin she is smiling
like a little princess.

(588)

Salomé herself aspires to be like the moon, which she calls "a little silver
flower," "cold and chaste," "a virgin" who has "never defiled herself. She has
never abandoned herself to men, like the other goddesses" (586). Salomé's
physique appears exquisite and precious, associated with the moon colors
white and silver: she looks "like a silver flower," her feet are "of silver," or
like "white doves"; her hands, equally small, white and exquisite, "are fluttering like doves that fly to their dove-cots. They are like white butterflies"
(586, 585). Perhaps echoing Mallarmé's image, Wilde also describes Salomé
as "the shadow of a white rose in a mirror of silver" (584). Throughout
Wilde's play, Salomé is presented in symbolic terms that indicate fragility,
virginity, vulnerability, and preciousness: "She is like a dove that has
strayed. . . . She is like a narcissus trembling in the wind" (586). Aside from
Mallarmé's influence, these are also typical traits of the literary *femme fragile,* another popular stereotype of femininity during the period.[14]

On the one hand, the moon signals Salomé's innocence and virginity; on
the other, it forecasts destruction. Throughout the play, Salomé's and the
moon's symbolic intertwinement functions as a structural device that fore-
tells impending turns of events via three phases—white, red, and black—
by slowly moving the plot toward its inevitable fatal conclusion, the escala-
tion into violence and murder. As the moon changes from white (bright
moon) to red (the phase of Salomé's passion and of the first blood, when the
Syrian kills himself) and ultimately to black (a cloud passes over the moon
and the stars and extinguishes their light; Herod orders the slaves to put out
the torches), so Salomé goes from innocence and purity (white), to feeling
passion and love for Jokanaan and inspiring Narraboth's suicide (red), to
the dark intrigue of the dance leading to Jokanaan's murder, the necrophilic
encounter with the severed head, and ultimately her own death (black).

Despite Salomé's and Hérodiade's innocent, virginal looks, Mallarmé's hymenic mirror and Wilde's moon embody the deceptive duplicity of femininity: Hérodiade and Salomé are suffering and sympathetic yet cruel and selfish, innocent yet fatal, inhuman monsters and lonely souls, victims as well as destroyers. Because they constantly oscillate between these positive and negative qualities, they also remain fascinatingly elusive. Mallarmé first mentioned his paradoxical conception of Hérodiade in an early poem from the *Parnasse Contemporain,* "Les fleurs," where he described her as a beautiful but cruel, blood-stained rose ("la rose / Cruelle, Hérodiade en fleur du jardin clair, / Celle qu'un sang farouche et radieux arrose!" [Mallarmé, *Collected Poems* 14]), linking the themes of precious beauty (the rose as the delicate queen of flowers) and violence, themes he would explore further in "Hérodiade." Hence Hérodiade is "at once a child and a woman; . . . simultaneously glacial and torrid" (Marvick 148).

Mallarmé's and Wilde's respective emphasis on their protagonists' double nature and innate inability to be whole, authentic, and fulfilled, as signified by the hymenic mirror and the moon, is at heart a modernist gesture. The image of a divided Hérodiade/Salomé in Mallarmé and Wilde encapsulates the crisis of the modern subject: she can neither bridge the split in herself that causes both her narcissism and her isolation nor forget her incompleteness altogether. Mallarmé and Wilde are acutely aware of humanity's tragic suspension in the space and the time between, hovering between the beckoning ideal and the sobering reality of the limited human condition, longingly imagining the possibility of transcending its own limits, knowing yet unable to forget (as Nietzsche would say) its inability to transgress those limits. Whereas Hérodiade remains a passive, artificial, self-absorbed, and conflicted figure, however, Wilde developed a shocking, crashing finish to Salomé's story that suggests the possibility of an individually willed escape route from the deadening ennui of Herod's court. While Mallarmé locks up Hérodiade in her tower in endless stasis, Wilde grants Salomé an awesome, triumphant moment in the spotlight before she is killed, investing her with perverse sublimity and empathy. In this regard, he learned much from Flaubert and Huysmans.

Gustave Flaubert's Models for Wilde's Sensual Sublime

Gustave Flaubert demonstrated for Wilde the potency of vivid literary representations of eroticism couched in terms of metaphysical longing, creating imagery that fused sexual lust with a desire for the divine and vice versa.

In Wilde's presentation of Salomé's yearning for Jokanaan's ideal body, one senses echoes of the Carthaginian priestess Salammbô's attraction to the moon goddess Tanit in Flaubert's historical novel *Salammbô* (1863); of the Queen of Sheba's sexual wooing of the chaste saint in *La tentation de Saint Antoine,* Flaubert's fictional account of Saint Antoine's visionary desert trials (final version published in 1874); and also of Salomé's dance in "Hérodias," Flaubert's Salome story in *Trois contes* (1877), in which the young dancer mimics the searching, yearning movement of a lost soul for God. In *Salammbô* in particular, Flaubert mixed decadent opulence and physical sensuality with the literary tradition of religious mysticism, as signified, for example, by the religious and meditative poetry of Teresa of Avila, Meister Eckhart, and Hildegard von Bingen. Flaubert was interested in religious subjects throughout his career. Religious mysticism often described the religious progression toward the divine in strikingly erotic terms by employing sexual language and imagery when describing supreme religious ecstasy or the imagined union with God.

In Flaubert's *Salammbô,* the Carthaginian priestess nightly implores the elusive moon goddess Tanit, an ambivalent deity of fertility and fatality, to answer her prayers and sweep her up in her divine, agile presence (53). Salammbô's yearning for the preternatural moon goddess is expressed via sexual imagery—in this case, via metaphors of volcanic heat and orgasmic intercourse.

> Sometimes, . . . the depth of my being gives off gusts of heat, heavier than the fumes of a volcano. Voices call me, a ball of fire rolls and comes up into my breast, it stifles me, I am about to die; and then something sweet, flowing from my brow down to my feet, passes over my flesh . . . it is a caress that enfolds me, and I feel crushed as though a God were stretched out on me. (54)

This erotic-religious fantasy culminates in Salammbô's fervent wish to literally melt or evaporate into the deity in her ecstasy. Salammbô yearns for a spiritual uplifting to take place so she can "glide, climb up," like air or light, into Tanit's divine presence, which she identifies with nature (a sexualized replay of the well-known Romantic trope): "Oh! I should like to lose myself in the mists of the nights, in the water of the springs, in the sap of the trees, come out of my body, be no more than a breath, a ray, and glide, climb up to you, oh Mother!" The passage culminates in an orgasmic, ecstatic moment, with imagery that fuses sex and prayer: "She raised her arms as high as possible, arching her body, pale and light as the moon in her long robe. Then she fell back on the ivory couch, panting" (54). Still, as much as she wishes to be made whole by an external, powerful force from which she re-mains painfully separated, Flaubert's heroine never comes close to complete satisfaction.[15] As Salammbô explains to the high priest Schahabarim, even when she is close, the deity seems to be "leaping to escape [her]," throwing her back upon her earthly existence so that she is sorely disappointed: "I seem to be about to hear her voice, see her face, I am dazzled by flashes of light. Then I fall back into the darkness" (56).

To the modern reader of Flaubert's tale and novel, such imagery arouses empathy for the female protagonist, who so desperately wants to experi-ence divine bliss but ultimately remains tragically unheard and alone.[16] This holds true even as Salammbô's behavior borders on the sacrilegious. The priestess secretly endorses the stealing of the zaïmph, the goddess's holy veil, from the temple—a criminal act that constitutes a supreme viola-tion of religious respect—because she inwardly rejoices at the chance to see and perhaps even touch it herself, eschewing the danger to her life. (The zaïmph eventually brings death to those who dare touch it, including Salammbô's lover Mathô, who stole it, and the priestess herself.) In her de-sire to merge with Tanit, Salammbô sometimes even resembles her closely—for example, in chapter 11, when Mathô wraps Salammbô in the stolen zaïmph and sleeps with her, wondering if she is really Tanit, the moon goddess herself. Throughout the novel, Flaubert humanizes, excuses, and elevates Salammbô's sacrilege by motivating it through the young woman's intense desire to get somehow closer to the goddess she adores and feels called to serve.

In a similar vein as Flaubert, Wilde portrays Salomé's intense yearning for Jokanaan; he embodies a spiritual other just as unattainable as Salammbô's moon goddess. Salomé is in love with the divinely inspired prophet and wishes to physically unite herself with him, but like Salammbô, she is rejected and disappointed by him time and time again, until at last she takes matters into her own hands and ruthlessly violates re-ligious and social law to possess the object of her desire. Wilde further sec-ularizes the trope, however, directing Salomé's yearning toward a purely aesthetic purpose and eschewing the moral and religious altogether (except for dramatic color and contrast). Wilde publicly compared his Salomé to Flaubert's virginal priestess and the sixteenth-century Spanish mystic Teresa of Avila: "My Salome is a mystic, the sister of Salammbô, a Sainte Thérèse who worships the moon" (quoted in Ellmann, *Oscar Wilde* 376). Yet Salomé reveres not the prophet's spiritual prophecies or religious authority but, rather, his *physical* qualities. She is enchanted with his body—Jokanaan's white skin, black hair, and red mouth—which to her is also the ideal embodiment of pure Beauty. Once Salomé has seen Jokanaan's beautiful body and taken in his overwhelming aesthetic appeal, she wishes to possess him with her entire being—but, crucially, without being touched, changed, or converted by Jokanaan's spiritual prophecies. She is simply not interested in the metaphysical contents he preaches, only in his sensual appeal. As the flesh-and-body version of the abstract ideal, Jokanaan becomes both an aesthetic and erotic attraction: the aesthetic becomes erotic, and vice versa. In her final monologue, Salomé testifies to her addiction to Jokanaan's physical beauty, making no mention at all of his spiritual aspect.

> Ah, Jokanaan, Jokanaan, thou wert the only man that I have loved. All other men are hateful to me. But thou, thou wert beautiful! Thy body was a column of ivory set on a silver socket. It was a garden full of doves and silver lilies. It was a tower of silver decked with shields of ivory. There was nothing in the world so white as thy body. There was nothing in the world so black as thy hair. In the whole world there was nothing so red as thy mouth. . . . Oh, how I loved thee! I loved thee yet, Jokanaan, I love thee only. (*CCW* 604)

Salomé's violation of Jokanaan arises from her unrelenting, passionate wish to physically take in his beauty at all costs (symbolized by the kiss to the severed head), just as Salammbô's transgression upon the goddess's veil resulted from her painful longing to touch the adored deity, if only by proxy. Like Flaubert and Mallarmé, Wilde creates empathy with the transgressive Salomé by portraying the intensity of her passion as a tragically impossible quest for pure beauty.

Flaubert's prose poem *La tentation de Saint Antoine* (which Wilde seldom traveled without and which he asked for when he was in Reading Prison) places a similarly ascetic male spiritual figure at its heart. Flaubert's Saint Antoine indulges in and struggles with morose delectation of all manners of physical sin and intellectual heresy, finally experiencing a vision of the radiant face of Christ that leads him back to spiritual authenticity in prayer—a main difference to the ending of Wilde's *Salomé,* in which the prophet is dead and a blasphemous, ecstatic human Salomé dies triumphantly. One scene in particular prefigures Salomé's decadent sensual-spiritual courtship of Jokanaan. After the appearance of the Seven Deadly Sins in part II, Saint Antoine is wooed by a dangerous erotic seductress intently pining for his love, the Queen of Sheba (actually the Devil in disguise). Like Salomé, she is a beautiful, sexy loner doggedly pursuing a chaste man who resists her. The queen's physical description in *La tentation,* especially her golden robe and "blue-powdered coiffure," may partly have inspired Sarah Bernhardt's costume in 1892 (which was also based on her costume in Sardou's 1890 play *Cléopatre* in London; see Tydeman and Price 22). Having looked for him everywhere and finally found him, the queen cries out, "Ah! handsome hermit! handsome hermit!—my heart swoons! . . . I love thee!—oh! how I love thee!" (37), "star[ing] at him, examin[ing] him closely," while he "remains motionless, more rigid than a stake, more pallid than a corpse" (38). Like Jokanaan, Saint Antoine rejects the temptress three successive times (39, 40, 42), even though she offers up not only material riches but herself as the ultimate gateway to sensual sublimity: "I am not a woman: I am a world. My cloak has only to fall in order that thou mayest discover a succession of mysteries!" (42). Like Salomé, she simultaneously embodies the heartbroken lover and the ruthless femme fatale: she "departs, uttering a convulsive hiccough at intervals, which might be taken either for a sound of hysterical sobbing, or the half-suppressed laughter of mockery" (43).

Just like the moon goddess in Flaubert's *Salammbô* and Saint Antoine in *La tentation,* Wilde's Jokanaan withholds himself from the adoring human eye and the thirsting soul. It is always Salomé who looks at and addresses Jokanaan, never the other way around; his rejections wound her sharply, so that she feels compelled to strike back at him. Salomé's final speech suggests that if the prophet had not refused to look at her, their relationship could have been different: "If thou hadst looked at me thou hadst loved me" (604). Salomé's decision to ask for Jokanaan's head in order to finally kiss his lips constitutes her attempt to unite herself with the unwilling sublime. What at first looks like Salomé's bloody vengeance, then, is actually the result of her unquenchable, mad thirst for the alluring, beautiful, ideal body that rejects her adoring eyes, hands, and lips. This God, through his prophet Jokanaan, doesn't offer what is most needed and desired: warm embraces and kisses rather than abstract moral warnings and religious verbiage.

Motivating the perversity of Salomé's desire for the prophet thus, Wilde cleverly uses it to create empathy for the rejected princess and to place some blame on the unresponsive prophet, who hurls moral warnings and attacks at her and has neither empathy nor patience. Thus Salomé's transgressions—ranging from her ruthless manipulation of all principal male characters to blasphemy and outrageous necrophilia—become eminently understandable and, despite their outrageousness, perhaps even somewhat excusable to the audience. The fatal dance and the murder of Jokanaan follow upon failed communication, failed faith, failed love. In Wilde's hands, the legend of Salome hence becomes a thought experiment of taking the pursuit of Beauty to its utter extreme, following it literally into murder and death, while distorting the moral and religious dimensions into aesthetic surfaces, divesting them of their guiding and regulating functions. This is where Wilde's aestheticism most brightly shines through and where *Salomé* most closely resembles *The Picture of Dorian Gray*. In *Salomé*, it is religion for aesthetics' sake, not the other way around.

In Flaubert's own rendering of Salomé's legend, his "Hérodias" tale from *Trois contes,* much admired by Wilde, there is a direct interplay of religious and erotic imagery as well, although Flaubert adds a potent dose of female fatality to the mix. The idea of using female sensuality as a powerful tool of seduction for a worldly ruler is already present in the original story as told by the gospels and previously in Josephus (the earliest source of the legend), but Flaubert dramatically expands the trope and provides an important model for Wilde's full-fledged focus on Salomé's visual appeal to Herod and the Young Syrian, Narraboth. Following the gospel accounts in interpreting Salomé as an obedient daughter to a power-hungry mother, Flaubert at first portrays Salomé's dance as the movement of an innocent soul searching for a lost god. Beginning her dance, the young woman seems to be yearning for a powerful Other who is either not yet or perhaps no longer present or responding to her: "Her rounded arms seemed to be beckoning someone who was forever fleeing from her. She ran after him, lighter than a butterfly, like an inquisitive Psyche or a wandering soul, always apparently on the point of fluttering away" (*Trois contes* 120). Like Salammbô, Flaubert's Salomé is alternately elated and desperate to unite herself with an elusive god, finally entering a state of ecstatic trance.

> The castanets gave place to the funereal sound of the pipes; hope was followed by despondency. Her poses now suggested sighs, and her whole body was so languid that one could not tell whether she was mourning for a god or expiring in his embrace. With her eyes half-closed, she twisted her body backwards and forwards, making her belly rise and fall and her breasts quiver, while her face remained expressionless and her feet never stopped moving. (120–21)

Just as in *Salammbô,* however, the religious imagery soon merges into forceful, impressive erotic language. From the dancer's spiritual yearning, Flaubert shifts the focus toward Salomé's erotic poses and the wielding of her feminine power, which seduces Herod and the rest of the male audience. At this point, Salomé's provocative dance becomes more directly sexual and almost pornographic.

> Next the girl depicted the frenzy of a love which demands satisfaction. . . . Without bending her knees, she opened her legs and leant over so low that

her chin touched the floor. And the nomads inured to abstinence, the Roman soldiers skilled in debauchery, the avaricious publicans, and the old priests soured by controversy all sat there with their nostrils distended, quivering with desire. (121)

Flaubert seamlessly connects religious and erotic imagery to portray female eroticism as a terrifying force to be reckoned with. In Flaubert's account, Salomé does not desire Iaokanann[17] (John the Baptist) as she does in Heine's, Huysmans's, Laforgue's, and, most pointedly, Wilde's versions; she even forgets his name when asking for the prophet's head according to her mother's wish. But Flaubert physically arranges the mother and the daughter as mirrors and extensions of each other, working together as the private orchestrator and public instrument to overpower Herod and ensure the inconvenient prophet's death. The maneuvering Hérodias is installed on a balcony above, from where she runs the show like the moon goddess Cybele with lions by her side, overlooking and directing the scene of the dance like a battlefield. The dancing Salomé on the floor below is a second Hérodias in training, sensual and ruthless; she even looks exactly like her mother.[18] Flaubert's emphasis on female spiritual-sexual power becomes particularly evident at the dance's climax, when Salomé "thr[ows] herself on her hands with her heels in the air, and in that position r[uns] around the dais like a great beetle." She stops dead in front of Herod, confronting him in silence and coolly measuring her erotic charisma against his worldly authority. Her face is described as a terrifying, inhuman mask, like that of a beautiful and terrible goddess demanding a blood sacrifice. The scene portrays a dangerous, serious contest: "Her lips were painted, her eyebrows black, her eyes well-nigh terrifying, and the beads of sweat on her forehead looked like vapour on white marble. She did not speak. They looked at one another. . . . The Tetrarch sank back in horror" (122). In Flaubert's version, the terrifying power of the young dancer is the result of the merger between her erotic and goddesslike appeal, turned around against Herod to overpower his senses and make him a slave to the female will.

The transformation of the religious aspect into a tool of seduction—and hence the fusion of the spiritual and the sexual—is a trait we find in Wilde's play as well. Wilde dramatically prolongs and relishes the central battles of will between Salomé and Narraboth and between Salomé and Herod, especially after the dance, as the desperate Herod repeatedly implores his stepdaughter to let up, pleading with her to accept any of his costly, precious material goods as substitutions for the head of the Baptist. Wilde's Salomé is acutely aware of her ambiguous spiritual-sensual appeal and paradoxical pairing of moonlike purity and smoldering fatality; she ruthlessly employs it to manipulate both Narraboth and Herod, while she fails with Jokanaan, who reads her, through his own foil, as the impure daughter of a disgraced mother.

Along with providing Wilde with a model for rendering the sensual sublime, Flaubert also dwelt on the political and religious conflicts connected with the biblical story, creating a meticulously researched, vivid, and realistic-seeming historical picture while elaborating on the orientalism of his biblical subject. For example, Flaubert provides rich geographical detail about Herod's citadel of Machaerus, overlooking the Dead Sea and the mountains of Judea; he also offers eye-popping descriptions of food and decorations at Herod's opulent birthday banquet and a visual walk-through of his imagined palace, which includes a secret stable of one hundred white horses with coiffed blue manes and hooves in espato mittens. Among Flaubert's many details are also religious disputes between some of the religious groups, including various Jewish factions, early Christians, and others (e.g., about the coming of the Messiah, the Resurrection, and Jesus' miracles), and it seems to be this kind of material that inspired Wilde's prominent use of similar theological tiffs and power struggles in *Salomé*.

Flaubert's historical and orientalist detail probably influenced Wilde's similar presentation of some warring religious factions in *Salomé,* but such arguments function differently: the contemporary religious and political war of ideas illustrates the confusing and paralyzing ideological and religious disarray of Herod's court. From the very beginning, Herod's court comes across as a fragmented one, in which there is no longer any overarching or all-encompassing framework of political, social, or moral values, meaning, or authority. In the very opening, this theme is introduced by the soldiers' and, later, by Salomé's report of religious conflicts between different Jewish factions, who are always "disputing about their religion" (*CCW* 583) and are "tearing each other in pieces over their foolish ceremonies" (586) or over the existence of angels. The Nubian and the Cappadocian then discuss the gods' nature and importance in their respective countries. The Cappadocian concludes that he thinks "[the gods] are dead," and on the Jews' worship of an invisible God, he comments that "[t]hat seems to [him] altogether ridiculous" (584). Shortly thereafter, two Nazarenes argue that the Messiah has come and is working miracles (something they only know by rumor), a belief that a Jew promptly denies.

By way of these accumulated dramatic vignettes, Wilde illustrates a lack of authority and of social and political unity and the resulting disagreements about even the most basic common truths and values. This conjures up a pervasive mood of existential uncertainty, insecurity, and superstition. There is no single comprehensive system of faith or meaning, and everything is uncertain or ominous. This is a mental universe in which the ground constantly shifts and nothing is stable, not even the metaphysical referent. Is there a god? Do angels exist? What do the gods want? Who is the prophet Jokanaan, and who is Elias? Are the gods alive and present? Do they care, or have they left? Are we alone?

Salomé's emphasis on divisions and lack of agreement on any kind of authentic truth or divine authority indirectly reflects skepticism toward a transcendental reality and faith in modernity, as marked, for example, by Nietzsche's programmatic pronouncement of the death of God, the birth of historical materialism in Marx and Engels's *Communist Manifesto,* or scientific and sociological theories by Darwin, Spencer, and others that describe a logical yet creator-free world marked by existential struggle. Arranging the religious conflicts as a backdrop for the characters' unresolved yearning, anger, or despair and contrasting this ineffectuality of religion with Salomé's postreligious erotic and aesthetic individualism, Wilde gives *Salomé* an essentially secular outlook. When the Voice of Jokanaan sounds from the cistern for the first time, proclaiming the impending arrival of the Messiah ("After me shall come another mightier than I" [584]), it inevitably does so against the cacophonous background of already skeptical, cynical human opinions that make an innocent reception of Jokanaan's prophesy impossible. This backdrop of religious discord immediately calls into question whether or not what Jokanaan offers could truly be God's saving grace and genuine revelation. Indeed, the Second Soldier promptly intones, "Make him be silent. He is always saying ridiculous things," and the First Soldier admits that "[s]ometimes he says things that affright one, but it is impossible to understand what he says" (585).

In addition, a lingering sense of impending existential danger and angst pervades the play. The Page of Herodias obsessively warns that "something terrible" will happen; the young Syrian captain of the guard, Narraboth, commits suicide, and Herod slips in his blood; and Herod superstitiously guards Jokanaan's life (in fear for his own life if the prophet's is taken) and repeatedly fantasizes about the beating wings of the Angel of Death, seeing bad omens everywhere. Herod is also terrified at the Nazarenes' belief that Jesus has raised the dead (because he secretly fears that the brother he murdered in order to take Herodias as his wife might come back to take revenge). Meanwhile, the bored realist Herodias, like the Cappadocian earlier on, finds all these religious debates tedious and pointless, sardonically ridiculing them: "These men are mad. They have looked too long on the moon" (595).

Despite its biblical setting and subject, the world of Wilde's play is thus at heart a posttheological and ironic one. It combines cultural pessimism and apocalyptic thinking with a rebellious, utopian modernist sensibility, the sober and liberating realization that humanity can find new ways of being in a world without the guidance of prophets, gods, or kings. As William Butler Yeats wrote in "The Second Coming," things have already "fall[en] apart; the centre cannot not hold" (*Collected Poems* 187). But at the same time as *Salomé* portrays a world on the abyss and discredits religion and worldly authority as sources of hope and stability, it also celebrates a secular modern individualism that transfers the fullness of ecstatic experience previously only associated with metaphysical transcendence to erotic and aesthetic transgression and sensuality. Where Flaubert's heroines yearn and strive, Salomé goes out to get and achieve what she wants.

Huysmans's "Goddess of Hysteria" in *À rebours*: Assembling a Decadent *Mysterium Tremens et Fascinosum*

Like Flaubert's *Salammbô* and *Trois contes*, Joris-Karl Huysmans's decadent novel *À rebours* (*Against Nature*, 1884) was another important influence on Wilde's conception of *Salomé*. (Wilde famously alluded to *À rebours* in *The Picture of Dorian Gray*, as the little yellow book Dorian is reading on his way to moral and mental corruption, illustrating for him the allure of a decadent life led solely on the basis of sensual, sexual, and aesthetic desires, with complete disregard for traditional morality.) If Wilde was inspired by Mallarmé's virginal, innocent, lonely Hérodiade for half of Salomé's character, he looked to Huysmans for the other half—her smoldering sensuality and ruthless femme fatale qualities. What stands out most about Huysmans's famous literary rendering of two Salomé pictures by Gustave Moreau in chapter 5—the oil painting *Salomé Dansant* (1876) and the watercolor *L'Apparition* (1874–76)—is Huysmans's development of the Salome figure into one of the most famous femmes fatales of the fin de siècle. He presents her as a cold, cruel, supremely powerful *vagina dentata;* a superhuman, monstrous, irresistible being who devours and destroys all that cross her path.

> She had become, as it were, the symbolic incarnation of undying Lust, the Goddess of immortal Hysteria, the accursed Beauty exalted above all the other beauties by the catalepsy that hardens her flesh and steels her muscles, the monstrous Beast, indifferent, irresponsible, poisoning, like the

Helen of ancient myth, everything that approaches her, everything that sees her, everything that she touches. (65–66)

In this description of Moreau's *Salomé Dansant,* Huysmans conjures up a cruel and indifferent Salomé, dazzling in her splendor, who radiates the power and invincibility of an irresistible and indifferent goddess and embodies both beauty and terror. Compared to Flaubert, Mallarmé, and other literary predecessors, Huysmans intensifies the aura of perversity and evil surrounding the dancer, developing Salomé into a flagship of decadent sublimity and moving her even further away from the innocent, obedient, nameless daughter of the gospel accounts.

To Huysmans's neurotic male protagonist Des Esseintes, a weakly aristocrat whose physical and moral decay symbolizes the decline of nineteenth-century bourgeois culture as well as the beginning of the decadent aesthetic, the two Moreau pictures encapsulate his quest for sensual ecstasy. In chapter 5 of the novel, Des Esseintes stations himself in front of these two paintings, which he owns, every night, pondering their steamy sensuality and intriguing religious atmosphere: "Huysmans' revery of Salome is the attempt to come close to the immortal, to the superhuman, to that which is indifferent to time and history" (Meltzer 42). Des Esseintes is Huysmans's ultimate eclectic, decadent consumer who explores alternative mental, erotic, and aesthetic worlds of self-indulgence in vain pursuit of a fuller, more satisfying sense of self. Bored by mass consumption and mass taste, he embarks on a highly idiosyncratic project to create an artificial domestic paradise of sensuality in his fantasy villa Fontana, a sort of fin de siècle Hearst Castle. At Fontana, Des Esseintes collects and assembles an expensive bricolage of the history of thought and culture through rare books, strange objects, and a series of odd scientific and behavioral experiments; decrying the normal and the popular, he worships the artificial and bizarre as the truly beautiful and sublime. In Huysmans's novel, Moreau's Salomés model a mixture of sexual transgression and quasi-metaphysical sublimity similar to that we find in Wilde's *Salomé,* adding elements of horror and pathology that may have influenced Wilde as well.

Salomé's outrageous moral rebellion and assertiveness bear witness of the influence of the overt femme fatale stereotype popularized by Huysmans. They also exemplify Wilde's modernist aesthetics of transgression, which focuses on the powerful utopian individualism of a fearless loner whose gender heightens the outrage of her rebellion. Wilde's princess of the moon is not cut of the same cloth as Huysmans's hothouse flower Salomé, the pathological flower of venereal sin, but she does possess strong femme fatale traits inspired by Huysmans's decadent imagination. Throughout the play, Salomé lives by her own rules and wishes, repeatedly ignoring Herod's orders (e.g., to return to the banquet inside, to drink from his cup, to bite into his apple, to sit next to him, and initially to dance for him, petulantly answering him, "I am not thirsty," "I am not hungry," "I will not dance," etc.). She also stubbornly and haughtily demands that others (Narraboth, Jokanaan, the soldiers) abide by her will against their earnest protestations and resistance, and she engages in ferocious battles of will that she is determined to win, proudly establishing her authority if she feels insulted ("I am Salomé, daughter of Herodias, Princess of Judaea" [*CCW* 589]) or striking back viciously as she is repeatedly rejected by Jokanaan. She shows ruthless egocentrism and disregard for others and does not shy away from (indirect) murder, as in the case of Jokanaan's execution and arguably also in the case of the Young Syrian's desperate suicide. Most obviously, there is Salomé's outrageous vampiric and necrophilic behavior in the final scene, which I discuss in detail in the last section of this chapter.

Wilde found in Huysmans's Salomé passages another model for his re-placement of metaphysical ecstasy with physical ecstasy and unabashed sen-suality. Like Flaubert in *Salammbô* and Wilde in *Salomé,* Huysmans merges erotic imagery with a vaguely religious aura from the beginning, bathing the scene of Salomé's dance at once into a decadent sexual as well as spiritual light as she dances in a cathedral-like setting. Huysmans's text dwells deli-ciously on Salomé's transgressions and her splendid, albeit hysterical-patho-logical, seductive body; she becomes a true goddess of perversity. Salomé dances amid the clouds of incense and bathed in light in the "overheated at-mosphere of the basilica" while Herod watches from a "throne like the high altar of a cathedral," "frozen like some Hindu god in a hieratic pose" (*Against Nature* 63–64). The mental image of her seductive, sweating body merges with the room and the precious jewels she wears on her skin: she "slowly glides forward on the points of her toes" to begin her "lascivious dance," with hardened nipples and seductively "moist flesh . . . ablaze with little snakes of fire" from the glittering jewels whose multicolored reflections "swarm[] over the mat flesh, over the tea rose skin," like "gorgeous insects" (64). The jewel-insects suggest Salomé's inhuman traits, her body being one with the strange forces she seems to command at will, like a goddess. The narrator stresses the autoeroticism and trancelike isolation of this iconic mo-ment, with Salomé in a "disquieting delirium," dancing "[w]ith a withdrawn, solemn, almost August expression on her face," as if "lost in a mysterious ec-stasy far off in the mists of time." Her "eyes fixed in the concentrated gaze of a sleepwalker" (64), she is encapsulated in her trance.

Huysmans portrays Salomé's ecstasy with some recourse to the popular medical-cultural discourses of the time, especially hysteria. He links her erotic and spiritual intensity with the typically fin de siècle interest in mental and physical pathology, "the maddening charm and the potent depravity of the dancer" (65). In Huysmans's text, Salomé takes on a withdrawn, swooning, somnambulist quality that suggests hysteria, the mental disease that became a focal point in the fin de siècle cultural worship of pathological mental and physical conditions.[19] Hysteria functions as a discourse of physical otherness that is worshiped as a form of ecstasy or madness, a spiritual as well as physical, perverse experience.[20] As Ellis Hanson has shown, Huysmans was intensely interested and knowledgeable in the scientific beliefs and practices surrounding the study of hysteria in his time, including Charcot's famous medical experiments at the Salpêtrière. The medical literature of hysteria often linked the phenomenon of the medieval mystics' ecstasy to hysteria, so it is not surprising to see Huysmans combining pathological with religious imagery in the Salomé passages.[21] In Huysmans's time, "[t]he religious and the psychological discourses existed side by side in highly politicized opposition, and Huysmans appropriated elements of both in defining his own decadent aesthetic, . . . celebrat[ing] the distinctly *fin de siècle* conjunction of the mystic and the neurotic" (Hanson 109). The intense out-of-body experiences supposedly experienced by the hysteric or neurotic were believed to lead to quasi-religious, spiritual revelations otherwise inaccessible to the rational or healthy mind. Hence Des Esseintes believes in *À rebours* that only a neurotic mind like his is attuned to a figure like Salomé: he is convinced that this paradoxical female idol is unfitted to ordinary sensibilities and instead is "accessible only to brains shaken and sharpened and rendered almost clairvoyant by neurosis" (*Against Nature* 65). Des Esseintes is portrayed as a classic male hysteric who fetishizes Moreau's Salomé as the "Goddess of Hysteria," a kindred spirit, larger than life, the epitome of physical-mental excess and ecstasy. In her, he literally personifies and idolizes the disease that has taken over his own body and brain. Her glorified trance models the quasi-metaphysical rapture for which Des Esseintes longs so keenly.

Des Esseintes's desire for such ecstatic experience of the metaphysical is not about religious transport or contemplation of the divine love, however; it is purely aesthetic. Moreau's Salomés, despite their biblical connections, do not appeal to him on a religious level. Des Esseintes is not a believer; in fact, his earlier strong affection for religious ritual (the wonderful pomp and circumstance of Catholicism observed during his Jesuit schooling as a boy) has morphed into a preference for the decorative aspects of religion only—

its secular artificial, eccentric, and decadent sensualism.[22] In fact, Huysmans writes, Des Esseintes's "penchant for artificiality and his love of eccentricity" signify his "ardent aspirations" toward an aesthetic ideal equivalent to the religious one, presenting his striving "towards an unknown universe, towards a distant beatitude, as utterly desirable as that promised by the Scriptures" (88–89). In Huysmans's presentation of Salomé in particular, we can observe a tendency, later fully unfolded by Wilde, to elevate the aesthetic and erotic to the level of religion or religious experience, preparing the way for Wilde's focus on aesthetic and erotic transgression as a new form of sublimity.

Des Esseintes's aesthetic desires vaguely cite yet entirely transform metaphysical experience into tangible physical ecstasy; he only invokes the aura of the sacred but does not adore the sacred itself any longer. In chapter 5, Moreau's Salomés create a state of mind for Des Esseintes in which he can experience himself wholly at one with his imagined ideal and leave his real, diseased, pathological, decadent body behind. Moreau's hypersexed Salomés appeal to Des Esseintes not in the typical pornographic sense, as an exciting visual-erotic stimulus, but for their transgressive sensual qualities, their ability to incite physical ecstasy in him that can mimic, if not replace, the lost connection to the divine. Ironically, Des Esseintes's sexual taste for real women has already abated at this point ("[o]ne passion and one only—woman—might have arrested the universal contempt that was taking hold of him, but that passion like the rest had been exhausted" [22]). It has been replaced with his desire for artificial, abstract feminine sexuality, such as Salomé's, or the two locomotives' "bodies" in an earlier chapter.[23] Ironically, Des Esseintes's periods of sexual impotence become another metaphor for his loss of religious faith; both sexual orgasm and religious ecstasy are replaced with aesthetic sensationalism.

In Huysmans's text, a complex picture emerges of Salomé as an invincible, terrible, gorgeous female idol who is also a vulnerable, terrified human being; a strong, sacred goddess and a weak human harlot; a cruel destroyer and guileless woman. In their astonishing oscillation between pathological perversity and human vulnerability, the Salomé passages in *À rebours* model another essential quality of Wilde's conception of Salomé, the intertwinement of horror with empathy and of danger or tragedy with satisfaction. Des Esseintes adores Moreau's Salomé like a powerful perverse deity. In her ornamented nakedness, her artificial and symbolic poses in these paintings, Salomé appears both infinitely, remotely sublime, and horrifically human and vulnerable, a mixture we find in Wilde and later in Georges Bataille as well. In his description of *L'Apparition,* Huysmans emphasizes Salomé's vulnerability and fear as she is faced with a frightening vision of the severed, bloody head of John the Baptist that seems to haunt and attack her.

> With a gesture of horror, Salome tries to thrust away the terrifying vision which holds her nailed to the spot, balanced on the tips of her toes, her eyes dilated, her right hand clawing convulsively at her throat. . . . In the unfeeling and unpitying statue, in the innocent and deadly idol, the lusts and fears of common humanity had been awakened; the great lotus-blossom had disappeared, the goddess vanished; a hideous nightmare now held in its choking grip an entertainer, intoxicated by the whirling movement of the dance, a courtesan, petrified and hypnotized by terror. (67–68)

To Des Esseintes, this Salomé is "less majestic, less haughty, but more seductive" than the first, because of the apparent humanity underneath her invincible, gorgeous exterior and perhaps also because, as an "entertainer," "courtesan," and "true harlot," she is more easily consumable and possessable to the male onlooker: "Here she was a true harlot, obedient to her passionate and cruel female temperament; here she came to life, more refined yet more savage, more hateful yet more exquisite than before; here she roused the sleeping senses of the male more powerfully, subjugated his will more surely with her charms—the charms of a great venereal flower, grown in a bed of sacrilege, reared in a hot-house of impiety" (68).

Not only does Huysmans prepare the way for Wilde's outrageously decadent, vampiric, necrophilic finale by making his Salome figure the iconic, seductive fin de siècle femme fatale, but he also introduces as her foil a quintessentially weak, pathetic, dependent male counterpart who lusts after her. Des Esseintes can be seen as an important model for Wilde's superstitious, insecure, deeply unhappy Herod, who, like Des Esseintes, is constantly on the lookout for something or someone else who could give him a stronger sense of self. There are several obvious parallels between the weakly aristocrat and the confused, insecure, vulnerable ruler of Judea, but the most important of these is each male's overwhelming wish to unite himself (physically and mentally) with Salomé, to become happy and whole by the proxy of her alluring femininity and independence. In fact, Des Esseintes and Herod willingly seek to *subjugate* themselves to Salomé's overpowering sensual femininity, her irresistible power and awe-inspiring independence; they wish not to be healed or changed by her but, instead, to drown themselves in her hypersensuality and quasi-divine being, as if in a powerful flood that can wash away all their unfulfilled desires and existential doubts. Each male protagonist seeks in Salomé ultimate forgetfulness, longing to merge completely with a supreme power that effectively erases him, leaving behind only ecstatic sensation and relief of rational thought and action.

Similar to Des Esseintes's escape into decadent consumerism in an attempt to drown out his own physical decay and mental and emotional dissatisfaction, Wilde's Herod is a restless, insecure, and deeply unhappy character driven by superstitious fears and visions (e.g., the beating of wings of the Angel of Death—a black bird—or having slipped in Narraboth's blood); he constantly tries to divert himself through wine, entertainment, and, most important, his erotic and (by Mosaic law) incestuous obsession with his stepdaughter Salomé. Herod is not in control, either of himself or of the complicated political and religious world around him. Where Flaubert's Herod in "Hérodias" engages in a visceral mental and emotional battle with Salomé and loses against his will, Wilde's Herod is completely enslaved to Salomé's awesome sexual and political power; he stands no chance against her. As Jean-Paul Riquelme puts it, Wilde's Salomé not only usurps and completely reverses the power of the male gaze at her but "turn[s] the tables on Herod by putting permanently out of his purview what he wants most. . . . As a matter of power relations, that resistance is political. . . . Because of Salomé, Herod is effectively already as dead as Jokanaan" (602). Like Des Esseintes, Herod—not Salomé—is the truly tragic character in Wilde's play. He embodies the ultimately impossible quest for the divine in an already fallen, abandoned world in which only human senses reign and only extraordinary, ruthless beings, such as Salomé, can revel in their Paterian moment of fulfillment.

Humanizing this essentially modernist crisis of faith, Huysmans inscribes empathy for the human condition into Moreau's Salome figures as well as into Des Esseintes's character, linking them to his earlier portrayal of Moreau's work as daringly modern, deeply haunted by the existential crisis of being. All of Huysmans's novels (before and after his 1892 conversion to Catholicism) "are ultimately about the failure of faith in a modern context" (Hanson 167). For Des Esseintes, the defining and attractive quality of Moreau's two Salomé pictures is precisely that it feels to him thoroughly secular and modern, not anchored in the gospels. His work features "the morbid perspicuity of an entirely modern sensibility"; Gustave Moreau "remain[s] downcast and sorrowful, haunted by the symbols of superhuman debaucheries and superhuman perversities, of divine debauches perpetrated without enthusiasm and without hope" (*Against Nature* 69).

Huysmans's novel seems as delicately perched on the edge of a fatal abyss as is the stylized, divided world Wilde creates in *Salomé*. Even though, at the end of the novel, Des Esseintes makes a final attempt to combat his existential despair by converting to Catholicism, so that *À rebours* effectively becomes a conversion narrative, this heavily ironized ending provides no true relief or salvation. In contrast to the *Bildungsroman* tradition, the novel's narrative drive toward self-created aesthetic paradises of the senses is always already undermined by Des Esseintes's continuing restlessness and disappointment, his never-ending search for the ultimate experience. Hence Des Esseintes's fate ultimately carries tragic overtones. As he moves from anticipation and hope for new thrills and stimulations to despondency, from one fragment of experience to the next, there is, in effect, no change of self. In fact, despite Des Esseintes's titanic efforts to stem the tide of the petit bourgeois style and taste, there is no rescue from the infusion of the ordinary in his life; it is always present. It comes as no surprise that Des Esseintes's project in *À rebours* is ultimately frustrated, that he is forced to return to the conventional world in the end. This ironic anticlimax of the novel marks it as a distinctly modern text, in that the hero himself abandons his commitment to individuation in the end: "Well, it is all over now. Like a tide-race, the waves of human mediocrity are rising to the heavens and will engulf this refuge, for I am opening the flood-gates myself, against my will" (219–20).

Huysmans ironically abandons his hero to normalization and mediocrity, but he does not seem to let him go without regret. Des Esseintes very unwillingly gives up his "ardent aspirations towards an ideal, towards an unknown universe, towards a distant beatitude" (89). In the final prayer with which the novel closes, Des Esseintes implores the Lord to take pity on him: "Ah! but my courage fails me, and my heart is sick within me!—Lord, take pity on the Christian who doubts, on the unbeliever who would fain believe, on the galley-slave of life who puts out to sea alone, in the night, beneath a firmament no longer lit by the consoling beacon-fires of ancient hope!" (220). Hanson writes,

> The final passionate prayer of *A Rebours* is by no means a resolution to Des Esseintes's oscillations. It is, rather, an inconclusive repetition in a circular narrative that rearticulates over and over the same eccentric sensibility in different words, through flowers and perfumes and fragrant books, in chapters that are virtually interchangeable. For an embrace of the faith, the prayer is oddly desperate and hopeless: . . . less a conclusion to *A Rebours* than a final repetition, we might even say a hysterical repetition, an outburst, of the same improbable longing after faith. (133–34)

With this, the novel reveals Des Esseintes's dreams of Salomé and the elaborate seductions through her image before his mind as a shallow hope, a utopian failure. Unable to forget his own role in creating his aesthetic object and his own vested interest in the female body, Des Esseintes cannot transport himself beyond himself, and the intoxicating potion of Moreau's Salomés does not lend such permanent forgetfulness. Like Mallarmé's Hérodiade, he remains suspended between his high aesthetic ideal and a banal material reality, circling obsessively around his desires without ever being able to satisfy them. Des Esseintes seeks happiness in what he has assembled, but still he is never able to fully enjoy the moment of consuming the fruits of his own, furiously active imagination. This tension implicates Huysmans's decadent novel in the project of skeptical modernist individualism. Des Esseintes's modernist gesture of investing Salomé's body and female sexuality in general with the aesthetics of sublimity is ultimately frustrated and ironized in *À rebours*.

Yet *À rebours* does more than simply add another flagship figure to the misogynistic gallery of fin de siècle femmes fatales. The novel effectively transforms Moreau's Salomés into an artistic and literary *mysterium tremens et fascinosum,* a mystical puzzle that inspires both horror and fascination, powerfully seducing Des Esseintes and the reader along with him. Starting with Huysmans's influential description of Moreau's Salomés, which was unfolded fully in Oscar Wilde's play (and, shortly thereafter, in Richard Strauss's opera), the Salome figure came to signify a courageous, amazing, godlike being who leaps forward into the unthinkable and unknown in striking and shocking new ways, extending and stretching her humanity to unheard-of, fantastical, and frightening new realms. Refusing to be bound by habitual norms and limits, Wilde's Salomé asserts self-confidence and independence; she models a fundamental assertion of the fully secular individual subject against a deadening, imprisoning sense of loneliness, stasis, and death in a universe without any transcendental direction or meaning. For all its transgressive, blasphemous, shocking daring, Wilde's play is a thoroughly utopian modernist text.

Salomé's Modern Apotheosis: Wilde, Pater, Nietzsche

Mallarmé's, Flaubert's, and Huysmans's texts already pointed toward the emerging metaphysical and aesthetic crises that Wilde's play emphasizes. Hérodiade's isolation and hymenic split in Mallarmé, Flaubert's yearning priestess Salammbô and ecstatically mourning Salomé, and Des Esseintes's fascination with the perverse goddess-woman in Huysmans all suggest an acute struggle for the unity of the self with an ideal other, for wholeness, and for agency. All three authors also shrouded their subjects in sensual aesthetic styles, aching to counteract this sense of crisis—Mallarmé through beautiful, abstract, poetic symbolist language; Flaubert by enveloping his Salammbô and Salomé in mythical, orientalist dances, prayers, and sexual imagery; Huysmans by piling up imaginative and linguistic ornaments and sensual fantasies through decadent language designed to capture and overwhelm the senses. Offering different poetic takes on achieving self-forgetfulness and aesthetic sublimity in the face of ontological and epistemological exigency, none of these writers and texts presents Herodias/Hérodiade/Salomé as a positive or hopeful figure. Compared with Mallarmé's struggling, aloof Hérodiade, Flaubert's pining Salammbô and childish Salomé, or Huysmans's pathological idol of perversity, Wilde's portrayal of Salomé in his play is distinctly more utopian and individualist.

Nowhere is Wilde's difference from his predecessors more obvious than in the play's infamous last scenes, in which a lawless Salomé kisses the severed head of Jokanaan before she dies an ecstatic *Liebestod*. In his ending, Wilde effectively transforms her into an unforgettable modern icon of transgression, extreme aesthetic affect, and erotic excess. In the iconic last scene, Salomé addresses, caresses, and kisses the bloody head of John the Baptist while symbolically bathed in radiant moonlight ("A moonbeam falls on Salomé, covering her with light" [*CCW* 605]). As a dramatic text, *Salomé* charts the trajectory of its heroine's two burning desires, erotic and aesthetic (Salomé's longing to kiss Jokanaan's mouth and her thirst for ideal beauty), up to the shocking climax in which these desires merge ecstatically, spectacularly, in a moment of erotic and aesthetic ecstasy and sublimity. Here Wilde grants his heroine a prolonged moment in the spotlight as she savors the taste of her prey and mourns her loss, a perverse atonement of erotic bliss paradoxically lined with love, vengeance, and tragedy. The scene attests to Salomé's genuine passion and invites sympathy: Salomé has murdered the man she loves, because there is no other way to conquer and subdue him after he has awakened her passion but rejected her: "Thou wouldst have none of me, Jokanaan. Thou didst reject me. Thou didst speak evil words against me. Thou didst treat me as a harlot, as a wanton, me, Salome, daughter of Herodias, Princess of Judaea! . . . I was a princess, and thou didst scorn me. . . . I was chaste, and thou didst fill my veins with fire" (604). Unlike the eternally isolated Hérodiade, or Salammbô, who never gets to see or touch her beloved moon goddess Tanit, Wilde's Salomé is al-

lowed to relish and ravish the object of her desires in the final moments of
the play. Salomé's decadent kiss and her death in her moment of triumph
are sure to linger on in the audience's mind even as the disgusted Herod
suddenly orders her execution (605).

It is worth recalling in this context that none of the major nineteenth-
century Salome versions prior to Wilde's included such a decadent tête-à-
tête during which Salome earnestly addressed and then amorously possessed the severed head. Heinrich Heine and Jules Laforgue previously
showed the figures of Herodias or Salome playing with the object, but neither of their heroines truly posed a threat to the moral order: in Heine's
"Atta Troll: A Midsummer Night's Dream," Herodias is a damned and mad
figure of the Wild Chase, and Laforgue's "Salomé" ironizes the princess to
the point of utter absurdity.[24] Wilde, by contrast, provides a prolonged dramatic effusion of Salomé's supreme bliss mixed with grief. She remains a
strangely attractive figure at the end, putting forth, in this moment of perverse tenderness, an unsettling vision of self-fulfillment and personal triumph. Her last words indicate that she has attained what she wanted and is
satisfied: "They say that love hath a bitter taste. . . . But what matter? What
matter? I have kissed thy mouth, Jokanaan" (*CCW* 605).

Salomé's final monologue embodies aestheticism's most important
tenet—the idea of putting one's whole being into the ecstasy of one perfect,
if fleeting, moment—which Walter Pater, father of English aestheticism and
Wilde's teacher in Oxford, enshrined in his famous conclusion to *Studies in
the History of the Renaissance:* "[t]o burn always with this hard, gem-like
flame, to maintain this ecstasy, is success in life. With this sense of the splendour of our experience and of its awful brevity, gathering all we are into one
desperate effort to see and touch, we shall hardly have time to make theories
about the things we see and touch" (Pater 152). For Pater and the aesthetic
tradition that followed, sensory fulfillment, not moral utilitarianism, was the
primary goal of art: "Not the fruit of experience, but experience itself is the
end" (ibid.). The ecstasy of the fully lived and felt moment is inextricably
connected to a looming sense of impending loss and death, however: sensual impressions are "in perpetual flight," and "each of them is limited by
time," with "all that is actual in it being a single moment, gone while we try
to apprehend it" (151); "we have an interval, and then our place knows us
no more" (153). Pater urges us to concentrate on "expanding that interval, in
getting as many pulsations as possible into the given time" (ibid.), intensify-
ing sensation and experience to the utmost degree.

Salomé's outrageous triumph suggests that unlike in Mallarmé's,
Flaubert's, Huysmans's, or Laforgue's versions, it is possible for the aesthetic

self to achieve blissful ecstasy not despite but because of erotic and aethetic transgression and death. This notion was at the heart of Wilde's aesthetic individualism, Jonathan Dollimore writes: "Wilde's notion of individualism is inseparable from transgressive desire and a transgressive aesthetic" (8). In keeping with Pater's and Wilde's program of aesthetic individualism, the final scene brings Salomé's defiance of traditional moral or religious goodness to fruition. Salomé's yearning for Jokanaan transforms metaphysical and moral ardor into mere physicality. In Salomé's deadly pursuit of Jokanaan's beauty, Wilde effectively reconfigures and secularizes the Enlightenment and Romantic traditions of the sublime that identify ideal beauty with the morally good. Provocatively reversing the teachings of another of his teachers at Oxford, John Ruskin, and those of Matthew Arnold, Wilde treats beauty as aesthetic surface, devoid of moral or religious depth. As in Pater's conclusion, the sublimity Wilde's Salomé achieves is a secular one, wholly come by through erotic and aesthetic transgression. Because she dares to transgress and seize what she wants (claiming the head of Jokanaan and finally kissing his mouth), Salomé can ultimately be at one with herself, freely inhabiting and claiming her ideal. Whereas Mallarmé's Hérodiade was haunted, objectified, and isolated, Wilde's Salomé asserts her independence and individual will. She turns herself from a passive object of desire into an active subject, successfully manipulating the mental, emotional, material, and political forces around her to her advantage.

Arranging for Salomé a spectacular execution center stage at her most intense moment of triumph and then immediately closing the curtain on her lifeless body, Wilde grants her the glamorous death of a heroine rather than that of a despised villain. I disagree with critics who interpret Salomé's execution as the just punishment of the femme fatale or as Wilde's indirect admission that aesthetic individualism was ultimately doomed (similar to Dorian's gruesome end in *The Picture of Dorian Gray*). Rather, I concur with Zagona that Salomé's thunderclap execution feels more like "the stroke of a dramatist than of a moralist"; it is "an appropriately crashing finish not intended to teach a lesson but shock and bewilder the audience" (128–29). Wilde lets Salomé die at the absolute height of her ecstasy, at the moment of her highest triumph that no earthly experience could match afterward, which is dramatically necessary and logical at this point. In *Salomé* as well as in his critical essay "The Soul of Man under Socialism" (also written in 1891), Wilde suggests that the philosophy and practice of individualism is a utopian goal that can be only approximated but not fully inhabited in modernity.

Critics who interpret Salomé's execution as the stereotypical death of the femme fatale and the restoration of order tend to underestimate the cloud of unease and fatality hovering over Wilde's finale. Unlike typical femme fatale stories ending with the defeat of the female evildoer and providing satisfying resurrections of human mastery over an otherwise uncontrollable and angst-inducing modern fate,[25] *Salomé* does not offer a reassuring reordering of the moral universe and restored sense of safety and comfort. The end remains unsettlingly sudden, ambiguous, and open. The abrupt royal execution—just three words ("Kill that woman!") and a stage direction, "The soldiers rush forward and crush beneath their shields Salomé, daughter of Herodias, Princess of Judaea" (*CCW* 605)—exacerbates, rather than solves, the question: does Salomé lose, or does she triumph? Where Flaubert ends his version with a hopeful religious outlook forecasting the rise of Jesus, while Huysmans provides Des Esseintes with an ironic conversion to Catholicism and sensual quietism, Wilde ominously stops with symbolic darkness and silence after Salomé's sudden and swift execution. The moon and stars are hid by a great cloud, the torches are put out, and Herod orders Herodias and the rest of the court inside with the words, "Let us hide ourselves, Herodias. . . . I begin to be afraid" (605).

Salomé thus purposefully stops short of making sense of its own ending and leaves audiences with an unsettling sense of shock and wonder. There is no triumph or sense of relief provided by this finish. After Salomé's transgressive torrent of violence and eroticism, it is not a satisfactory resolution to the existential questions raised by the play. *Salomé* has a dark, unsettling, and apocalyptic quality at the same time as it establishes the utopian idea of individual transgression as a way out of a fragmented, bleak universe without order or transcendental meaning. In place of a venerated God and his prophet, Wilde installs Salomé's ecstatic human body on a blasphemous, violent, ecstatic theatrical throne.

Despite the biblical subject, Wilde's play does not suggest any metaphysical authority that might intervene or adjudicate with finalizing resolve. Throughout the play, there is no genuine quest for a religious absolute; on the contrary, the one figure in the play who constantly urges it, John the Baptist, is superstitiously misunderstood (by Herod), despised (by Herodias), and outrageously violated (by Salomé). The paradoxical irrelevance, idiosyncrasy, and impotence of Christ's precursor do not make him a sympathetic figure; religious proselytism was clearly not the author's goal. Not only does Salomé disrespect the religious taboo the prophet presents, but she completely recasts his being as erotic and aesthetic rather than spiritual and holy. Not only does her sensual interest in a prophet have blasphemous overtones, but her merely erotic savoring of his body insults his earnest spiritual intent. In Wilde's final monologue, Salomé even challenges Jokanaan's choice of seeing and loving only God instead of her: "Well, thou hast seen thy God, Jokanaan, but me, me, thou didst never see. If thou hadst seen me thou wouldst have loved me" (*CCW* 604). Salomé has not only killed the prophet but insulted and reinterpreted everything he stands for. What better allegory for the programmatic displacement of God in modernity than the story of a female protagonist for whom a religious prophet's spiritual dimension simply adds to his erotic and aesthetic attractiveness?

With its blasphemous violence and glaring lack of religious faith, Wilde's play indirectly echoes Friedrich Nietzsche's proclamation of the death of God in modernity, introduced for the first time just about a decade earlier in Nietzsche's *The Gay Science* (1882). There is no proof of a direct influence of Friedrich Nietzsche's idea of the death of God on Wilde (Nietzsche was also not widely read in England at the time, as Oscar Levy lamented as late as 1909), but general affinities of ideas and themes between Nietzsche's and Wilde's work have long been noted.[26] In Nietzsche's *The Gay Science*, a visionary madman establishes the momentous nature of this killing of God, portraying it as a daring deed with unforeseen consequences.

> What was holiest and mightiest of all that the world has yet owned has bled to death under our knives: who will wipe this blood off us? What water is there for us to clean ourselves? What festivals of atonement, what sacred games shall we have to invent? Is not the greatness of this deed too great for us? Must we ourselves not become gods simply to appear worthy of it? There has never been a greater deed; and whoever is born after us— for the sake of this deed he will belong to a higher history than all history hitherto. (181)

Similarly, in *Salomé,* the killing of the prophet and his erotic-aesthetic consumption is portrayed as an extraordinary, superhuman, even inhuman deed that exceeds all moral and religious boundaries. Wilde's Herod, always fearful of divine wrath, finds Salomé "altogether monstrous"; he is convinced that "what she has done is a great crime. I am sure that it was a crime against an unknown God" (*CCW* 604).

Indeed, Salomé looks like a conceptual sister to Nietzsche's free spirits of the future (in *Human, All Too Human*) and to his *Übermensch*, a transgressive, postreligious figure Nietzsche ties to the death of God in *Also Sprach Zarathustra.*[27] Nietzsche's *Übermensch* scorns the old codes that must be overcome, including conventional morality and religion. He (or she, since *der Mensch* is a gender-neutral concept in German) is a visionary who acts not out of nihilism or despair at the world but with self-affirming purpose, creating new, controversial, entirely secular values. Similarly, Nietzsche's free spirits scorn human or divine law and radically remake themselves in their own image and to their own liking only, while willfully violating the laws and beliefs of the powers that be. As Nietzsche writes in the preface to *Human, All Too Human,* they are self-reliant, rebellious, and bold; they live dangerously and experiment with transgressive thoughts and deeds as they follow a strong inner calling. Nietzsche's utopian, postreligious beings have freed themselves of metaphysical and moral ballast, openly embracing the earth instead of the heavens as the site of final meaning and happiness. For Nietzsche, they modeled a way out of Enlightenment philosophy's failure to completely free humankind from conventional belief systems and codes, especially religious ones that falsely promised meaning and freedom but only imprisoned humans in their own ignorance, like Plato's prisoners in the cave.

Like Nietzsche and Pater, Wilde captures, in *Salomé,* a symbolic turning point away from religion and toward a modernist amoral anthropocentrism. Salomé celebrates and relishes the body, not the soul, turning full attention to the physical, sensual, aesthetic, and erotic world, rather than to the metaphysical sphere. In presenting an individual wholly devoid of spiritual longing yet full of erotic and aesthetic desire, half-mad in her passionate pursuit of beauty, Wilde establishes a utopian opening for human agency as he redirects Salomé's energy from religion (ironized by a prophet whom Wilde represents as a phrase-mongering, ineffective madman) to the search for physical and aesthetic ecstasy. It is a new, daring, anarchic beginning, just as it was for Nietzsche, who insisted that the death of God was ultimately a positive and hopeful relief ridding humankind of a dangerous liability. According to Nietzsche, the prospects of a world without God were

> not all sad and gloomy but rather like a new and scarcely describable kind of light, happiness, relief, exhilaration, encouragement, dawn. Indeed, we philosophers and "free spirits" feel, when we hear the news that "the old god is dead," as if a new dawn shone on us; our heart overflows with gratitude, amazement, premonitions, expectation. At long last the horizon appears free to us again, even if it should not be bright; at long last our ships may venture out again, venture out to face any danger; all the daring of the lover of knowledge is permitted again; the sea, *our* sea, lies open again; perhaps there has never yet been such an "open sea." (*Gay Science* 280)

As a strong literary image of erotic and aesthetic excess and ecstasy, Wilde's play echoes and incorporates important tenets of Pater's radical aesthetic individualism and equates Nietzsche's antimetaphysical, transgressive moral philosophy. Salomé's individuation is achieved and celebrated in the full-ness of a perverse erotic encounter that echoes Pater's idea of the ecstatic moment, suggesting that there is, indeed, ecstasy after the death of God. It is be found in free spirits, like Salomé, who hurl their desires, courage, and defiance at their world in stunning excess and transgression and who experience individual satisfaction and secular ecstatic sublimity in the process.

Salomé and Bataille's *Madame Edwarda*

At the same time as it shows the influences of nineteenth-century literature and philosophy, *Salomé* already looks forward to later modernist thought. In particular, a conceptual line leads from Wilde's play to Georges Bataille's literature and philosophy in such works as *The Story of the Eye, My Mother, Epinone, Erotism,* and *Madame Edwarda.* Bataille proposes inextricable links between physical excess and sublimity, on the one hand, and outright horror, on the other, a conceptual connection that is crucial for Wilde's *Salomé* as well. The strange amalgam of erotic ecstasy, excess, and violence in Salomé's final moments—where her triumphant joy commingles with the horror of blood and a dead, severed head—is a hallmark of Wilde's bold, shocking transformation of Salome's age-old story.

For Bataille, the conceptual relation of ecstatic joy and horror was not paradoxical. In the preface to *Madame Edwarda* (a later addition to his philosophical and pornographic novella, which he published under the pseudonym Pierre Angélique in 1937), Bataille views ecstasy and horror as fundamentally alike in their effect on the subject. Since both are experiences of emotional excess and loss of control, they establish a similarly complete reign of affect over reason. Horror and ecstasy do not contradict but, rather, enhance each other.

> If we are to follow all the way through to its last the *ecstasy* in which we lose ourselves in love-play, we have got constantly to bear in mind what we set as ecstasy's immediate limit: horror. . . . [W]hen horror is unable to quell, to destroy the object that attracts, then horror *increases* the object's power to charm. . . . We do not attain *ecstasy* save when before the how-ever remote prospect of death, of that which destroys us. (Preface to *Madame Edwarda* 140)

The vision of physical-metaphysical transcendence that Bataille articulates is apocalyptic yet also inherently utopian. It is based on the mingling of excess, violence, and physical ecstasy, which allow for a new experience of sublimity. Excess (which Bataille defines in quasi-religious terms as "the marvelous, the miraculous") possesses an inherently utopian and visionary quality because it points toward the unknown; it "designates everything which is more than what is, than what exists" (145nl). Excess and ecstasy allow the self to leave the circle of "all circumscribing restrictions" (ibid.) in moments of intense sensuality, terrific yet often blissful, that can lead one to "rediscover God" (141).

> Our minds' operations . . . never reach their final culmination save in excess. What . . . does truth signify if we do not see that which exceeds sight's possibilities, that which it is unbearable to see as, in ecstasy, it is unbearable to know pleasure? what [sic], if we do not think that which exceeds thought's possibilities? At the further end of this pathetic meditation . . . we rediscover God. (ibid.)

Salomé's final monologue can be seen as excessive, horrendous, and sublime according to Bataille's sense in *Madame Edwarda* and other writings. Salomé conquers, masters, and, for a brief interlude, experiences her aesthetic and sexual fulfillment as she confronts the severed head; in its horror, it presents the most powerful of charms that catapults her into a state of ecstasy. Bataille encapsulates this connection in a few lines that read like a commentary on Salomé's daring, blasphemous final moments: "the unreservedly open spirit—open to death, to torment, to joy—, the open spirit, dying, suffering and dying and happy, stands in a certain veiled light: that light is divine. And the cry that breaks from a twisted mouth may perhaps twist him who utters it, but what he speaks is an immense *alleluia*, flung into endless silence, and lost there" (143).

Bataille's literary character Madame Edwarda bears an intriguing conceptual resemblance to Wilde's Salomé. *Madame Edwarda* is not a version of the Salome story itself, and we don't know if Georges Bataille ever read or saw Wilde's *Salomé* or attended a Paris performance of Richard Strauss's operatic adaptation. Nevertheless, Wilde's transgressive princess certainly seems right up Bataille's alley. Both writers put forward a vision of erotic transgression and physical obscenity as a kind of secular ecstasy, where physical suffering and horror are identical with the highest joy and hope possible. *Madame Edwarda* is a provocative revision of the relationship of the human body and soul to the divine spirit; it is a secular modernist transformation of the religious ecstasy of the Christian mystics. Even the title of the collection in which Bataille originally intended to publish *Madame Edwarda,* "Divinus Deus" (which remained incomplete at the time of Bataille's death), encapsulates the metaphysical metaphor at its heart.[28]

At first sight, *Madame Edwarda* is the banal story of a male narrator's visit to a brothel, but this visit quickly turns into a much more profound and unsettling mystical-philosophical encounter. Madame Edwarda, the bored but "ravishing" prostitute the narrator picks, unexpectedly reveals herself to him as "GOD" by showing him her gaping vagina, the "'old rag and ruin,' . . . hairy and pink, just as full of life as some loathsome squid" (*Madame Edwarda* 150). A riveting series of obscene sexual encounters between the drunk and deeply unhappy narrator and the beautiful, merciless, cruel Madame Edwarda follows. Images of burning physical desire, jealousy, disease, and despair commingle with nightmarish visions of metaphysical impossibility and epistemological uncertainty. Ecstatic orgasms, which resemble epileptic fits in their utter abandonment, let the narrator and Madame Edwarda forget momentarily that the skies above are empty, "mad and void" (152). Despite her awe-inspiring perversity and physical allure, however, Madame Edwarda is not omnipotent, nor does she offer satisfaction or refuge or salvation to the desperately infatuated narrator. Repulsive yet irresistible, Madame Edwarda sends the narrator in desperate pursuit of her into the night as she madly roams the streets outside, experiences epileptic fits along the way, and picks up random men with whom she has sex right in front of him. She reminds the narrator of "death-shrouds" as he pursues her through the deserted streets into the "black night hour of the being's core no less a desert nor less hostile than the empty skies" (154–55). He feels insecure and lost, "as though [he] were borne aloft in a flight of headless and unbodied angels shaped from the broad swooping of wings, . . . painfully forsaken, as one is when one is in the presence of GOD" (149), reminiscent of Herod's nightmarish visions in *Salomé*. Signifying the very "absence of meaning" (154), Bataille's goddess-whore is metaphysical denouement incarnate. Yet the very horror of her emptiness only increases the narrator's infatuation with her; he cannot let go.

Madame Edwarda's behavior and the narrator's alternation between exquisite joy and utter dejection recall a long series of cultural images of horny femmes fatales on the prowl, *vaginae dentatae* with their shark jaws wide open to devour their terrified and awed male victims. If there is a certain recognizable Eve-like or biblical quality to the figure of Madame Edwarda, however, it does not exhaust itself in the misogynistic cultural history the text inevitably evokes, just as Wilde's *Salomé* is not just another femme fatale text. As a blasphemous new testament to the powers of physical desire and the horror of finding that God is neither benevolent nor omnipotent, Bataille's story does not speak but shriek, ecstatically proclaiming the death of God into "the empty sky curved above us" (154). *Madame Ed-*

warda does not lend itself to rational analysis so much as it tries to engage the reader affectively, aesthetically—to draw the reader into its irrational universe of sexual excesses and desperate bodies. The text pours forth a visceral flood of images, words, and evocative silences, capturing, in Bataille's style as well as the subject matter, not only the fundamental ontological disorientation of modernity but also its anarchic freedom. Bataille understood from reading Nietzsche that man's awareness of the death of God still carries with it an "extreme, unconditional yearning," an irascible burning, an unquenchable thirst for the divine ("On Nietzsche" 331), comparable to Nietzsche's warning of God's persistent shadow in *The Gay Science* (book 3, section 108).

Wilde's play and Bataille's novella unabashedly attack the Judeo-Christian God and his attendant religious and moral authority. Both the play and the novella implicitly assume the pathetic powerlessness and irrelevance of a transcendent metaphysical force and unfold a literary modernist aesthetics of transgression instead. Specifically, they replace the male divinity with an unabashedly blasphemous, excessive spectacle of postmetaphysical, ecstatic femininity. Salomé's and Madame Edwarda's transgressions include shocking violence and pathology, a complete disregard for social or moral rules, and an irrational pursuit of physical pleasure and sensation. In their lawlessness and dangerous idiosyncrasy, Salomé and Madame Edwarda are disturbingly independent, idol-like figures, strange mixtures of goddess and woman, who mark the irrational, postmetaphysical turn to erotic transgression and excess as new sites for the sublime in modernity.

The aesthetic and philosophical forces at work in both *Salomé* and *Madame Edwarda* speak to the important paradigm shift from religious faith to erotic transgression that Michel Foucault has described for late nineteenth-century and twentieth-century modernity. In "A Preface to Transgression," which builds on and quotes Georges Bataille, Foucault outlines the larger cultural discursive movement toward and obsession with physical sensation, with sexuality and transgression as the ambiguous utopian replacements of metaphysical experience in modernity. After Nietzsche's proverbial death of God in modernity, the previously strong bonds between erotic, ecstatic language and the experience of divinity (which had still been omnipresent in the writings of the medieval Christian mystics) were severed. The language of sexuality and eroticism became a purely secular, physical affair. Foucault explains that desire, rapture, ecstasy were no longer seen as continuous and leading directly, "without interruption or limit, right to the heart of a divine love of which they were both the outpouring and the source returning upon itself." With the loss of the metaphysical referent, the language of sexuality was thus thrown "into an empty zone, where it point[ed] to nothing beyond itself, no prolongation, except the frenzy that disrupts it" (69). According to Foucault, the language of sexuality in modernity thus carries a heavy cultural burden, one that paradoxically reminds us of the painful absence of the divine in everyday life at the same time as it replaces it with intense experience of a different (physical) kind. Sexual transgression in particular becomes conceptually central as a replacement for religious ecstasy in Western cultural and philosophical modernity, as it allows the self to step outside of itself and experience a momentary suspension of its boundaries. Foucault argues that instead of embodying a connection, a passageway from the physical to the metaphysical, modern sexuality became a marker of the *loss* of metaphysical anchorage, "a fissure . . . that marks the limit within us and designates us as a limit," a threshold that arrests rather than enables the passage into a beyond (69–70).[29]

Foucault's figure of the threshold or fissure addresses a limit that can be neither overcome nor forgotten; transgression can provide a brief ecstatic limit experience, but it "does not transform the other side of the mirror, beyond an invisible and uncrossable line, into a glittering expanse" (74). Because sexuality designates the threshold, the limit, and the fissure as the last zones of subjective experience, it becomes so central to the experience of modernity. The modern subject craves the experience of the limit, as a mirror by which to assure itself of its own existence now that God is absent. Hence it tries to re-create and recompose the limit experience, which becomes the modern substitute for the sacred. In the absence of the metaphysical, the physical turns back upon itself, while still searching for the experience of the depth of the beyond by relaying it onto the surface of the body. The modern discourse of sexuality, Foucault asserts, "will say that [man] exists without God; . . . [T]he language of sexuality has lifted us into the night where God is absent, and where all of our actions are addressed to this absence in a profanation that at once identifies it, dissipates it, exhausts itself in it, and restores it to the empty purity of its transgression" (70). Sexual transgression, then, is a new kind of utopia, defined by Foucault as physical, limited, and aware of its postmetaphysical condition.

> [T]he interrogation of the limit replaces the search for totality, and the act of transgression replaces the movement of contradictions. . . . On the day that sexuality began to speak and to be spoken, language no longer served as a veil for the infinite; and in the density it acquired on that day, we now experience finitude and being. In its dark domain, we now encounter the absence of God, our death, limits, and their transgression. (85)

According to Foucault, in modernity, sexuality thus comes to replace God, and the sensational limit experience of physical excess is all that remains of the formerly religious experience of ecstasy, or the attempt to experience a being beyond (oneself). In Foucault's view, sexual transgression and excess mark "the moment in which being necessarily appears in its immediacy and in which *the act that crosses the limit touches absence itself*" (86). Figurations of sexual transgression become both a marker of the perceived *absence* of the divine and a way to express and recompose the experience of a rest experience of the divine aura through aesthetic means. In modern texts from Sade to Freud and beyond, the imagination of the violation of limits with or through the body (one's own or that of others) becomes, as Foucault explains, "the sole manner of discovering the sacred in its unmediated substance, but also a way of recomposing its empty form, its absence, through which it becomes all the more scintillating" (70).

Wilde's *Salomé* and Bataille's *Madame Edwarda* closely echo these concepts, conjuring up the tension, despair, and fascination inscribed in the original theological concept of the *mysterium tremens et fascinosum* through their excessive, perverse, idol-like heroines. We see Wilde and Bataille making similar investments in aesthetic figurations of female eroticism and excessive erotic consumerism as a substitute for the lost connection to the divine in modernity. The fantasy of the excessive and ecstatic coupling with the divine is acted out in their texts but already presented from a disillusioned, thoroughly modern perspective that accepts the death of God in favor of the life of erotic and aesthetic excess.

One important aspect of this literary-philosophical relationship has gone unmentioned so far: the obvious problematic relevance of Salomé's excessive, ecstatic, and perverse femininity for *feminist* modern literary and cultural criticism. I will turn to this perspective in detail in chapters 3 and 4, where I examine the paradoxical intersections between Salomé's misogynous history and her feminist potential in the work of two female modernists, dancer Maud Allan and film producer and Hollywood star Alla Nazimova. Let it be said in the general context of this chapter, though, that feminist interpretations add a crucial perspective to the analysis of Salomé as a cipher for the modernist aesthetics of transgression. Alice Jardine, for example, has unveiled the identification of sexual transgression with femininity as a distinctive feature of modernity and has analyzed transgressive figurations of Woman as central epistemological embodiments of that crisis: "In the search for new kinds of legitimation, in the absence of Truth, in anxiety over the decline of paternal authority, and in the midst of spiraling diagnoses of Paranoia, the End of Man and History, 'woman' has been set in motion both rhetorically and ideologically" (36). Salomé can be understood as a catalyst and symbol for a culture and literature in crisis—an elusive, oscillating figure that points toward an imagined utopian direction, a way out of the crisis of the modern subject and a diversion from the death of God.

In *Salomé,* Wilde offers a bold aesthetic and philosophical thought experiment that pushes modern individualism to the extreme, the emphatic and ecstatic assertion of a transgressive individual. In Salomé's final moments, Wilde conjures up a postmetaphysical, self-sufficient self able to satisfy her own needs recklessly and triumphantly by savoring her own aesthetic and erotic desires and consuming herself in her own pleasure, transforming a biblical story into a testament to modern individualism and erotic transgression. Sublimity becomes purely immanent and tied to physicality, experienced through erotic and aesthetic excess and transgression. Outside the self, there is no divine eternity to conquer, but through erotic and aesthetic transgression, the present is transformed into an ecstatic, excessive moment of fullness that more than makes up for eternity. Salomé lives an excessive, extreme, ruthless, and yet ultimately ecstatically satisfied individualism, willfully violating the laws of the secular as well as spiritual powers that be; beyond the heroine's death, however, neither God nor eternal Fate are waiting to redeem her ultimate violation of humanity. In this sense, Wilde conceives of his Salomé as a decidedly modern character. Later versions of the Salome theme seem to have been particularly drawn to this distinctly radical, shocking, individualist utopian quality of Wilde's Salomé figure. Upon her, they build their own visions of the nexus of eroticism, aesthetics, and transgression in modernity.

2

"The Brutal Music and the Delicate Text"? Richard Strauss's Operatic Modernism in *Salome*

In October 1905, two months before the astounding premiere of his *Salome*, Richard Strauss received an enthusiastic letter from friend and peer composer Gustav Mahler, who had just reviewed the completed score.

> I absolutely must tell you of the overwhelming impression your work made on me when I recently read through it! . . . Every note hits its mark! As I have known for a long time, you are a born dramatist! I admit that through your music you have made me understand for the first time what Wilde's play is all about. (Quoted in Grasberger, *Der Strom der Töne trug mich fort* [henceforth cited as *ST*] 163–64)[1]

That Strauss's operatic adaptation "made [Mahler] understand" Oscar Wilde's original "for the first time" may come as a surprise to many scholars today. The familiar view of Strauss's music drama, established through decades of scholarship and commentary, is that his revolutionary modernist score, with its spectacular orchestral effects and jarring bitonality, fails as an artistically sensitive adaptation of Wilde's 1891 symbolist-decadent tragedy (available to Strauss in Hedwig Lachmann's German translation as well as in the original). Rather than transpose the play's airy, evocative, and subtle poesy to appropriately gentle and suggestive harmony, many critics have argued, Strauss fiercely appropriated and subjected Wilde's play to his own purposes, effectively erasing Wilde's original in the process. The perceived aesthetic abyss between the poetic language and the modernist music has particularly interested literary and cultural comparatists, for whom the opposition between "the brutal music and the delicate text" (Hutcheon and Hutcheon 209) or between the "direct, brutal, and modern" score and the "dark allure" of the more "impressionist" fin de siècle play (Schmidgall *Literature as Opera* 286, 266) often symbolizes the different directions of the operatic and the theatrical stages at the turn of the century. Despite different approaches and degrees of interest in the Wilde-Strauss relationship, literary critics and musicologists have shared the sense that the modernist music and the symbolist-decadent text do not go together, judging Strauss's work to be a clear antithesis to Wilde's.

This view seems based not only on the obvious difference of genre but also, importantly, on assumed disparities between the symbolist-decadent aesthetic, on the one hand, and modernism as a budding new cultural-artistic era with distinctive concerns, on the other. Wilde's *Salomé* features a typically symbolist theatrical style and language characterized by synesthesia, evocation, and verbal repetition (similar not only to Mallarmé's "Hérodiade" but also to Maurice Maeterlinck's 1889 symbolist play *La princesse Maleine*), paired with blatantly decadent subject matter and gender politics. *Salomé* also hints at the pervasive sense of an ending accompanying the nineteenth century's close, with its prominent themes of ennui and immorality in a corrupt world, Herod's decadent and divided court. By contrast, Strauss's achievement in *Salome* has generally been seen not as an end but as a revolutionary beginning, reinventing Wagnerian music drama with its dazzling orchestral technique and stunning bitonal harmonies.

While musicological studies of Strauss's opera abound, most musicologists have not concerned themselves with the aesthetic relationship between the music and Wilde's text. They have tended to restrict their analyses to the changes Strauss made to his libretto source, pinpointing the excision of certain passages and some marginal dramatis personae, as well as discussing the anti-Semitic quintet of the Jews and Strauss's innovative interpretation of Wilde's leitmotifs. Yet John Williamson notes that the "critical appraisal of [Strauss's] *Salome* has yet to reconcile the restless, innovative and often brutal technical triumph of the music with the aesthetic roots of the subject," *Salome's* symbolist-decadent genealogy (143–44). Indeed, more than one hundred years after Strauss sat down to compose the first bars of *Salome,* the fundamental question remains unresolved: why did he pair *this* text with *this* music?

Conversely, literary critics have not yet systematically examined the important forward connections of Wilde's *Salomé* to some of Strauss's modernist ideas or techniques.[2] Although modernist studies has started to recognize and scrutinize the modernist elements of Wilde's work, even the most recent scholarship still presents *Salomé* as a composite bricolage of 1890s symbolist and decadent aesthetics rather than a budding modernist aesthetics (see my introduction). In the present chapter, I suggest that, contrary to the established perception that Strauss's modernism is very different from Wilde's symbolism and decadence, the composer and the author have important formal stylistic and thematic elements in common. First, I attempt to identify clearly and analyze these elements to develop a new account of the two works' relationship. Second, I recast the literary-historical relationship between the two movements that the play and the opera are often taken to stand for, symbolism-decadence and modernism. In the fluid period of the works' composition, these movements respond in tandem to the metaphysical crisis of modernity in which the various writers examined in chapter 1 also participated. The common roots of Wilde's and Strauss's Salome versions can be found in the developing modernist aesthetics of transgression. This aesthetics is expressed in both the play and the opera despite their seeming difference, and the overall goals and effects of each work are fundamentally the same.

In approaching these concerns, I delve into the rich trove of contemporary reactions to Wilde's play and Strauss's opera in Germany and Austria from 1905 to 1907. Some of these appraisals I translate here for the first time and thus hope to make more readily available to Anglo-American scholarship. In particular, I draw extensively on two German collections of contemporary letters and reviews concerning the opera's Dresden premiere in 1905—one edited by Franz Grasberger (*ST*), the other Franzpeter Messmer's *Kritiken zu den Uraufführungen der Bühnenwerke von Richard Strauss* (henceforth cited as *KUB*)—and on Leon Botstein's compilation of feuilleton pieces about the opera's first Vienna production in Bryan Gilliam's *Richard Strauss and His World* (henceforth cited as *RSHW*), as well as on W. Eugene Davis's essay and bibliography on the play's reception in the early twentieth-century German press. Although some have occasionally been cited, the contemporary reviews have not received the scholarly attention they deserve. They yield fresh clues about the essential compatibility between Wilde's and Strauss's projects at a time when the relationship between the symbolist-decadent and modernist aesthetic was very much in flux. The stylistic and thematic similarities that escaped late twentieth-century scholars were often discussed by Wilde's and Strauss's contemporaries, which suggests that the transitions between literary-cultural periods are often more complex than we may care to acknowledge.

While historical readers' reactions become part of the cultural story of any work of art, they also constitute a doubly interesting, if fraught, agency in the case of a work such as *Salome,* which is itself a reading and an interpretation of another's work that critics viewed through the lens not only of

Wilde's earlier piece but also, to some extent, of his life. This is where the artistic and erotic dimensions of the modernist aesthetics of transgression first meet the cultural reception of Wilde's scandalous 1895 trials, which influenced almost all subsequent adaptations and many stage productions of both the play and the opera. The unusual avant-garde style and provocative subject matter of both works were immediately read as artistic masks and indirect endorsement of Wilde's personal transgressions, or, to use the favorite contemporary word, Wilde's "perversity." Reviewers were divided on the artistic merits of Strauss's *Salome,* some praising it, some condemning it in the strongest terms, often on moral grounds. Still, both the negative and the positive reactions demonstrate an interesting sense of continuity between Wilde's play and adaptation. Many early opera reviewers understood Strauss's musical decisions as aesthetic corollaries to Wilde's: these decisions point to important conceptual correspondences between the symbolist-decadent play and the modernist opera, rather than identify one as the radical overhauling of the other.

Wilde's Symbolist Style:
The Corporalization of Affect

Initially, their mutual contact with Richard Wagner's nineteenth-century *Gesamtkunstwerk* aesthetic provided the cultural and intellectual connection between Wilde's play and music drama. Like Strauss, Wilde was strongly influenced by the fin de siècle Wagnerism championed by the French symbolists he sought to imitate and emulate in *Salomé.* Wagner's ideal of stimulating all the senses in a total work of art spoke to the symbolists' search for new principles by which to immerse readers in intense experiences of aesthetic beauty—the perfect corporalization of affect through words. The same goals are at work in Oscar Wilde's *Salomé.*

Wilde's play achieves a powerful dreamlike atmosphere through its stylized, dense, repetitious poetic prose, which unfolds at an exaggeratedly slow pace and creates an almost ritualistic effect, building up hypnotic force over time. A good example of Wilde's symbolist technique is found in the opening scene between the Page and the Young Syrian, discussed in chapter 1, which Strauss cited as his initial inspiration (*CCW* 583).[3] The scene mesmerizes the spectator through short verbal phrasings and incantory parallelisms, introduces the main themes (beauty, fatality, fragility, dance, death), and conveys the sense that "something terrible" will happen. *Salomé* is a play about erotic and aesthetic obsessions, and Wilde's language in this scene therefore feels obsessive in its circling around two central mysteries, the moon and Salomé. The circling, almost fetishistic effect returns many times, especially in Salomé's alternating invocations of the beauty and the horror of Jokanaan's body and her fanatical insistence that he let her "kiss [his] mouth, Jokanaan . . . I will kiss thy mouth" (590–91). Such repetitions are contemplative, self-centered, and affirmative rather than informative; they prey on the object of desire as a distant, unwilling participant whose mystery obstinately refuses to be pierced. The symbolic imagery of unfulfilled desire, mysterious beauty, and fatality becomes the evocative emotional center of *Salomé's* stylized universe, provoking a response that is sensual and instinctive rather than rational, inducing a dreamlike enchantment of the audience.

Wilde's approach can be explained by the goals of Wagnerian-symbolist aesthetics, as well as by the sensory and rhetorical effusion of decadent novels he read and championed, such as Joris-Karl Huysmans's *À rebours* (1884), famously alluded to as the seductive yellow book in *The Picture of Dorian Gray* (1891). As in Huysmans's sensual Salome passages, the novel's overall style creates the impression of sensual and material details in excess. The text itself is a thrilling rhetorical microcosm designed to overwhelm its readers with verbal and imaginary synesthetic thrills. Symbolist evocation and synesthesia and decadent sexual and sensual excess were intended to produce an erotic fullness in the here and now: the corporal affect of art took center stage as this literature expounded an almost erotic relationship to poetic aesthetics. As described in chapter 1, Stéphane Mallarmé was painfully aware of language's mimetic inadequacy, no matter how much he yearned for poetic purity, ahistoricity, and *nullité,* or nothingness (a line of argument Jean-Paul Sartre pursued in his interpretation of Mallarmé as the poet of nothingness). At its best, Mallarmé felt, symbolist poetry could evoke and conjure up certain moods and feelings that would ring true in a purely visceral, emotional and aesthetic sense but not in a strictly descriptive or cognitive one. Ideally, readers would lose themselves as if in a trance and would enter a higher state of intense mental and physical experience. In a famous letter to Henri Cazalis, the symbolist *maître* Stéphane Mallarmé described this goal: "I'm inventing a language which must of necessity burst forth from a very new poetics, which I could define in these few words: *paint, not the object, but the effect it produces.* Therefore the lines in such a poem mustn't be composed of words; but of intentions, and all the words must fade before the sensation" (*Selected Letters* 39).

Alongside Mallarmé's work, the Belgian poet and dramatist Maurice Maeterlinck's *La princesse Maleine* (1889) provided a model for Wilde's dramatic idiom and synesthetic effect in *Salomé*. Like Mallarmé, Maeterlinck aimed at theatrical synesthesia, the sensual evocation of spiritual and existential mystery, and a dreamlike, Schopenhauerian atmosphere of fatalism. Influenced by the contemporary interest in pantomime and puppets, Maeterlinck placed slowly moving actors on a dimly lit stage, where they seemed like symbolic ciphers rather than human beings. Wilde was familiar with Maeterlinck's work, lauded and read in the circle of symbolists in Paris that Wilde frequented, and *La princesse Maleine* (1889), which received glowing reviews at the time, predates Wilde's *Salomé* by only about one year. Not only does *La princesse Maleine* bear symbolist stylistic hallmarks, such as verbal repetitions and the leitmotif-like use of symbols, but it probably also suggested specific dramatic and symbolic building blocks to Wilde. These include the strong presence of the moon and the sky throughout Maeterlinck's play; the fatalistic atmosphere beset by ill omens (e.g., 71, 91, 99, 118, 160–61); and his tripartite color symbolism, that is, white for innocence and death (Princess Maleine's pallor [e.g., 98–99, 102, 115]), red for violence (a comet looking "as though it dripped blood on the castle," presaging "great disasters" [18]; light streaming from the chapel door after Maleine's murder [186]; murderess Queen Anne's bloodred coat [200]), and black (a black and menacing sky [21, 63]). The opening scene in particular, with two royal officers outside in a moonlit garden while a feast is going on inside, is often mentioned as the blueprint for *Salomé's* opening.

The fatalistic atmosphere of *La princesse Maleine* is shot through with prominent religious symbolism, such as seven nuns, a cross, a chapel, and two tapestries depicting the Slaughter of the Innocents and the Last Judgment (182–83), but as in *Salomé*, spirituality has no specific moral function. Instead, it simply serves to underscore the play's nihilism, its thorough undermining of religious as well as worldly authority. At the end of Maeterlinck's play, King Hjalmar is an emasculated, frightened, weak and confused old man, like Wilde's King Herod, and Fate reigns powerfully as an omniscient force that doesn't help humans but pursues its own, possibly evil designs. The spectator may sigh, with King Hjalmar, "I am glad it is over; for I had the whole world on my heart" (206). Where Maeterlinck's play ends with the seven nuns chanting the prayer for forgiveness, *Miserere*, indicating human culpability and an existential plea for mercy, Wilde creates a powerful vision of the triumphant erotic-aesthetic individual Salomé. Still, both endings are similar in that they do not offer a reassuring restabilization of meaning.

In *Salomé*, Wilde managed to adopt the symbolist idiom perfectly and create an atmosphere and expressionism that captured Mallarmé's and Maeterlinck's most central goals. To his delight, both Mallarmé and Maeterlinck wrote to praise Wilde's skills in producing that essential symbolist quality, a dreamlike evocation of mysterious realities. Mallarmé stated, "I marvel that, while everything in your *Salome* is expressed in constant, dazzling strokes, there also arises, on each page, the unutterable and the Dream." Maeterlinck thanked Wilde "for the gift of your mysterious, strange, and admirable *Salome*. I expressed my thanks to you today as I emerged, for the third time, from this dream whose power I have not yet explained to myself. I assure you of my great admiration" (trans. Ellmann, *Oscar Wilde* 375).

In light of Wilde's own description of *Salomé* in "De Profundis" as a "beautiful, coloured, musical thing" whose "refrains" reminded him of "old ballads" (*CCW* 1042, 1026), Wilde scholars have hardly considered the play's symbolist style and language sensational, overwhelming, or excessive. Instead, *Salomé*'s form is often implicitly understood or presented as a beautiful, deceptive veil behind which Wilde hides a roaring beast—never as the roaring beast itself.[4] Wilde's choice of form, however, was geared at an excess of style. Symbolist theater, with its notions of synesthesia and *Gesamtkunstwerk,* sought to provoke a cumulative overflow of sensual impressions, so that linear reason could give way to free-floating, sensual responses rather than cognitive ones and could transport the audience into a strange, fascinating aesthetic universe of emotional excess.[5] Similarly, Wilde's achievement in *Salomé* was the creation of intense, overpowering affect in the audience—the corporalization of art.

Wilde's original plans for staging *Salomé* illustrate that Wilde envisioned a highly stylized stage set, costumes, and performance style that would produce such comprehensive sensation and synesthesia. Designer Charles Ricketts recounts Wilde's detailed ideas for the stage and color scheme.

> I proposed a black floor—upon which Salome's white feet would show; this statement was meant to capture Wilde. The sky was to be a rich turquoise blue, cut across by the perpendicular fall of strips of gilt matting, which should not touch the ground, and so form a sort of aerial tent above the terrace. Did Wilde actually suggest the division of actors into separate masses of colour, to-day the idea seems mine! His was the scheme, however, that the Jews should be in yellow, the Romans were to be in purple, the soldiery in bronze green, and John in white. Over the dress of Salome the discussions were endless: should she be black "like the night"? or— here the suggestion is Wilde's—"green like a curious poisonous lizard"? I desired that the moonlight should fall upon the ground, the source not be-

ing seen; Wilde himself hugged the idea of "some strange dim pattern in the sky." (Quoted in Tydeman and Price 45–46)[6]

Ricketts later added that Herod and Herodias were to have been clad in "blood-red" and that an additional alternative costume solution for Salomé would have resulted in making her "silver like the moon" (Raymond and Ricketts 53). With set and costumes thus symbolically colored in different matching or opposing shades, the symbolic colors discussed in chapter 1 (white and silver for innocence and purity, red for violence and blood, black for death and fatality, etc.) are thus supported and enhanced by symbolic yellow for the jealousy of the bickering Jews and black or green for the dangerous "poisonous lizard" Salomé. Charles Ricketts returned to these original design ideas, of which sketches by both Wilde and Ricketts survive, in a June 1906 private production by the Literary Society at King's Hall, Covent Garden (Tydeman and Price 44–57), as well as in a later Japanese production (1919).

The rich sensuality and symbolism of the color scheme would have fed nicely into the acting style and even the olfactory sensations Wilde had planned. During rehearsals, Wilde reportedly demanded a particularly slow, sensuous recital of his lines by the actors and had arranged for "scented clouds [of perfume rising from incense basins] rising and partly veiling the stage from time to time—a new perfume for each new emotion!" (quoted in Raby, *Oscar Wilde* 116–17). Another designer, W. Graham Robertson, mentions that the London production was to have included, "in place of an orchestra, braziers of perfume. Think—the scented clouds rising and partly veiling the stage from time to time—a new perfume for each new emotion!" (125–26). Thus targeting the eyes, ears, and even noses of the audience, Wilde clearly imagined *Salomé* as a feast for the senses, combining Wagner's and the symbolists' synesthetic ideals for a *Gesamtkunstwerk* production. Even in mere book form (the only version in which the play was available to Victorian audiences after the theatrical censor had banned it from the stage), *Salomé* struck Oscar Wilde's 1890s friends as a sensual Dionysian feast with a power to touch and transport the audience into a realm of ecstasy. Max Beerbohm declared himself helplessly "enamoured" of Wilde's play: "It has charmed my eyes from their sockets and through the voids has sent incense to my brain; my tongue is loosed in its praise" (quoted in Beckson, *Oscar Wilde* 134). Wilde's friend Edgar Saltus described the strong sensation of "shudder" and "sacred terror" it elicited in him (quoted in ibid. 132).

In 1902–3, after Wilde's public humiliation, imprisonment, and death, the budding German star director Max Reinhardt followed Wilde's stage conceptualization when he mounted his landmark Berlin production with a private theater troupe, Schall und Rauch, with Gertrud Eysoldt and, later, Tilla Durieux in the title role as Salomé and with set designs by Max Kruse and Lovis Corinth. Strauss attended Reinhardt's 1903 production, which offered *Salomé* and *The Importance of Being Earnest* as a double bill, and the performance moved him to set Wilde's text to music. (Strauss later saw another Reinhardt play, Hofmannsthal's *Elektra,* which inspired his 1907 opera and his subsequent collaboration with Hofmannsthal.) Reinhardt's theatrical experiment provided another link between the styles of Wilde and Strauss in light of the Wagnerian aesthetic. Deeply influenced by Wagner's monumental music dramas yet craving to modernize and reinvent his mythical stagecraft, Reinhardt was keenly aware of its limitations and challenges. Which direction should theatrical innovation take after Wagner? How could one apply *Gesamtkunstwerk* notions and synesthesia to the modern stage, moving away from Germanic legend and toward modern experience?

Max Reinhardt envisioned modern theatrical production in terms of musical metaphoricity and harmony derived from Wagner. During his early Berlin years, Reinhardt was interested in transforming the naturalist, realistic theater he had himself experienced as an actor. Conceiving of drama as an overwhelming, pleasurable sensory experience, Reinhardt wanted to reinvent the theater as a space that would speak to all the senses and provide a stage for "the music of the word."

> I wish for a theater that gives people joy again. That takes them beyond themselves and out of the gray misery of the everyday, into the cheerful and pure air of beauty. . . . There is but one purpose to the theater, and that is the theater, and I believe in a theater that belongs to the actor. . . . I want to see beautiful people around me; and more than anything I want to hear beautiful voices. A sophisticated art of language . . . infused with the pathos of our own day, . . . so that one can hear the music of the Word again. . . . What I have in mind is a sort of chamber music of the theater. I cannot tell you how much I long for music, and color. I intend to attract the best painters. . . . Just as I will welcome everything that has the power to expand those capabilities of the theater which are yet unknown. (Quoted in Fuhrich and Prossnitz 29–31, my trans.)

A theater that belongs to the actor, that emphasizes and celebrates the musical qualities of language and literally paints with words and gestures—in his manifesto, Reinhardt uses a plethora of synesthetic metaphors to describe his ideal theater. Reinhardt's productions generally paid a great deal of attention to the visuals of the stage (set design, costumes, and lighting). They also included music, strategically placed to support the action or mood of the play, steeping the audience in the intensely emotional world of the stage.

Wilde's *Salomé* was an ideal find for Reinhardt's theatrical enterprise. The original 1901 German premiere in Breslau, at the Freie Literarische Vereinigung, had already inaugurated a reappraisal of Wilde in German intellectual circles. But Reinhardt's avant-garde and visually beautiful interpretation made the play an exhilarating experience and an instant smash hit.[7] Reviewers highlighted the sensually exalting quality of the play under Reinhardt's direction; they compared it to "a drink blended from the most pungent essences" and spoke of "the delight of the intoxication and color which the painter and poet use[d]" (quoted in Davis 157, 160). As another Berlin critic remarked, *Salomé* offered a "richness or excess of visual images which pass by in rapid succession," "excessive emotion," "suggestive power," and "peculiar dark splendor" (quoted in ibid. 164). Robert Ross, Wilde's loyal friend and the executor of his will, spoke in his preface to *Salomé* and *La Sainte Courtisane* of the importance of Reinhardt's production for the subsequent wide success of Wilde's play: "In 1901, within a year of the author's death, it was produced in Berlin; from that moment it has held the European stage. It has run for a longer consecutive period in Germany than any play by an Englishman, not excepting Shakespeare. Its popularity has extended to all countries where it is not prohibited" (x).

As realized by Reinhardt and admired by reviewers, Wilde's symbolism thus anticipated modernism in its goal of triggering extraordinary sensation. Strauss responded to Wilde's sensual form and style with his own modernist means but with the same symbolist-Wagnerian ends in mind.

Interpretive Response to Wilde: "Music Which Must Crash"

Strauss's music drama premiered at the Dresdner Hofoper on December 9, 1905, and hit the German cultural scene like a bombshell. The early critics expressed astonishment and marvel at the "thunder," "noise," and orchestral "cacophony" Strauss had in store for them. As Lawrence Gilman writes in the first monograph on the opera (1907), *Salome* presented "a harmonic *tour de force*—a practically uninterrupted texture of new and constantly varied sequences and chord formations" that created the impression of "sheer noise, intentional cacophony," modernist sounds hitherto unheard on the operatic stage. At several moments, notes Gilman, the orchestra was "literally divided against itself, and thunders simultaneously in two violently antagonistic keys" (55). Although the Dresden premiere was a smashing success (there were thirty-eight curtain calls, and subsequent performances sold out for weeks), the critical reaction was mixed. Fellow composers Gustav Mahler, Maurice Ravel, Gabriel Fauré, Paul Dukas, Ferruccio Busoni, and, later, Arnold Schönberg, Alban Berg, and Anton Webern admired the score's revolutionary technical accomplishments: the tonal and rhythmic daring, the independence of line from harmony, and the complex arrangement of forty-nine instrumental and voice parts (John Williamson 139–41). But many reviewers were simply baffled. The *Dresdner Nachrichten* critic concluded that Strauss wanted to create a "sensation, . . . something yet unseen and unheard on stage, something monstrous, stimulating the nerves in the extreme" with its "huge, sensational-artistic and technical apparatus . . . which drastically changes moods on cue" (*KUB* 37–38). Paul Pfitzner of the *Musikalisches Wochenblatt* argued that through *Salome's* "choice ugliness of the most garish disharmonies" and its "admirable accumulation of effects and means of expression," Strauss had "arrived at the limit where . . . there really is nowhere else to go" (ibid. 46). In the *Musikalische Rundschau,* Paul Zschorlich described the score as a "labyrinth," a thick "underbrush of dissonances" that would confound and exhaust even the most experienced listener, whose "ear finds no points of rest" (ibid. 53).

Dissonances, bitonal surprises, and dramatic orchestral effects are ubiquitous in Strauss's score, but two examples clarify what appeared so new and strange to these first audiences. First, in *Salome's* famous opening, the curtain rises suddenly and surprisingly right on the action. There is no orchestral prologue or prelude, only a one-bar rising clarinet scale followed by two shimmering measures of woodwinds and violins that establish the C-sharp minor chord famously associated with Salome (m. 2), before Narraboth intones (m. 4), "Wie schön ist die Prinzessin Salome heute Nacht" (How beautiful the Princess Salome is tonight). While the tempo is moderate for the first twenty-nine bars, measure 30 (fig. 4, "etwas lebhafter," a bit more vivacious) introduces a flurry of sound: while the first soldier sings of tumult ("Aufruhr") inside, with the Jews fighting over their religion, Strauss whips up the orchestra as an echo of the action, exemplified by his descriptive notation "heulend" (howling) for the cellos, basses, and violins (fig. 4, mm. 31–37). A good example of the thickets of dissonance is the second interlude (at the end of scene 3, after Jochanaan's retreat to the cistern), following Salome's ominous oracle that she will indeed kiss his mouth (figs. 141–49), where impenetrably thick orchestration portrays extreme agitation and foreboding. Similarly exciting, a "bitonal racket . . . greets the appearance of the head" once Salome's will is about to be fulfilled (fig. 314) (Puffett 78).

Wilde's emphasis on strong sensation in his symbolist-decadent text is echoed in some of the comments early opera reviewers made about the modernist score as they marveled at the opera's aggressive assault on their nerves. Robert Hirschfeld, a conservative reviewer of the opera's first Vienna performance in 1907 for the *Wiener Abendpost*[8] and a prominent opponent of Mahler, one of Strauss's admirers, disliked the "presumptuous curiosity" and "stimulating sensation" of Strauss's operatic spectacle. He complained that *Salome*

> ceaselessly electrifies and discharges the spirit; it rattles and bangs until the emotions are worn out; it no longer wants anything but explosions, and the dynamic of these has no effect but that of dynamite. . . . Cleverly worked-out series of tones that calculatedly resist every ordinary comprehension rob the ear of its powers of discretion: the most far-flung notes are rubbed together so that it rains sparks. . . . . art has become nothing but a great pestle. (*RSHW* 334–36)

Hirschfeld's electricity and combustion metaphors highlight the monumental force of Strauss's explosive score with its sudden, intense, yet passing moments of forceful illumination, violent surprises, and drastic harmonic twists and turns. Other early reviewers repeated this impression of forceful affect in similar words, complaining, like Friedrich Brandes of the *Dresdner Anzeiger,* that Strauss's music "tortures and tickles, almost destroys, it brutalizes and exerts us to the point of exhaustion" (*KUB* 51). For Strauss himself, the operatic Salome could actually not be outrageous, extreme, and excessive enough. During a rehearsal at Prague, he reportedly encouraged the orchestra to increase the din, because the impression was "too gentle—we want wild beasts here! This is no civilized music: it is music which must crash!" (*RR* 151–52).

The thematic similarities between Strauss's music and Wilde's text are brought out and emphasized by the formal arrangement of Strauss's provocative score. *Salome's* thundering orchestra highlights the conflicts and contrasts between Wilde's characters, worldviews, ideas, and desires, blasting into the open the deep conflicts and longings inherent in Wilde's contemplative, sparkling prose. The opera portrays solitary individuals on the edge of the abyss and a world in disarray, musically as well as dramatically out of joint. Some of Wilde's antithetical pairs include Narraboth and the Page, Herod and Herodias, Herod and Salomé, Narraboth and Salomé, and, of course, Salomé and Jokanaan. In a December 1906 letter, Lachmann praised Strauss for "extracting from much that was unspoken" in Wilde's play "a quite unprecedented dramatic power" that highlighted not only the inner conflicts of characters but also the tensions between them; Strauss had transposed their battles of will into the orchestra (ST 174). For example, when Salome first woos Jochanaan and is repeatedly rejected by him, the score quickly switches between different musical moods and tempos to contrast her seductive attempts with his violent resistance (figs. 83–88); and similar battles of will exist between Narraboth and Salome and, later, between Salome and Herod or Herod and Herodias. Paul Mittmann of the *Breslauer Zeitung* fittingly called Strauss Wilde's musical "illustrator" or "colorist," whose palette illuminates the characters' most extreme passions and agonies, from "intense sensual rapture" to "the twilight of horrific inner suffering," to produce an "almost palpable effect" (KUB 30).

Some of Strauss's listeners also stressed the irresistible pull of his sensational musical modernism, echoing the earlier reactions to Wilde's beguiling symbolism. The audience was inevitably "drawn into the delirium [*Taumel*] of this music" (KUB 53), which had "an intoxicating effect" (ibid. 51), so that one could but follow Strauss wherever he wanted to go: "With daring energy the genius storms across chasms and ravines in Dionysian rapture, and even though we are at first diffident and indecisive, we follow him" (ibid. 38). In the eyes of many contemporaries, Wilde's and Strauss's goals, notwithstanding superficial differences, turned out to be essentially the same: corporal affect and aesthetic intoxication. Overwhelming the senses with crashing waves of orchestral turmoil, Strauss's modernist score acted similarly to Mallarmé's ideal poetry, Maeterlinck's and Wilde's symbolist drama, and the deliberate excesses of literary decadence: the aesthetic style took over and eliminated rational thinking, laying bare unmitigated affect and intense passion.

A Secular Spectacular: Sublimity in Wilde and Strauss

Wilde's and Strauss's shared formal and stylistic interest in sensation and physical stimulus can partly be explained by the larger cultural-historical secularization of art in the late nineteenth and early twentieth centuries. The displacement of metaphysical morality by a new secular physicality was an important feature of post-Wagnerian symbolist theater as well as Strauss's radically refashioned music drama.[9] Wagner's idea of *Gesamtkunstwerk* had been marked by his nineteenth-century religious humanism: "Ultimately, [he] saw the music drama not merely as an aesthetic phenomenon but as the vehicle of a religious experience" (George Williamson 181). *Der Ring des Nibelungen, Tristan und Isolde,* and *Parsifal* offered mythical grandeur that connected the fate of his heroes and heroines to a transcendental plan. Like Wagner, the symbolists and decadents regarded art as a gateway to sublimity, but they did not share his religious anchoring of it. Instead, they elevated art itself to quasi-religious status: language and literature became sublime. ("It is all an attempt to spiritualise literature, . . . for in speaking to us so intimately, so solemnly, as only tradition had hitherto spoken to us . . . [literature] becomes itself a kind of religion, with all the duties and the responsibilities of the sacred ritual," Wilde's contemporary Arthur Symons explained in *The Symbolist Movement in Literature* [8].) The ideal work of art overwhelmed its recipient with sensation, producing an all-enveloping atmosphere of quasi-transcendental, evocative reverie—blissful, ecstatic, aesthetic dreaming independent of a god. Rather than imitating the mythical-metaphysical direction of Wagner's anticipated beyond, symbolist and decadent literature fashioned art as an essentially amoral agency, in which the quest for physical ecstasy replaced metaphysical longing.

Similarly, as Bryan Gilliam notes, Strauss's operatic adaptation "exploited Wagner's 'sacred apparatus,' his 'sacred language,' only in order to demythologize the philosophy that gave us that very language" (viii). Strauss recharged and transformed Wagner's music drama according to his own creative designs.[10] He adopted only selected musical techniques, such as leitmotifs and dramatic key association, while stripping Wagner's form of its religious humanist content and purpose (*RSS* 58–87, 47). Wagner's music was "purifying, exonerating" to the soul, whereas Strauss's did not reach beyond the "utilitarian machinery," "the sounds coming together from [his] grandiose apparatus" (*KUB* 51).

To Theodor W. Adorno, Strauss's style marked a new conceptual quality of modern music.

> The treasuries of images are plundered, the booty transformed into objects of "viewing enjoyment"; the joy of great music in holding fast is debased to the hedonism of being in on the fun, as with the love of sensation, which similarly prefers stimulation as such to any content which might be enjoyed. Strauss was probably the first to transplant the notion of "sensation," already widespread in the literature of the time, to music.

Adorno, forever harping on Strauss's modernist consumerism, explains that his emphasis on sensationalism and entertainment moved *Salome* away from moral or metaphysical reference, reflection, or depth: in Strauss's music drama, "even the expression of extreme emotional states, such as Salome's, remains sensuously pleasant, culinary; the great happiness which music once promised metaphysically in the transcendence of the infinite idea, becomes practical, available here and now for consumption" ("Strauss: Part I" 22–23).[11] Adorno also explains that unlike Berg's *Wozzeck* or Schönberg's *Moses und Aron* and *Erwartung, Salome* is wholly stylistic surface and physical immanence, free of the didactic impulse that characterized the later musical modernists ("Arnold Schoenberg" 283).

Wilde's play was the perfect libretto for Strauss to use to keep alive the sacred aura and overwhelming sensual effect of symbolist synesthesia and total theatrical excess while severing Wagner's mythical-metaphysical chord and reflecting an anthropocentric view of art pursued for experience's sake rather than for moral or religious advancement. Early reviewers commented on Strauss's "musical glorification" and indirect endorsement of Salome's transgressions: he presented her as "a transfigured superhuman figure in the madness of love's passion," acting as if "forced by a higher power" (*KUB* 38). Thus this Salome becomes the center of a "deeply moving tragedy" with "purifying" effect (ibid. 50). Granting Salome an "abrupt metamorphosis" in her final aria, "the demure lament of a bride for her dead bridegroom," Strauss's music made visible "what Wilde leaves open as an unsolved mystery in Salome's soul"; "[t]hrough the composer's musical language we gaze more deeply into the soul of this woman," who becomes "humanly understandable" (ibid. 48, 32–33). Strauss made the audience "shudder" at her force and truth (ibid. 37). Similarly, Lachmann noted the "wonderfully shattering effect" of Strauss's ending, in her letter from December 6, 1906: "herrlich von erschütternder Wirkung ist der Schluß" (*ST* 174).

Despite the fact that Wilde's story presents a corrupt Jewish princess and her sexual obsession with an unattainable prophet, a decadent court, and an infamous dance of seduction leading to a necrophilic kiss (surely great material for yet another hothouse flower of decadent orientalism), Wilde and Strauss present a mythical heroine in search of beauty and passion, a paradoxical amalgam of fatal force and virginal fragility, ruthless desires and spiritual earnestness. They wanted the transgressive Salome to remain, despite her perversity and sexual daring, an attractive, tragic figure who would evoke "sympathy" rather than "terror and disgust" in the audience, as Strauss himself insisted when he described her as "a chaste virgin and oriental princess" tragically "defeat[ed] by the miracle of a great world" rather than as a monstrous femme fatale (*RR* 151). Strauss's description

Fig. 1. Maria Ewing in Richard Strauss's *Salome* (Pittsburgh Opera, 2001).
Copyright Suellen Fitzsimmons.

echoed Wilde's view of Salomé as "a mystic, the sister of Salammbô, a Sainte Thérèse who worships the moon" (quoted in Ellmann, *Oscar Wilde* 376), which reflects the influence of Flaubert (see chap. 1) as well as his sense that Salomé is an earnest seeker, albeit not for religion but for her own transgressive secular spirituality, the gospel of physical beauty. Strauss called his musical representation of Wilde's ending a "dreadful apotheosis," a religious term indicating his sense of Salome's physical-metaphysical exaltation in her final aria (see fig. 1) and the ambivalent Burkean sublimity she inspires in the audience (*RR* 154). Both Wilde's and Strauss's versions embrace physical violence and aesthetic transgression as sites of secular sublimity.

Strauss described his ideal Salome as a sixteen-year-old princess with the voice of Isolde, a powerful singer who could combine the *femme fragile* qualities of Wilde's Salomé with the vocal powers of a Wagnerian heroine, one of the most cruelly demanding and difficult soprano roles in operatic history (Wilhelm 168). According to Herbert Lindenberger, who met one of Strauss's early ideal Salomes, the American-born Marcella Craft (c. 1880–1960), in Riverside, California, in her later years, Strauss also "gave her his interpretation of Salome as an innocent girl who was driven to her actions because she was horrified by the corruption of the court."[12] Strauss had chosen Craft for the role in 1910 and wanted to convince her to perform the transgressive princess; he personally emended the vocal score for her high-voiced soprano.[13]

Like Wilde, Strauss was also not interested in Jochanaan as a serious religious-spiritual figure. He rather thought of Jochanaan as a comical target whom he could have satirized even more, as he wrote to Stefan Zweig in 1935: "I tried to compose the good Jochanaan more or less as a clown; a preacher in the desert, especially one who feeds grasshoppers, seems infinitely comical to me. Only because I have already caricatured the five Jews and also poked fun at Father Herodes did I feel that I had to follow the law of contrast and write a pedantic-Philistine motive for four horns to characterize Jochanaan" (quoted in Wilhelm 101).

With *Salome,* Strauss thus offered an essentially modernist aesthetic experiment that follows in Wilde's footsteps and pushes secular modern individualism to its extreme, emphasizing erotic and aesthetic transgression in place of metaphysical or religious humanism. In the final scenes of the opera, we see Salome "all alone" ("ganz allein") in the universe, just like Strauss's subsequent ancient but modern heroine Elektra. Salome achieves her shocking triumph and is neither saved nor sorry at the end.[14]

Popular Avant-Gardism

Adorno's reading of Strauss's unabashed consumerist "plunder[ing]" of musical treasures for pleasure and entertainment suggests another important parallel between Wilde and Strauss, their common interest in popular avant-gardism. For both Wilde and Strauss, the Salome theme provided ideal opportunities to be popular in subject and innovative in style. The fin de siècle Salome vogue provided a sufficiently alluring background and enduring public interest for another version, while offering a platform to do something different—to offer a new and even more tantalizing variation on an already well-known subject. Both artists wanted to gain a seat among the literary and musical avant-garde elites of their time while still appealing to a broader middle-class public. Highly sensitive to contemporary audiences' tastes, Wilde and Strauss acted as modern artist-marketeers interested in producing innovative art that would titillate, dazzle, and sell.

Scholars like Regenia Gagnier, Julia Prewitt Brown, Josephine Guy, and Ian Small have shown that Wilde responded very actively to the Victorian marketplace for aestheticism. He wished to ally himself with the symbolists in Paris by consciously writing his play in French, in the style of Mallarmé and Maeterlinck, and to become the first English symbolist. To further ensure the attention of the British public, Wilde engaged the famous actress Sarah Bernhardt as Salomé. Kerry Powell notes that when writing *Salomé* in French, Wilde may have had in mind the "by no means trivial . . . consideration that Sarah Bernhardt did not speak English" (Powell, *Wilde and the Theatre of the 1890s* 35). Setting his theatrical experiment in her native language, Wilde could not only appeal directly to the French symbolists but also hope to have his play performed by the *grande Sarah*. By the early 1890s, Sarah Bernhardt had become one of the most famous actresses on the European stage: she was the undisputed superstar of Paris and London, with several international tours to her credit; she had numerous personal connections to the Paris circles of writers, artists, and other cultural agents; and audiences and critics all over the world were enthralled with her unique talent.[15] Powell notes, "Galvanized by celebrity, athirst with ambition, fluent in French—how could Wilde have resisted breathing the charmed atmosphere of the Parisian actress who moved Londoners to tears with her performances in a foreign tongue? . . . Such was the glamour and acclaim in which Wilde sought to baptize his play" (ibid. 44). Bernhardt's acting style uniquely fit the synesthetic, excessive style of *Salomé:* her grand stage gestures and powerful, melodic voice highlighted emotional extremes;

she could combine dreamy sweetness and torrid violence. According to Elaine Aston, Bernhardt's "histrionic performance style . . . swept her into a whirlwind of passion that seemed, at times, to border on delirium." Bernhardt's strong stage presence relied on "the contrast between the sheer power of her acting and the slightness of her physical build, between her portrayal of awesome heroism and the abiding image of tenderness" (Aston 24, 21).

According to Powell, submitting a play in French to mandatory London theatrical censorship also significantly enhanced Wilde's chances to evade the censors and increased the chances for unimpeded commercial success with London audiences, who not only would come to see Sarah Bernhardt but would less likely be offended if the scandalous lines were in a foreign tongue (*Wilde and the Theatre of the 1890s* 35–40). In asking Bernhardt to apply her talent to Salomé, Wilde combined his genuine admiration for her art with a strategic positioning and marketing of his own: her acting would contribute to the strong artistic impression that Wilde hoped *Salomé* would make; Bernhardt's approval would enhance his own reputation and ensure that the play would attract attention from serious critics as well as the paying public.

Contemporary reviewers quickly detected Richard Strauss's active catering to audiences' tastes as well. Friedrich Brandes called him "an artist of musical attitudes" ("musikalischer Attitüdenkünstler") who knew how to "make his compositions the sensation of the day" and "follow[ed] the fashion of the times" just as Wilde did: "just a few years ago everyone was talking about Wilde and his most daring paradoxy, *Salome*," and so Strauss, as "an educated man with open eyes and ears," wrote his "newest sensation as a response to the spirit of the times" (*KUB* 36). According to Sander Gilman, with *Salome's* caricature of Orthodox Jews, Strauss wooed the fashionable secular German-Jewish avant-garde in Berlin, Strauss's home at the time, and the theatrical elite around Max Reinhardt. Strauss's calculated appeal to this peer audience influenced not only his choice of subject but also the infamous quintet of the Jews, which satirizes the *Gemauschel* of the Orthodox Eastern Jews (*Ostjuden*) held in disregard by the assimilated German-Jewish left (Gilman, "Strauss and the Pervert").

That the anti-Semitic allusions of Strauss's opera did not escape German-speaking audiences at the time and featured prominently in their reception of Wilde's and Strauss's works is strikingly illustrated by a little known (and, to my knowledge, never translated) anonymous play held in the archives of the Clark Library, Los Angeles. Entitled *Salome: Moralisch-musikalisch-hysterisch-altjüdisches Sittendrama frei nach Oskar Wilde,* the play was apparently first performed in 1904 (a year before the premiere of Strauss's opera) but was entirely rewritten for its publication around 1911.[16] It is best characterized as a bawdy parody of Wilde's play; in it, anti-Semitism intermingles with sexual jokes. After the opening scene depicts various Jewish soldiers who are comically dumb and parade up and down in aimless military pursuit, the second scene shows the Jewish princess Salome wooing the German gentile Jochanaan (who speaks in Bavarian dialect) and makes ironic references to the kosher taboo against eating pork. Salome's desire for Jochanaan's head is changed to her desire to listen to Jochanaan's pseudoreligious hymns praising pork and her obsession with snatching from him the huge (pork) "sausage" that he loves eating. The dialogue insinuates phallic and Freudian themes. Salome has a doubly forbidden desire, both as a Jewess and as a woman: "He is a German, I am told, with red-golden hair. And of what does he sing? He praises the meat of the pig, whose flesh we are forbidden to eat. Oh, I am sure that must be particularly good, like everything that is forbidden. *(Ruminates for a while.)* Let me see Jochanaan!" (16, my trans.). Taking the bad joke even further, Herodias is also after Jochanaan's "sausage," but Salome finally gets and eats it. Worried about the lady's reputation, Herod makes sure that Salome and Jochanaan marry at the end, much to the hilarity and relief of all the characters. That a burlesque play like this could make fun of Jews and play up the sexuality of Salome's and Herodias's relationship with Jochanaan, with audiences most likely understanding and enjoying these references in performance, is surely due to the fact that the scandalous sexuality of Wilde's play and the anti-Semitism of Strauss's opera were common knowledge by 1911.

Like Wilde, Strauss fused avant-garde ambition with commercial appeal, catering to the audience's popular, political, and religious tastes, which included, in the case of his *Salome,* the secular Jewish avant-garde's disdain for the allegedly backward ways of their Orthodox Jewish brethren. Biographer Matthew Boyden explains, "Strauss's attraction to Wilde's heady symbolic perfume was determined as much by business as by aesthetic considerations. . . . In setting Wilde's *Salome* . . . , Strauss discovered the [Jewish] avant-garde and was in turn discovered by them" (165). He knew that his *Salome* could build both on the popularity of Max Reinhardt's recent smash hit production of Wilde's play and on the enduring popularity of the Wagnerian genre of music drama, which he wished to innovate while he imitated many of its features, such as leitmotifs and dramatic dialogue.

Orientalism was another popular feature of the Salome theme on which Strauss could build. It was already firmly established via Jules Massenet's *Hérodiade,* which was based on a whitewashed libretto of Flaubert's "Hérodias." Massenet's opera, in which Salomé becomes John's spiritual disciple and tries to save him, featured a richly oriental thematic background and music. Richard Strauss stated that he wished to create a different kind of operatic orientalism than he observed in Massenet, however—more exciting, more evocative, and modern. In his 1942 autobiographical collage *Recollections and Reflections,* Strauss wrote, perhaps commenting indirectly on Massenet's pseudo-orientalist, pious opera: "I had long been criticizing the fact that operas based on oriental and Jewish subjects (*Orient- und Judenopern*) lacked true oriental colour and scorching sun." For his own opera, "[t]he needs of the moment inspired [him] with truly exotic harmonies, which sparkled like taffeta particularly in the strange cadences" (*RR* 150). Strauss's choice of words and the simile he uses to describe his vision of musical orientalism reveal that he imagined his interest in alienation as well as familiarization; like precious silk from faraway lands, this music was to "sparkle," to be "truly exotic" and "strange." What could be more orientalist than an opera about a beautiful Jewish princess in love with an unattainable outsider? Yet Massenet had failed: Strauss thought that representing the orient to modern turn-of-the century audiences called for something more "strange," "exotic," and innovative than Massenet had offered. Strauss desired exoticism and vague atmospheric color to create an imagistic mood, an abstract, stylized sensual experience, much like Wilde had envisioned. Ultimately, the opera's modern orientalism would help to sell the work to turn-of-the-century audiences who were already richly acquainted with fashionable orientalist structures of representation.

Strauss's modernist approach to orientalism features prominently in the Dance of the Seven Veils, prepared throughout by Strauss's leitmotif use of the tambourine (which always sounds at the mention of *Tanz* or *tanzen,* "dance"). Musically, Strauss embodies Salome's wordless wielding of her will to power in the dance, combining familiar, waltzlike orientalist harmonies and rhythms with more eerie modernist passages that break up the comfort and hint at the presence of danger and the coming of disaster; hence, Lindenberger notes, "the avant-gardism of [Strauss's] opera cannot be separated from its orientalism" (*Opera in History* 186). According to Robin Holloway, Strauss's mixing of the familiar—the "genuine corn" (Holloway 157) and "bargain-basement orientalism" (149)—with the truly innovative element results in Strauss's original contribution, his "rais[ing of] kitsch to *Kunst* by sheer genius" (157). Nowadays the operatic Salomes handle their own dancing, but historically the representation of the dance on stage was one of the most challenging elements of any *Salome* production.

Though the dance scene was brief, it was crucial to any production; and most sopranos, it was discovered, could not dance the part. Either they were entirely too heavy, or they had no dance training, or both. So in most early instances a professional dancer traded places with the singer for the one scene. In the New York Metropolitan Opera Company's aborted 1907 production, the transition from the 250-pound Olive Fremstad to the diminutive Bianca Froelich, and back again, was so startling a spectacle that Franklin Fyles said it was 'as if some anti-fat remedy had worked wonders for a few minutes and then suddenly lost its potency.' . . . Scores of other dancers found work in productions of the opera, though seldom was their existence acknowledged in the program. (Bizot 73)

In 1930, Strauss commented to the producer Erich Engel that he preferred the dance very measured and simple; he "would rather not have any dramatics in the dance at all. No flirting with Herod, no playing to Jochanaan's cistern, only a moment's pause before the cistern on the final trill." Salome's dance should be performed "purely oriental, as serious and measured as possible, and thoroughly decent, as if it was being done on a prayer-mat." There should only be the occasional "pacing movement" and a "slight orgiastic emphasis" in "the last 2/4 bar." On the whole, it should be "done really aristocratically and stylishly" (quoted in Wilhelm 102–3).

In contrast to Walter Benjamin's concept of an authentic, metaphysical aura of art, both Wilde and Strauss aimed at creating a synthetic, physical aura in their respective *Salome* versions—a cleverly manufactured, secular sublime experience evoked purely by aesthetic and stylistic means. According to Benjamin's famous essay "The Work of Art in the Age of Its Reproducibility," the "cult value" of art—the metaphysical reference point, the organic connection of human aesthetics to divine law and order—was effectively replaced by "display-value" (or "exhibition-value," in Harry Zohn's and Edmund Jephcott's translation) in late nineteenth- and twentieth-century modernity. To Benjamin, modern art irrevocably shifted its focus from a metaphysical to a physical and anthropocentric reference point: the concept of authenticity that celebrated and identified the artistic image and its human creator had replaced the organic aura of art (the image's former religious function and its supposed organic connection with a divine origin). Adorno recognized this and ingeniously applied Benjamin's categories to his analysis of Strauss's modernism: "If Walter Benjamin's category of 'display-value' as opposed to 'cult-value' has any relevance at all to music, it is to Strauss" ("Strauss: Part I" 22). Strauss moved away from metaphysical and toward spectacular, *secular* physical experience through art that was oriented toward popular entertainment and avant-garde appeal rather than moral edification. Wilde and Strauss employed aesthetic shudder and thrill not to bring about a catharsis of the soul but to furnish momentary stimulation and enjoyment, the "tickle" of aesthetically innovative and provocative spectacle. The play and the opera provide quick, intense, shocking yet pleasurable, ultimately inconsequential dips, never more than skin-deep, into the physical experience of the limit, the sensational, the excessive. Nowhere is this clearer than in the provocative subject matter of the play and the opera, in which the popular sensationalism of the content fuses with the innovative sensationalism of their styles.

Perversity's Allure and the Specter of Wilde's Trials

Against the backdrop of their sensational form, contents, and popular avant-gardism, we may now understand better why Wilde's and Strauss's works both appalled and fascinated contemporaries. An additional element of the impression Strauss's opera made in 1905, however, was the memory of Wilde's trials, his internationally publicized prosecution and incarceration for "acts of gross indecency" just one decade earlier, and his lonely death in exile in 1900. Read through the lens of Wilde's life, Salome was understood as the author's alter ego who challenged the moral as well as the metaphysical order openly, and Strauss seemed to endorse rather than condemn her in his version. Although Germany had embraced rather than condemned Oscar Wilde after the trial (his works were widely performed), the cultural debate about Wilde's immorality and perversity was directly associated with the opera as well. For many reviewers, this association inevitably tainted Strauss's work and drew it into the eddy of sensual perversity. According to Leopold Schmidt of the *Berliner Tageblatt,* Strauss's "accumulation of garish effects" and "deliberate preference for the abnormal" formed "the musical correlation to [Wilde's]—to use the favorite word of our time—perversity" (translated and quoted in Seshadri 124). To Max Kalbeck (*Neues Wiener Tageblatt*), Strauss's music presented a "voluptuously disgusting feast for the senses" that brought Wilde's dark secrets to light.

> Excesses that were previously cloaked in seven veils of darkness are staggering around today free and unfettered in the light of day, having thrown off one veil after the other in their dance. First denied and then persecuted, then described and discussed, then understood and excused, then beautified and imitated, they are finally praised and glorified. . . . Adultery,

incest, and sexual madness are the motives; suicide, execution, and necrophilia the consequences of this drama, which spends itself in brutal effects. (*RSHW* 339)

Kalbeck's language operates through sexual signifiers, equating the music with orgasm ("spends itself") and conferring on it sadistic qualities ("brutal"): sexual and stylistic excesses are linked. Kalbeck's colleague Julius Korngold employed similar sexual-pathological language to describe his experience of Strauss's orchestra in the first 1907 Viennese staging of the opera as musical hell: "It is as if it were saturated with the fumes of this dreadful Salome world. Vague reveries, dark rushes of feeling, brutal lust, the failure of sick nerves, delirium, paroxysms, sharp screams, bellowing, howling—everything in this orchestra. What inexhaustible mixtures, what mysterious, satanic, orgiastic, bacchantic sounds!" (ibid. 347).

The emphasis on the pathological excess of the orchestra in these statements encapsulates a simultaneous fear and fascination with the perverse physical body that cannot be rationally controlled as it consumes itself in dangerous erotic pleasures that become aesthetic and vice versa. Romain Rolland, Strauss's collaborator on the French translation of the libretto, wrote to Strauss in May 1907 that Strauss's "strange" and "truly exotic" musical style sustained the sickness of cultural decadence and thus actually held back his modernist aspirations: "In spite of the pretentious affectations of the style, there is an undeniable dramatic power in Wilde's poem; but it has a nauseous and sickly atmosphere about it: it exudes vice and literature. . . . [Y]ou transcend your subject, but you cannot make one forget it" (*Richard Strauss and Romain Rolland: Correspondence,* ed. Myers, 82–83). As John Williamson notes, this reasoning "remain[ed] rooted in the belief that *Salomé* was intended at face value as a case-study in evil and perversion; for Rolland, as for so many otherwise intelligent critics, Wilde had never left the dock" (132). One poignant commentary to this effect was offered by Adam Röder, a local critic for the *Rheinischer Kurier.* After the opera's premiere in Wiesbaden in 1907, Röder wrote:

That Mr. Wilde is homosexual, is unfortunate; he is not responsible and is worthy of pity. Even when he follows his perverse inner drive—his whole way of thinking and feeling is sick, you see—and writes plays that mirror his thoughts and world of the senses, one cannot intervene; but when such things are put on stage and presented within the framework of normal art, then one has to protest in all seriousness. We are no fans of censorship. But if the sadists, masochists, lesbians, and homosexuals approach us demanding that we understand their crazy world of thought and sensibility as expressions of art, then we have to intervene in the name of the healthy. Art has no interest in sanctifying the dirty things that have grown in the soil of sexual madness. One thing only counts in that case: to cry, out with them! It will be the task of our psychiatrists, doctors, politicians, and elected officials to draw attention to the terrible dangers that arise for the physical and mental health of the public at large, if one gives free rein to the army of perverts and they launch themselves on the public via the tools of art. (3, my trans.)

The well-known examples of official censorship of Strauss's opera in Berlin, Vienna, London, Chicago, and New York that followed in the next few years indicate the strictly guarded yet volatile balance of sexuality, aesthetic representation, and morality in the transitional cultural phase between symbolism, decadence, and modernism.[17] In Germany and England, censors sometimes demanded ludicrous changes to the libretto and dramatic presentation, geared at toning down or subverting *Salome's* offensive qualities. In Berlin, Kaiser Wilhelm asked that the last scene be "Christianized": the star of Bethlehem was to appear at the end, to transform a disturbingly open-ended drama of sex and death into a safe allegory of Christian redemption. In London, the English censors only gave permission for the opera's London premiere (of December 8, 1910) after bowdlerizing the libretto and especially Salome's final aria, which incidentally carried dangerous overtones in the context of the contemporary English suffrage movement.[18] Salomé's claim "If thou hadst looked at me thou wouldst have loved me" became a preposterous "If thou hadst looked at me thou wouldst have blessed me," turning Salomé's physical desire into a safe metaphysical quest for spiritual guidance and transforming "a lurid tale of love and revenge" into "a comforting sermon that could have been safely preached from any country pulpit," as conductor Sir Thomas Beecham recalled in *A Mingled Chime* (169).

In New York, *Salome* initially fared not much better. After the Metropolitan Opera premiere under conductor Alfred Hertz on January 22, 1907, reviewers and puritan lobbyists immediately decried the performance as having a "moral stench" (quoted in Tydeman and Price 128). The comment in the *New York Sun* that "[t]he whole story wallows in lust, lewdness, bestial appetites, and abnormal carnality" summarized the reigning moral outrage and highlights the perception of the excessive nature of the piece, especially its final scenes. A 1907 review by Hermann Klein in *Theatre* magazine recounted the swift censorship action by the owners and directors of the Met (including John Pierpont Morgan, W. K. Vanderbilt, and August Belmont), adding that "[i]t was not the character of Salome nor her voluptuous dance [*sic*] of the Seven Veils which offended. It was the repulsive grewsomeness [*sic*], the shuddering horror of the woman fondling a decapitated head, that sickened the public stomach" (70). The opera was withdrawn after just one performance, and despite rapidly following successful productions at the Manhattan Theater as well as in Philadelphia and Boston, the Metropolitan only dared to stage *Salome* again in 1933, twenty-six years later.

In their focus on sexual pathology paired with blasphemy, these acts of censorship also echo the reasons that Wilde's play was banned from the British public stage in 1892. The court censor in Vienna, where Gustav Mahler had worked hard but failed to secure the premiere of Strauss's *Salome* for the Wiener Hofoper in 1905, prohibited the opera for "religious and moral reasons," his notice explaining that "the representation of events which belong to the realm of sexual pathology seem to us not suitable for our court stage" (*Richard-Strauss-Ausstellung zum 100. Geburtstag*, ed. Grasberger and Hadamowsky, 149). In the eyes of many critics and reviewers, the association with Wilde's art and presumed perversity both elevated and disgraced Strauss. In any event, it did not keep his opera, which premiered five years after Wilde's death, from attaining ever greater commercial success than Wilde's original. On the contrary, the subject's scandalous appeal helped situate Strauss firmly in the avant-garde even as he appealed to middle-class tastes. Early audiences gave Strauss's *Salome* an enthusiastic reception:, the work was staged in fifty German opera houses from 1905 to 1907 alone and all over the world shortly thereafter. As Strauss gleefully pointed out, the huge financial success of *Salome* finally enabled him to build his luxury villa in Garmisch (*RR* 152).

In this chapter, I have argued that despite their seemingly divergent styles, Wilde's symbolist-decadent play and Strauss's modernist opera featuring Salome both evince an earnest attempt to manufacture a secular sublime experience by aesthetic means. Strauss emerges as a composer whose emphasis on physical sensation rather than inner depth—on the intensely stimulated body instead of the calmly contemplating soul—connects him to Wilde and the symbolist-decadent attempt to transport the rational self, if only momentarily and purely immanently, outside itself, to a secular ecstatic realm. Art that erases its individual components as it thrusts itself forward, leaving only one overpowering effect of sensation, while treating subject matter that is unabashedly secular, individualist, and rich in appeal to both avant-garde aesthetics and modernist consumerism—this is the fundamental aesthetic connection between Wilde's symbolist-decadent affiliations and Strauss's modernism. In this sense, Mahler was right to point out that Strauss's music enabled his audience to understand "what Wilde's play is all about."

My study of the intersections between Wilde's play and Strauss's opera has several implications for Wilde and Strauss studies, as well as for the transitional phase between late nineteenth-century aestheticism and early twentieth-century modernism. For Wilde scholarship, it demonstrates the need to examine *Salomé* systematically in the light of the otherwise well-established discussion of Wilde as modernist—to make the play less an exception and more a modernist variant in the canon of his works. The secular anthropocentric, even blasphemous individualism and fragmentation of final "meaning" that *Salomé* puts forward are quintessential modernist traits, and so, one might add, is Wilde's popular avant-gardism (his dual appeal to mass consumer culture and to more select artistic circles). For Strauss scholarship, both the contemporary reviewers' opinions and my own theoretical conclusions suggest the need to look at Strauss as a serious musical interpreter rather than a butcher of his literary source, as well as at his relationship with fin de siècle aesthetics, including decadent Wagnerism, which lives on in Strauss's emphasis on corporal affect and synesthetic sensation.

Regarding the proposed aesthetic relations between symbolism-decadence and modernism, my argument endorses and underscores recent developments in both fin de siècle and modernist literary studies by illustrating the problems with critical attempts to define decadence or modernism solely in terms of opposition or "difference" from earlier or later periods.[19] We would be better off, I believe, to think of symbolism-decadence and modernism not as periods (even periods of transition) but as an interrelated dynamic of cultural themes, ideas, and techniques that participate, to greater or lesser degrees, in the development of twentieth-century modernity. Suspending the artificial temporal and cultural binaries between fin de siècle and modernist studies and challenging the disciplinary barriers between literary and musicological analytic discourses (as well as, e.g., visual, cinematic, and artistic ones) may shed new light on what, for artists such as Wilde and Strauss, "being modern" was all about.

3

Perverts in Court: Maud Allan's *The Vision of Salomé* and the Pemberton-Billing Trial

This chapter considers the first influential modernist female interpreter of Wilde's play, the Canadian American dancer Maud Allan, who shot to international fame with *The Vision of Salomé* in London in 1908. Scholars studying dance or lesbian legal and cultural history and scholars of Wilde's cultural afterlife have been very interested in Allan because of her tragic involvement in the 1918 Pemberton-Billing Trial, in which Allan and the avant-garde theatrical producer and director J. T. Grein became the targets of a sexual-political smear campaign against their private staging of Wilde's *Salomé.* Despite the well-established scholarship on the trial and Allan's previous dance career, however, the complex connections between Allan's pioneering professional, inherently feminist work as a dancer and Oscar Wilde's transgressive *Salomé*, as well as the momentous cultural conflation between artistic and sexual "perversity" in Allan's art, have not been systematically explored.

Like Wilde's, Allan's art crossed established boundaries of art, morality, and gender, challenging social, cultural, and political conventions, and it is no coincidence that she chose *Salomé* as her platform. Adapting *Salomé* for modern female solo dance gave Allan a chance to make her mark as an avant-garde artist by following in the footsteps of Wilde, Reinhardt, and Strauss. To her "goes the distinction of performing the first important Salome dance in the post-Strauss era, independent of the play and the opera—in Europe at any rate" (Bizot 74), and she was the first female adapter of Wilde's scenario for the stage. This was all the more daring because her provocative subject matter and revealing stage attire prompted contemporaries to identify Allan with the suffragettes' calls for women's greater social,

83

cultural, and political independence, though Allan was never actually involved with those campaigns and vigorously denied the association. Even though the public was enamored with Allan's grace, physical beauty, and marketing as a serious artist, *The Vision of Salomé* was understood as gender rebellion against women's traditional morality and modesty, especially since it was put forth by a financially, legally, and sexually independent woman. Contemporaries also feared that Allan's popularity would corrupt her enthusiastic female audiences. In the public's eye, Allan's half-naked Salomé dangerously merged the specter of Wilde's homosexuality with "perverse" feminist ideas that threatened the very fabric of society. Transgressive art became synonymous with transgressive sexualities.

Maud Allan's *The Vision of Salomé*

Born in Canada and growing up in the United States and in Europe, Allan's ambition was to make a serious impact and build a name for herself as an artist. She had originally planned to become a classical pianist and studied with excellent musicians in Berlin (including composer Ferruccio Busoni), but when her music career did not really take off as much as she had hoped, she decided to switch career paths to modern dance. As much as Allan's talent, shrewd business sense, and independent artistic spirit were unmistakable factors in her career, she was spurred on by personal factors as well. One reason for Allan's keen wish for personal and professional success was a dark and tightly guarded secret in her recent family history that put keen pressure on her to ease her family's shame. In 1895, shortly after Maud Allan had left to start her classical piano lessons in Berlin, her beloved brother Theo Durrant had murdered, raped, and mutilated two young women in a San Francisco church, a much-publicized crime for which he was first imprisoned and then executed at San Quentin in 1898. As a consequence, Maud Allan (born Beulah Maud Durrant) changed her name and followed her mother's urgent entreaties to stay in Europe, where Theo's horrible deeds had not made the headlines the way "the crime of the century" had in the United States. In an 1899 letter, her mother, Isabella, wrote, "You must make a name for yourself if you wish to gladden our last days, or nothing else in the world will make up for our loss but showing the world that you as well as he were ambitious. Now, my dear, close your teeth tight and say I WILL, even if it takes every minute of my time, I will, I shall I MUST and NOTHING will prevent it!" (quoted in Cherniavsky, *Salome Dancer* 118).

Although she had had no prior formal dance training and was already twenty-seven years old at the time she started to dance at private house performances for friends and acquaintances, Allan recognized the opportunities of the developing field of modern dance for aspiring female artists. Due to Isadora Duncan's recent successes as a performer and teacher, modern dance was a fashionable and welcoming new field of opportunity for talented young women, even untrained ones: "Not only were late starters welcome [in modern dance], but, with no tradition behind it, this new art form was, by definition, begun with dilettantes with big ideas. . . . An amateur like Maud could be not only a pioneer in this newfound profession but a leader" (Bentley 57). Even though Isadora Duncan was a clear influence on Allan's barefoot dancing style, Allan denied the association, probably to establish her independence.[1]

Maud Allan and Marcel Rémy, the Belgian composer for *The Vision of Salomé,* had both seen Max Reinhardt's avant-garde production of Wilde's *Salomé* in Berlin and, like Strauss, been inspired by it.[2] Now following in Reinhardt's and Strauss's footsteps and capitalizing on their success, Allan's *The Vision of Salomé* courted comparison with these trailblazers and marked Allan's ambition to be perceived as a pioneering innovator of modern dance. The association with Reinhardt, Strauss, and Wilde helped place *The Vision of Salomé* in the context of avant-garde art while simultaneously demonstrating its aesthetic independence from them, as well as from the only previous famous Salome dancer, Loïe Fuller.[3]

The most important female solo dancer of the late nineteenth century, Fuller had performed a Salome routine in a *pantomime lyrique* at the Comédie-Parisienne in March 1895, with music by Gabriel Pierné and designs by Georges-Antoine Rochegrosse, but it was based on Massenet's *Hérodiade* rather than Wilde's play.[4] Allan knew Fuller's piece well, and it is possible that Fuller's innocent, childlike, spiritually seeking Salomé influenced her somewhat in conceiving of her own version. Still, Allan's *The Vision of Salomé* was clearly an independent work of art.[5] In May 1907, both Fuller and her protégée Maud Allan were dancing their separate versions at the Théâtre des Variétés and the Théâtre des Arts, strategically scheduled to coincide with the premiere of Strauss's *Salome* at L'Opéra Paris. While Allan's *The Vision of Salomé* received glowing reviews, *La Tragédie de Salomé*— a 1907 revision of Fuller's earlier routine that dance scholar Rhonda Garelick describes as "an over-the-top extravaganza complete with 4500 feathers, 650 lamps, and 15 projectors"—met with scorn: "Reviews were unkind toward this middle-aged, overweight woman playing seductress. . . . It was the last time she ever allowed her body to appear onstage, and the first and last time she ever placed herself in an overtly sexual role on-stage" (*Electric Salome* 93). Allan quickly surpassed Fuller as the iconic Salome dancer of the 1900s. *The Vision of Salomé* (1906) was loosely based on the two transgressive highlights of Wilde's play, the dance before Herod and Salomé's speech of love and grief to the severed head, reimagined as a dream scene in which Salomé relives the brutal destruction of her innocence. Allan's piece recognizably alluded to Salomé's necrophilic love monologue in Wilde, performed as a dance of love, horror, fear, and triumph addressed to John the Baptist's head, which Allan handled and caressed.

From the beginning, Allan insisted on her artistic originality, citing the poses she had observed and studied in ancient Greek art as her main inspiration. To friends, she explained that she had "sought all [her] attitudes and movements in the art galleries of Europe, on Etruscan vases and Assyrian tablets . . . model[ing her] attitudes and motions on their crude perspectives" (quoted in Blathwayt 296).[6] Allan was silent on another, more scientific source of influence, however, the Delsartean movement technique and body culture then wildly popular in North America, which "linked [Allan] to the American women's health reform movement and to the amateur tradition of *tableau vivant*" (Walkowitz, par. 35). This influence did not escape J. T. Grein: "Good old Delsarte, . . . forgotten in Europe, is having his day. For the Duncans and Maud Allans, *what else are they* but Delsartians. If proof were needed it would be easy to harmonize their every movement with the doctrines of the French aesthete and the fact that both ladies hail from the American continent where the Delsartian theory is taught in many girls' schools" (quoted in Walkowitz, par. 37).[7] Referring only to her ancient and mythological models as official sources of her art and not specifically acknowledging Delsarte's somewhat more mundane modern influence had the advantage that Allan could place her revealing costumes into a long accepted cultural tradition of the beauty of the nude or natural human form. This tradition ideally helped her justify her rather daring appearance on the public stage, "at a time when actors and actresses had only recently become socially acceptable and the association between actresses and prostitutes was still common, despite the influx of middle class women into the theatre in the 1890s" (Koritz, "Dancing the Orient" 75). Allan's appearance as Salomé, as documented in many surviving promotion photographs and postcards (see fig. 2), was shocking for a time when Edwardian ladies still wore full-length gowns and did not show bare legs or feet in public: "She wore nothing above her waist but breastplates of pearls and jewels held in place by a [*sic*] open mesh of gold and pearls. Around her hips hung more strings of pearls over a transparent black ninon skirt, its

4946 C ROTARY PHOTO, E.C   MISS MAUD ALLAN,
AS " SALOME."   FOULSHAM & BANFIELD.

Fig. 2. Postcard featuring Maud Allan in *The Vision of Salomé* (c. 1908)

hem embroidered with gold and jewels," a "jangling, swaying costume" that enthralled or scandalized viewers (Hoare 76).

Maud Allan's bare legs in particular caused a sensation, since women's legs and feet were still commonly concealed objects of erotic fantasy. The Duchess of Sermoneta wrote in her memoir, "I remember Maudie Ashley writing to me when I was in Rome: 'I have seen this new dancer, Maud Allan, at the Palace. I examined her most carefully through my opera glasses and—*she does not wear tights!*' It seemed incredible!" (91–92). Arthur Compton-Ricketts, a literary critic and historian who had known Allan since her first season at the Palace Theatre, commented, "For any dancer to appear stockingless on the stage was unknown—almost inconceivable. . . . bare legs! Horrible! [But] Maud Allan showed how lovely the human body can be with a yard or two of *crêpe de Chine,* and bare legs and arms" (199). Eager to establish and maintain her moral reputation as an Edwardian lady, Allan was careful to signal a clear break between her public art and her private appearance, by dressing with impeccable and demure style offstage.

After her initial professional debut as an aesthetic dancer at Vienna's highly respected Conservatory of Music on December 24, 1903—with a program of Mendelssohn's "Spring Song," Schubert's "Ave Maria," and Rubinstein's "Valse Caprice"—and after another appearance in Brussels in late 1904, *The Vision of Salomé* premiered at Vienna's Carl-Theater on December 26, 1906, in front of an invited audience that included Max Beerbohm and other cultural luminaries. After a subsequent tour that took her to Budapest, Munich, and Paris from January to May 1907, Allan's big break came in September 1907: she was invited to perform privately for King Edward VII, who was vacationing at the Hotel Weimar in Marienbad. "The King expressed a wish to see her dance," the king's private secretary Sir Frederick Ponsonby wrote in his memoirs, "but I was rather doubtful whether it would be right for His Majesty to do so. I had been told that she danced more or less naked . . . with only two oyster shells and a five franc piece." Perhaps to defend the king's taste, Ponsonby stressed Allan's artistry and modesty: "Her dance as Salome with the head of John the Baptist was really most dramatic, and although I cannot say she wore many clothes, there was nothing the least indecent about her performance" (341–42). The king was thoroughly enchanted, and his open endorsement won Allan a lucrative contract at one of London's major music halls, the Palace Theatre. There Allan appeared in over 250 sold-out performances starting in March 1908, after further tour stops in Prague, Hamburg, and Berlin. Ironically, the venue in which Allan performed was the same in which Sarah Bernhardt had been scheduled to perform *Salomé* under Wilde's direction in

1892 (it was then still a theater and not yet a music hall).[8] By a fortunate twist of British censorship rules, public performances of mere dance versions of biblical matter were permissible even though plays were not: the theatrical censor did not have jurisdiction over music halls. In any case, the king himself had already signaled his keen approval, so censorship must have seemed unwarranted.

Allan's Success at the Palace Theatre

The royal endorsement of Maud Allan's performance was a particular bonus for the Palace Theatre, as nothing could really be offensive about an artistic presentation even the king had praised. At the time, popular music halls, such as the Palace or the Alhambra Theatre of Varieties, were still controversial for their eroticism, alcohol, bawdy songs, jokes, and general association with immorality. Derived in the 1850s from the tradition of pubs and singing saloons, music halls offered a variety entertainment program with food, drink, and public dancing. As Dagmar Kift shows in *The Victorian Music Hall,* the combination of alcohol and bodily contact together with a reputation for often raucous and bawdy performances that satirized traditional Victorian values and morals made music halls a prime target for moral reformers and a frequent subject of passionate political debate as well as official intervention or closure.

Coincidentally, when Allan appeared on the scene, London's music halls had started to seek out a more respectable clientele to counter political and cultural criticism, by offering a more appealing middle-class program that included scenes from currently fashionable and popular middle-class plays, famous opera arias or duets, and ballets (Bailey xii). At her public debut at the Palace Theatre on March 8, 1908, Allan presented a twenty-minute program consisting of three dances set to Rubinstein and Mendelssohn, as well as *The Vision of Salomé,* her most popular routine. She was programmed as one "'turn' on the venue's variety bill alongside acts such as impersonators, caricaturists and educated sea lions" (Carter 40). Nevertheless, Amy Koritz argues, "Allan's middle-class status, Continental education, and elite sponsorship distinguished her from the typical music hall performer"; the artistic tone and demeanor of her dance presentations elevated not only her own erotic performance but the reputation of the music hall as well (*Gendering Bodies* 31). Allan's dance was also a welcome replacement for the wildly popular *tableaux vivants,* which had been banned as recently as 1907 for their controversial erotic quality (Walkowitz, par. 26). Allan presented Salomé as "a mystifying mixture of the erotic and the exotic, artfully shrouded in a veil of Edwardian discretion and good taste," playing on the thin line between art and sex (Cherniavsky, *Salome Dancer* 167). Hence *The Vision of Salomé* ideally combined the sensual allure of the music hall with the moral and artistic respectability that lured middle-class audiences. It presented a highly successful marriage of artistic innovation and popular eroticism: "Whether through luck or shrewdness, Maud Allan had hit upon a highly marketable formula, composed of sexuality and pseudo-spirituality, apparent innocence, a transparent skirt, and thinly-disguised lust, the whole package wrapped up in the rhetoric of High Aesthetic purpose" (Bizot 76).

Palace Theatre manager Alfred Butt prepared Allan's appearance with an extensive marketing campaign that included an exclusive matinee preview performance in front of selected invitees (on March 6, 1908) and a fully illustrated advertising pamphlet that suggested the eroticism of Allan's performance and body while stressing that she was a great artist who had won royal endorsement (see Cherniavsky, "Allan, Part III" 121–23). In this pamphlet, the sexual allure of Allan's potentially offensive performance was channeled back into the realm of intellectual art and regal femininity that downplays overt sexual appeal as a mere expression of aesthetic refinement.

Contemporary reviewers picked up on the same tension between promiscuity and art in Allan's performance. The *Observer*'s reviewer wrote that Allan's dance embodied "the most graceful and rhythmic forms of classic Greece" while suggesting "the whole voluptuousness of Eastern femininity" (quoted in Cherniavsky, *Salome Dancer* 164). On March 10, 1908, the London *Times* called Allan's performance "voluptuous" but took care to point out that it was far from "lascivious": "every movement was beautiful. There is no extravagance or sensationalism about Miss Allan's dancing; even when crouching over the head of her victim, caressing it or shrinking away from it in horror, she subordinated every gesture and attitude to the conditions of her art." Probably responding to the public controversy about Allan's costume, the reviewer saw the need to add that both her costume and her performance were "absolutely free of offense" and "completely . . . justified in her art" (quoted in Cherniavsky, "Allan, Part III" 126–27). The *Daily News* also praised Allan's "beautiful work. . . . The dancing itself is a poem, and none but the most prurient could see the slightest appeal to any sense but that of beauty of motion and pose" (quoted in ibid. 125). In an article in *The New Age* entitled "The Maud Allan Myth," which compared Maud Allan to Isadora Duncan but was critical of her claim to true artistry, W. R. Titterton mildly praised Allan's less provocative dances but wrote, evidently disappointed at her lack of lurid appeal, "The Salome is detestable.

I cannot imagine anything more immoral and less artistic than this pas-
sionless aping of the gestures of lust, this intoxication hammered out cold.
Was that why they stopped her dancing in Vienna? Vienna never places em-
bargo on the merely nude" (quoted in ibid. 137). On July 4, 1908, Max
Beerbohm countered in the well-respected *Saturday Review,* "For my part, I
cannot imagine a more ladylike performance" (quoted in ibid. 138).

Lingering memories of the transgressions of Wilde and his 1890s circle
accompanied the sight of Allan's risqué attire and her talk of her own artistic ambitions, however, just as they had Strauss's opera. Although Allan's
routine did not include any direct references to Wilde's figure or his homosexuality, the simple fact that it was based on one of his works caused some
critics to condemn *The Vision of Salomé.* The *Spectator* openly disapproved
of Allan's choice of Wilde as a literary source: "Unless we are greatly mistaken the notion of [Salomé's] love for John the Baptist had its origin in the
depraved imagination of one whose literary gift was in essence flashy and
mechanical, and who cannot rightly be called a poet and a man of letters,
unless the notoriety of impudence, scandal and aberration is held to confer
that title" (quoted in Koritz, *Gendering Bodies* 36–37). Walter Higgins of the
Labour Leader thundered even more loudly,

> London has never seen such a glorification of the flesh. . . . Night after
> night this comely girl from Toronto dances before appreciative crowds, the
> lower limbs clad in the thinnest of veils, the rest of her body naked save for
> a few trinkets. . . . In the soft blue light Miss Allan's white limbs, gleaming
> through the clinging draperies of dusky gauze, reminded me of nothing so
> much as the pestilential mists rising from Eastern tropical swamps. . . . Al-
> ways the fascination is animal-like and carnal. . . . She kisses the head, and
> frenzy comes upon her. She is no longer human. She is a Maenad sister.
> . . . In the "Vision of Salome" there is nothing redeeming, nothing that
> purges, nothing that lifts the thoughts above and beyond the beauties of
> the body. It is the incarnation of the bestial in Oscar Wilde and Aubrey
> Beardsley. (Quoted in Cherniavsky, "Allan, Part III" 127–28)

Coincidentally, Lord Alfred Douglas, Wilde's former lover, also joined the
chorus of Maud Allan's critics. *The Academy,* a magazine Douglas edited, ran
an article entitled "All We Like Sheep" by Christopher St. John (Christabel
Marshall), which called Allan's act "grit" and "fluff." According to the article,
which appeared with Douglas's sanction, Allan was a fraud, since she was
neither original nor well trained in dance: "There is very little art in Miss Allan's performance" (quoted in ibid. 131). This was the first in a series of
fateful animosities between Lord Alfred Douglas and Maud Allan (Hoare

78), which did not bode well for their legal battle in the Pemberton-Billing Trial almost one decade later.[9]

Still, Maud Allan's engagement at the Palace Theatre was an overwhelming popular success that, for a while, made her one of the biggest stars in London. Her contract was extended from the initial two weeks to eighteen months. Her performance "saw the biggest box-office receipts in the history of the Palace, and thanks to Maud's popularity, its shareholders received a 33 percent dividend" (Bentley 65). Allan herself earned the princely sum of £250 a week at the Palace and asked at least £200 for private performances; *Salomé* made her a rich woman. In 1909 and 1911, she returned to the Palace Theatre for another series of engagements that broke box office records; between 1910 and 1915, she also went on tours to the United States, Russia, South Africa, India, Singapore, Hong Kong, New Zealand, and Australia.

Burlesques, parodies, and popular music hall songs attest to Allan's iconic status at the time. In London, a highly successful *Sal-oh-Mee!* revue was playing at the Alhambra Theatre. *Sal-oh-Mee!* (called *Sal Oh My!* by some scholars) followed quickly on Allan's *The Vision of Salomé* (Allan opened on March 8, *Sal-oh-Mee* on March 30). Parisian dancer La Belle Leonora satirized Maud Allan's Salomé (Carter 38). As *The Era* described, "The Baptist's head must have presented a somewhat more farcical image in the Alhambra's burlesque of *Salomé,* for here it was crowned by a trick wig which allowed the 'hair to stand on end at suitable moments'" (ibid. 43).

A wealth of original music hall songs of the period also satirized Allan's popularity and the Salome dance vogue she helped inspire in 1908. My recent research in the British Library turned up a host of popular music hall song parodies of this wave of Salome imitators, most of which have not yet been studied.[10] One of these, "Salome (The sheep's head and the tin-tack)," portrays a man's "crazy wife Naomie" who becomes one of the promiscuous Salome imitators. Increasingly mad, she threatens to take the man's own head, prompting him to take defensive measures. The song illustrates the cultural association between the Salome dance craze and the perceived dangers to male authority, as well as to female modesty and sanity.

VERSE:
My crazy wife Naomie,
Took me out one night to show me
A lady fair with feet all bare,
The rage of Town—Salomé.
To some music wild and weird

She danced about promiscuous,
But what was great, upon a plate
She'd an old man's head with whiskers.
It drove my poor wife off her head,
And now at night when I'm in bed—

CHORUS:
Salomé, Salomé, My old girl's Salomé!
Night and day with her feet all bare
On a tintack here, and a tintack there
She's gliding and sliding, Salomé up to date;
Like Maud Allan in the picture,
With a sheep's head on a plate!

VERSE:
While all the neighbours clap her,
She will dance with that sheep's napper,
Upon a dish, meanwhile I wish
That I'd been born a scrapper.
When she falls down feeling faint,
If I run up to fan her,
She says my head she'll have instead,
So that she can save a "tanner."
And then that sheep's head looking glum,
Will drop its jaw and bite her thumb. (*Repeat Chorus*)

VERSE:
I'd like to bet a gallon,
Not a halfpint, a gallon,
Without the rows of beads she'll pose,
And spiflicate Maud Allan.
Now the sheep's head's run away,
At night you'll hear her holloa,
For my poor head, but while in bed
I wear a cast-iron collar.
She's lost her "nut," now that's the sign,
For me to watch I don't lose mine. (*Repeat Chorus*)

Several short Salome-themed films also appeared at the height of Allan's fame in 1908 and 1909: "Salome; or, The Dance of the Seven Veils" (United States: Vitagraph, 1908); "If You Had A Wife Like This" (United States, exact date unknown), a comedy in which a jealous wife chases her Salome-obsessed husband and transforms the dance into a husband-beating domestic "dance"; "The Saloon Dance" (United States, 1908), a burlesque;

"Salome Craze" (United States: Phoenix Film Company, 1909), satirizing the Salome dance craze; "The Salome Dance Music" (Britain, 1909), synchronized to Strauss's Dance of the Seven Veils on gramophone; and two different shorts entitled "Salome Mad" (Britain, 1909), one a comedic portrayal of a man's obsession with the Salome dance and the other a chase film in which a man chases a Salome poster underwater. Most of these films are now extinct (see Bizot 78, 82; Simonson 9–10). A later silent movie, *The Rugmaker's Daughter* (1915), described in detail by Elizabeth Weigand, featured Maud Allan in the title role and followed an orientalist plotline during which Allan performed three of her dance routines (but not *The Vision of Salomé*).

Allan's popularity was so great that "[i]n the burgeoning Edwardian consumer society, Maud was a marketing dream" (Hoare 80). Flowerpot statuettes of Allan were sold as souvenirs in London's gift shops; "[c]artoons, monographs, sonnets, essays, interviews, burlesques, and satires surfaced, all featuring Maud as Salome. A photograph of her in costume, seated and pensive, became a popular greeting card of the day, its caption reading, 'Thinking of you'" (Bentley 66). Hamburg sculptor Artur Bock (briefly Allan's fiancé) sculpted an erotic statue of her that depicted her kneeling in front of the severed head, bare-breasted. She also modeled for Kaulbach, Grutzner, and Franz von Stuck's three well-known oil paintings of a semi-nude Salome dancing ecstatically next to the prophet's severed head.[11] The dandy novelist Ronald Firbank mentioned Allan in one of the two prefaces he drafted for *The Artificial Princess* (originally entitled *Salome; or, 'Tis a Pity That She Would*), a posthumously published, satirical modernist novel that adapts Wilde's *Salomé* as a comedy in the vein of Laforgue's ironic style: "It was about the time of the Maud Allen [sic] boom & the Straus [sic] cult (a little previous to the Russian Ballet) & the minds of young boys turned from their Greece to the Palace Theatre, Vienna & Berlin" (quoted in Benkowitz 115). As Louise Wright has shown, D. H. Lawrence also loosely based a literary character on Allan, Miss Maud Callum in his novel *The Lost Girl,* further attesting to Allan's overwhelming visibility in the popular culture of the 1900s.

Maud Allan's innovative artistic dance interpretation of Wilde's play, paired with her remarkable musical talent and attractive looks, ensured that she stood out among the crowd of Salome dancers. The so-called Salome dance craze, or "Salomania," was hitting European and U.S. vaudeville stages at this time, partly due to Allan's own success in 1908. "Salomania" developed simultaneously on both sides of the Atlantic between approximately 1907 and 1914. It was fueled by the orientalist dance vogue already present as well as by the scandalous successes of Strauss's opera throughout Europe.[12] In New York, theater and vaudeville impresario Oscar Hammerstein first took note of Allan's success and sent the talented vaudeville performer, imitator, and dancer Gertrude Hoffman to London to study and plagiarize Allan's routine. They named their work *A Vision of Salome*. According to the *Hartford Courant*, Hoffman's costume was even more outrageous than Allan's: "Miss Hoffman had on, above her waist, first a black wig and a good make-up, second a lot of jewelry and chains [*sic*] and there is no third" (quoted in Bizot 78). In fact, Hoffman did wear "a pair of tight, thigh-length trunks under her filmy skirt, but these were often not visible beyond the footlights" (ibid. 82). Ironically, Hoffman's creative imitation was so successful that it overshadowed and eclipsed Maud Allan's original when Allan finally arrived for her first U.S. tour in January 1910 (going from Boston to Carnegie Hall, New York, and on to her former hometown, San Francisco): imitator and imitated traded places as "Salomania" raged across the United States.

Most of Allan's Salome dance rivals hailed from vaudeville or opera stages. One popular Salome dancer, Bianca Froelich, had been scheduled to perform the Dance of the Seven Veils in the banned 1907 Metropolitan Opera's production of Strauss's *Salome* before taking her routine to New York's Lincoln Square Variety Theater. Froelich's success set off a wave of vaudeville Salomes in the United States, starting with La Belle Dazié (Daisy Peterkin of Detroit) who shot to fame in 1907 in a Salome parody at the Ziegfeld Follies, mainly by wearing very little clothing. Dazié even opened her own Salome dance school for amateurs and "was sending approximately 150 Salomés every month into the nations' vaudeville circuits, each armed with the same routine—an incoherent mix of gestures and undulations addressed to a papier-mâché head" (Kendall 75). Other noteworthy U.S. vaudeville and opera Salome dancers of the time include Eva Tanguay, a white Salome who included risqué racist-sexual imagery alluding to the minstrel tradition in her version and who parodied Hoffmann (see Glenn 108–10); Aida Overton Walker, a black Salome with considerable choreographic talent and artistic originality who alluded to black women's struggles but was eclipsed by her white female rivals (see Krasner 193, 199–206); Gertrude Hoffman, a Maud Allan imitator from New York (see Simonson 5–8; Glenn 102–6; Kendall 75–76); Mary Garden, an opera singer at Oscar Hammerstein's Manhattan Opera House who sang as well as danced the part in 1909 (see Kendall 77; Simonson 11–12); and Julian

Eltinge (born William Dalton), a female impersonator and musical and film star who parodied Salome's hyperfeminine appeal and also made a career giving ladies fashion advice (see Glenn 111–12; Senelick, *Changing Room* 307). Ruth St. Denis, who had made a career of orientalist eroticism in dance, also started a Salome dance project at the same time as Allan did, about 1906.[13] Ida Rubinstein starred in a scandalous St. Petersburg production of Wilde's *Salomé* in 1908 (performed completely in mime, with dance choreography by Michel Fokine and costumes by Leon Bakst, who soon went on to Ballets Russes fame). She identified strongly with the role, but the production was severely censored and then shut down by the Holy Synod of the Russian Orthodox Church after just one performance (see Townsend, "Staking Salome" 171). Rubinstein was not to perform the Dance of the Seven Veils again until 1912, during six performances of Wilde's *Salomé* in a gala at the Théâtre du Chatelet in Paris.

Allan's Artistry

Maud Allan's performance situated itself on the dangerous threshold between the patrolled limits of the private erotic body and the public domain of art. This precarious liminality constituted her success but also her risk to be taken seriously as a female artist who publicly displayed her body as the main artistic instrument. One of the first women artists to take on Salomé as a career-defining role, Maud Allan had not only to reckon with the transgressive associations the name of Oscar Wilde brought up but also to contend with the sultry and sexy orientalist visual and literary heritage from Flaubert to Moreau to Huysmans. While this heritage surely increased Allan's box office appeal to crowds who came to see an almost-naked, sexy Salomé, it also endangered her personal reputation. Just as Wilde's queer body was read and traced in hindsight through his aesthetic creed, Maud Allan's gender-transgressive body entered into a bewitching fusion with her art in the eyes of the public and was easily mistaken as sexual spectacle. Allan commented on this in a 1907 interview with the *Augusta Herald*.

> It takes tremendous courage . . . to come out on stage before hundreds with feet bare, with little dress. . . . Every time I appear, until the spirit gets into me, it is as though I were about to undergo martyrdom. Don't you think that is courage—to fight down and go out and face the thing you dread? . . . Hundreds peering at you from a darkened house. Eyes of men, eyes of women. In how many are there other lights of contempt—of desire? Each time I dance I think of it and I dread it. (Quoted in Cherniavsky, *Salome Dancer* 145–46)

Yet for Allan it was precisely the sensual appeal of the dancer's body that defined her art. In a letter to the newspaper *Magyar Szinpad* shortly after her acclaimed Budapest debut on January 4, 1907, she publicly defended it as a necessary tool for aesthetic creation: "The dancer's body is her instrument, the raw material, just as the violin is to the violinist, and clay is to the sculptor. Is it really possible to cover up this raw material when it is precisely this that brings about the desired artistic effect?" (quoted in Cherniavsky, *Salome Dancer* 145). Such public statements show Allan's genuine desire to be taken seriously as an artist. Time and again, she stressed her desire to transform, change, and innovate not only the techniques but also the reputation and reception of modern dance. Even before the Ballets Russes was beginning to revolutionize dance as highbrow artistic entertainment in cities all over Europe from 1909 to 1929, Allan's importance as an innovator of modern dance was recognized by such contemporaries as Arthur Compton-Ricketts: "Pavlova and the Russian Ballet were still things of the future, and nothing like Maud Allan's classical dancing had ever been seen on the English stage . . . she was, so far as London was concerned, a pioneer" (199). In her own profession, Allan was just as interested as Wilde was in innovating the stage.

Maud Allan's autobiography *My Life and Dancing,* published and marketed strategically on the occasion of her 250th performance at the Palace Theatre in 1908, concludes with a chapter entitled "Salomé," in which Allan comments extensively on *The Vision of Salomé* and explains her creative interpretation of Wilde's play. Scholars have generally either ignored or dismissed *My Life and Dancing* as a highly unreliable, fabricated text—a "cliché-ridden, overblown narrative" (Bizot 76). It is true that the text whitewashes aspects of Allan's childhood and family background to shield the awful family secret about Theo; she also seizes the opportunity to defend her moral reputation as an artist. Nevertheless, there is no reason to assume that Allan outrightly lied about her aesthetic rationale and understanding of *The Vision of Salomé,* the work she regarded as the cornerstone of her career; and the autobiography provides important clues to her own understanding of her art. Allan writes that she is glad to write the book "if for none other [reason], that it gives me an opportunity to explain what is the meaning that I wish to convey by my dance 'The Vision of Salomé'; a meaning that has been dimly guessed by some, hinted at by others, and perhaps more widely misunderstood by what in Jacobean times were called 'the groundlings' than any dance in my collection" (120).

Like the dance itself, Allan's verbal description of it in her autobiography's final chapter is divided into two parts, entitled "This is the Dance of

Salomé" and "This is the Vision of Salomé." The latter is presented as a dream in which Salomé relives her dance and the encounter with the Baptist's head. The dream conceit allowed Allan to focus on Salomé, eliminating all other characters and focusing on Salomé's inner life, her memories and emotions. The first part describes a childlike, innocent Salomé ("hardly more than a child, fourteen I take her to have been") and draws the reader into her luxurious but prisonlike orientalist surroundings (120–21). Allan continues this theme after Salomé has danced and received the head: "Think of the terror of that moment to the child. She had heard of John as of a great, good man, who preached purity and higher things than she had ever known in the debasing luxuries of the court. Buoyed up by the excitement of her triumph she had put the ghastly trophy of her skill into the hands of her mother" (124). This final image of a terrified Salomé alone on the moonlit terrace precedes an intense inner vision, the centerpiece of Allan's dance.

> She stands panting, aghast, her hands pressed to her young breasts; she raises them, and, bowing her head to meet them, sees upon her naked flesh, upon the hands that seek her flesh, upon the hands that seek her smarting eyes, the purple, sticky stain that she has not been able to avoid—it is the blood of the Baptist, John. The sight turns her for a moment to stone. Then it brings the whole ghastly scene back, as in a vision. (Allan 124–25)

Allan's introduction sets the mood to trancelike, mysterious dreaming. Her description of Salomé's vision carries overtones of Flaubert's *Salammbô.*

> Drawn by an irresistible force, Salomé in a dream descends the marble steps leading from the bronze doors that she has just flung to, behind her frightened attendants. The sombre stone obelisks, backed by the inky darkness of the cypress trees, shut out the silver rays of the moon, and, save for the flickering red light of the cresset flames that the slaves have lit, all is mystic darkness, and to Salomé's overwrought brain all is fantastic, vague. (ibid. 125)

As she remembers the words of her mother and "the greedy glittering eyes of her stepfather," Salomé "lives again *the awful moments of joy and of horror* which she has just passed through" (ibid. 125, my emphasis). Like Wilde's princess, she experiences emotional extremes that take her from triumph at her own power and freedom to despair as she fails to achieve what she most longs for. When the severed head, "a pale, sublime face with its mass of long black hair arises before her," Salomé's "ecstasy mingle[s] with dread," and she physically experiences the absolute intensity of desire: "Every fibre of her youthful body is quivering; a sensation hitherto utterly unknown to her is awakened" (ibid. 126).

Allan's Salomé, like Wilde's, experiences irreversible individuation through the experience of intense sensual sublimity: "The awakening is that of her childish heart. The realisation of a superior power has so taken possession of her that she is spurred on to sacrifice everything even unto herself to conquer. . . . What passes in those few moments through this excited, half-terror-stricken, half-stubborn brain makes of little Salomé a woman!" (ibid. 126–27). When she kisses the Baptist, "the curtain of darkness that had enveloped her soul falls, the strange grandeur of a power higher than Salomé has ever dreamed of beholding becomes visible to her, and her anguish becomes vibrant. . . . The Revelation of Something far greater still breaks upon her, and stretching out her trembling arms turns her soul rejoicing towards Salvation" (127). Here we see Allan's narrative taking a dutiful turn toward religious orthodoxy. Perhaps to appease her critics, her verbal description of the performance channels Salomé's horror, joy, ecstasy, and sensual quivering into an unconvincing interpretation of Salomé's soul in need to submit to a higher force. Even in Allan's ostensibly chaste interpretation of Salomé's desires and actions as spiritually motivated, however, Allan's rhetorical emphasis echoes Wilde's transcendental, tragic realization of Salomé's final monologue: "It is gone! Where, oh, where! A sudden wild grief overmasters her, and the fair young Princess, bereft of all her pride, her childish gaiety, and her womanly desire, falls, her hands grasping high above her for her lost redemption, a quivering huddled mass" (ibid.).

In Allan's interpretation, Salomé's intense yearning and loss are a physical anguish not unlike the one Flaubert's erotic priestess Salammbô experienced for the moon goddess Tanit, and Salomé's dramatic giving in to the awareness of complete and utter loss does not diminish the powerful agency and freedom displayed in her dance with the head just moments earlier. Allan's dance effectively beautifies Salomé's mourning and longing, showing her horror at the deed and nostalgic longing for the dead prophet who is now paradoxically both within and beyond her reach. She undergoes a symbolic change at the moment of her most intense self-actualization (expressed by her falling to the floor in "a quivering huddled mass"), and we know that she will forever be transformed; there is no going back. Allan's explanation of Salomé's simultaneous experience of "joy and horror" connects her version to the modernist aesthetic of physical sensation and transgression, a line that runs from Wilde to Strauss to Bataille (see chap.

1). As this brief analysis shows, scholars have perhaps underestimated Allan's sensitivity to Wilde's (and, indirectly, Strauss's) versions in *My Life and Dancing*. Allan had a profound understanding of the modernist sublime, the connection of physical ecstasy to a nonreligious, entirely human apotheosis. It also suggests that even a spiritual interpretation of Wilde's princess held feminist potential for contemporaries. No matter how hard Allan tried, no attempted reinterpretation of Salomé's desire as spiritual or religious yearning could hide Salomé's or Allan's transgressive force from audiences.

Maud Allan and the Suffragettes

For many contemporaries, the strength of an aggressively sexual character like Salomé on stage evoked the aims and tone of the early feminists' forceful publicity of women's increasing demands for legal, political, and cultural enfranchisement and independence in their rebellion against traditional gender roles and sexual objectification. As a widely recognized "archetype of the sybaritic, bodily and sexual," Salomé became a potential "vehicle for appropriation by a second cultural force, feminism"; she was "a powerful symbol in the age of the *femme nouvelle*" because of her self-reliance and open rebellion against the patriarchal status quo (Caddy 38). Embodying rebellion, individualism, and violence, Allan's Salomé came dangerously close to and was openly associated with the causes of feminism and militant suffragism. Amy Koritz writes that Maud Allan's success coincided with the English suffrage movement's first mass demonstrations, which presented a strong public picture of large numbers of women demanding political and social visibility. On February 9, 1907, for example, an estimated three thousand women had participated in the so-called Mud March; the number of demonstrators increased to between ten and fifteen thousand in a rally held in June 1908; and two weeks later, a Hyde Park demonstration drew an estimated quarter of a million supporters, mostly female. In such a cultural climate, "the public representation of an aggressively sexual figure such as Salome would have a high ideological charge" (Koritz, *Gendering Bodies* 37).[14]

Allan's success was especially alarming to some because of her popularity and influence with some of the highest members of society, high-ranking politicians among them. At the height of her success in London, Allan was openly admired and courted by such personages as the Duke of Westminster and the prime minister Herbert Asquith and his wife, Margot. Sponsored by Margot Asquith, with whom Allan was rumored to have (and likely did have) a same-sex affair, Allan even moved into the west wing of the royally owned Holford House in Regent's Park (demolished in 1948), whose grand drawing room she equipped with floor-to-ceiling mirrors for her practice and teaching.[15] Her personal connections to powerful people constituted an alarming sexual-political nexus for those who feared Allan's allegedly loose morals and suspected feminist leanings.

Perhaps even more dangerously, Allan's popularity reached directly into the drawing rooms of fashionable ladies who admired her artistry and started to imitate her dress and demeanor. Edwardian socialite Lady Diana Cooper vividly remembered her mother sending her to the Palace Theatre as a girl to see Maud Allan.

> Greatly daring, [Maud Allan] had appeared in a wisp of chiffon and bare legs with pipes and cymbals. My mother . . . was enthusiastic about this new Grecian frieze form of movement. She sent us weekly to watch and learn, in spite of the number finishing with "Salome's Dance"—considered scandalous, for she was all but naked and had John the Baptist's head on a plate and kissed his waxen mouth (a business later forbidden on the Covent Garden stage [for Strauss's opera], where a dish of gravy was substituted). My mother was untrammelled by convention. (82)

At home, female socialites famously organized Salome dance and costume parties in Allan's honor and started to dress in Salome costumes and jewels; some even defied the boundaries of ladies' modesty in dress and went barefoot in public. During the International Dance Conference taking place in Berlin in 1908, the *New York Times* reported the goings-on in Mayfair with satirical alacrity.

> It seems that Miss Maud Allan's Salome Dance has so fired the imagination of society women that one of the great hostesses of the Metropolis a few weeks ago issued invitations to twenty or thirty ladies whose names figure in Court and other fashionable lists, to attend a "Maud Allan" dinner dance, which would be undesecrated by the presence of any man, and at which the guests were bidden to appear in Salome costumes. . . . Each of the ladies proceeded to outvie her sisters in providing herself with . . . the undress effect of Maud Allan's scanty attire. . . . It was the intention of the British delegates to the international terpsichorean conference to tell this story in horror stricken accents as convincing proof that the Classical dances make for public immorality. (Quoted in Cherniavsky, "Allan, Part III" 143)

Thus emboldened, Edwardian ladies could conceivably become public supporters of women's rights and fuel the debate about suffrage—or so it was feared. Even Maud Allan's stage costumes were seen as propaganda for the women's dress reform movement (contributed to by Wilde's magazine *The Woman's World,* among others) by revealing more flesh and freeing the female body from corsets, stays, high collars, and other movement-inhibiting fashion items.[16] Along with suggestive press comments about suffragettes' love of Allan and influential ladies' infatuation with her and along with the Salome dinner parties and with private and commercial imitations of Allan's erotic costume came fears of immodesty and immorality, which might easily be translated into threats to political and religious authority.

Some of the Salome-themed music hall songs of the period illustrate the public's mixture of amusement and alarm, especially since they associated Salome with promiscuity and scanty clothes. The first verse from the 1909 song "Salome" by two British songwriters illustrates the inescapability of "Salomania" and its association with nudity around 1909.

> She's come to stay!
> Won't go away!
> We've got Salome with us;
> She's made her home with us!
> She may have been a waitress, . . .
> She may have been a Gibson girlie dear;
> But, anyhow, she shows
> She's got no use for clothes!
> In fact we shudder at the bare idea!
> On ev'ry bill we see:
> S-A-L-O-M-E![17]

Allan's success also attracted very diverse groups of women into physical settings formerly associated with predominantly male, lower-class entertainment (the Palace Theatre in London's commercial West End), which increased public perceptions of an association between Allan's dancing and an alarming encouragement of female independence, political agitation, and social mayhem (Walkowitz, par. 19). Some activists against suffrage and for moral purity made "valiant attempts to stop the stampede of flesh and pearls" that was threatening to take over Europe and the United States (Bentley 40). The *New York Times* reported, for example, that actress Marie Cahill "issued a warning to President Theodore Roosevelt" in August 1908, "requesting that he monitor the outbreak of 'Salomania' and censor the appearance of such 'vulgar exhibition' on stage" as a matter of national security (Caddy 52). A worried representative of the Church of England, Canon Newbolt of St. Paul's Cathedral, spoke out against the Salome dance craze as late as August 1913: "the current evil is the indecent dance, suggestive of evil and destructive of modesty. I urge parents to assert 'I will not allow my daughter to turn into a Salome even though . . . [the] world has persuaded itself that immodesty is artistic and that anything is inartistic that removes the intolerable monitoring of its pleasures'" (quoted in Cherniavsky, *Salome Dancer* 185).

If moral protest was one mode of dealing with Allan's explosive political potential, satire was another. As Cherniavsky records, the weekly magazine *The Referee* published a satirical playlet entitled *Salome and the Suffragettes,* which showed Allan kidnapped by suffragettes and used as a political pawn: "The main characters in this silly symphony are the leading politicians of the day [including Winston Churchill and Lloyd George]—and Maud Allan." By attacking and pelting the flustered politicians with strawberry jam, rushing Allan away, and holding her hostage, the suffragettes ensure the prime minister's "solid pledge to bring in a measure for the enfranchisement of women at once." The distressed prime minister, Asquith, fears there will be "a revolution" if Salome does not appear at the Palace that night, and theater manager Alfred Butt calls for the army's intervention ("Sir, as Prime Minister of this country . . . you must restore Salome to the Palace, or I will not answer for the consequences"). Under all this pressure, the suffragettes win: Asquith gives in, and "Maud is rushed under police protection to the Palace Theatre at the horrendous speed of sixty miles an hour." Finally, England's women have the vote thanks to Allan's popularity, and all is well (Cherniavsky, "Allan, Part III," 154). A cartoon in the *Pall Mall Gazette* on July 8, 1908, at the height of Allan's Palace Theatre sensation, even outrageously put Asquith in Salome costume, indicating the prime minister's enslavement to Salomania and its supposed metaphorical influence on daily politics (ibid. 144; see fig. 3). Referring to a highly unpopular measure, the caption reads, "Pas de Fascination. Mr. Asquith yesterday moved his guillotine solution on the Licensing Bill."[18]

In 1909, Edith Nesbit, a novelist, Fabian socialist, and author of children's books, published a novel based on Maud Allan's London fame that also contains traces of Maud Allan's perceived New Woman persona. The novel was very popular in its time but has since been neglected by readers and critics, and I am not aware of any scholarly analyses of its Salome theme. Enticingly titled *Salome and the Head: A Modern Melodrama* (later republished as *The House with No Address*), Nesbit's work features a satirical romance plot and presents as the fictional Allan stand-in the gifted young dancer Sandra, with the stage name Sylvia. Sandra falls victim to men's desires and intrigues before she extricates herself and takes fate in her own hands by marrying a New Man. In its description of Sandra's dancing and

PAS DE FASCINATION

Mr. Asquith yesterday moved his guillotine resolution on the Licensing Bill.

Fig. 3. Cartoon depicting British prime minister Herbert H. Asquith in Maud Allan's Salome costume (*Pall Mall Gazette*, July 8, 1908)

details of her glamorous life and stage allure, the novel clearly alludes to Allan's career, personality, and reputation for snagging men's hearts (including, possibly, the prime minister's). Like Allan, Nesbit's heroine dances barefoot in bucolic settings and wears classically draped, loose outfits that bare her lovely shoulders and arms (similar to Allan's dress in one of the plates included in the original edition of *My Life and Dancing*); she practices in a room lined with floor-to-ceiling mirrors, a piano, and a music stand, which seems modeled on Allan's practice room in the west wing of the Holford House (Nesbit 35). She is a self-reliant New Woman who takes care of her family and her business herself by resolving to make her own fortune with her own hard work, as a dance star in London: "I've had enough of being under people's thumbs. I'm going to have people under *my* thumb. And the way to do it's money, money, money" (ibid. 89).

Apart from being a gifted and spellbinding artist devoted to her self-taught art, Sandra increases her independence by her expert handling of a crowbar, a revolver, a bicycle, and, in the climactic Salome dance scene,

even the head of a real dead man—twice. The novel's shocking onstage sub-
stitution of the waxen head with the dead man's head (that of Sandra's secret estranged husband, murdered by her admirer Denny) was evidently
based on a scandalous rumor about Maud Allan that circulated in London
at the time, which Nesbit most certainly knew. According to the rumor, a
prankster—most probably the Hungarian Count Zichy, who had a score to
settle with Allan—had once delivered into Allan's hands the head of a real
dead man as her stage prop, and Allan, smeared with blood, dropped the
head with a scream and fainted on stage (Hoare 75, 85). At the end of the
novel, Nesbit's fictional characters actually repeat the same popular rumors
about Maud Allan that inspired the playlet in *The Referee* and the *Pall Mall
Gazette* cartoon: that her Salomé dances introduced or supported immorality in general society and that even the prime minister was infatuated with
her. This insinuation gives the dancer's seeming innocence or victimization
an air of political intrigue and cunning. Sandra's former fiancé, Templar,
feebly defends her against his aunt's and uncle's derision.

> "Oh, well," says the Aunt, . . . "there's one thing I'm thankful for, these pro-
> fane Salome dances have been stopped by law. I can't think what the Gov-
> ernment was about not to stop it long ago."
>
> "Perhaps the Prime Minister admired the lady's dancing," suggests the
> Uncle with a decorous little chuckle.
>
> "You never know, do you?" the Aunt agrees. "These smart-set people.
> And that sort of girl attracts men." She speaks as though the attraction
> were a willful vice.
>
> "Well, whatever she's done she's paid for it, poor girl!" says the Uncle.
>
> And then Templar stands up.
>
> "She's done nothing," he says, "nothing. She's the victim of circum-
> stances."
>
> "They always are," says the Aunt, and sniffs. (Nesbit 303)

Even more scandalous than Edith Nesbit's fictionalization of Allan's independence was the anonymous pornographic novel *Maudie: Revelations of
Life in London Society* (1910). A notorious allusion to Allan's rumored bisexuality and New Woman–like independence, *Maudie* delivered well-placed
stabs at Allan's political and social clout, especially her supposed embroil-
ment with the suffragette cause and with the Asquiths. Setting the action in
a mansion turned brothel, the novel capitalized on rumors of Allan's affairs
with both male and female members of high society, most famously her presumed affair with Margot Asquith, alluding to the well-known fact that
Margot had rented an apartment for Allan in the west wing of the Holford

House, a real-life mansion. One core scene features "Maudie" (Allan's nick-name) performing a dance routine tellingly entitled the "Dance of Emanci-pation," which is no more than a striptease performed for the voyeuristic pleasure of Maudie's bawdy admirers. Even though the suffragist allusion is clear, Maudie's/Allan's "emancipation" is safely contained by satire and im-mediately reduced to harmless sexual titillation. The satirical portrayals of Maud Allan as a pawn for the political and sexual emancipation of women in *Maudie* as well as in the playlet in *The Referee* illustrate that comparisons were indeed drawn between women's political struggles and Maud Allan's performance. Both texts enlisted Allan's fame to ridicule the suffrage move-ment's aims, strategies, and rhetoric. In the playlet, Allan is helplessly car-ried off and deposited back by the suffragettes in a mock-heroic kidnapping that derides the suffragettes' political determination as militancy; in *Maudie,* Allan is condemned to the brothel.

The cultural association of Salomé with suffragism is also affirmed in a little-discussed British feminist production of Wilde's *Salomé* by the New Stage Players at the Court Theatre on February 27 and 28, 1911 (only the third private production of Wilde's play in London and the first to be pro-duced in a real theater), unearthed by Judith Walkowitz. This production was arranged by a "group of Edwardian women, feminist actresses" who felt "emboldened . . . to enact the 'modernity' of Salome and her dance . . . along lines more compatible with militant feminism. . . . The performance was organized by Adeline Bourne, the honorary secretary of the Actresses' Franchise League, who assumed the leading role" (Walkowitz, par. 56). Walkowitz points out that reviewers were quick to associate this *Salomé* production with feminism and suffragism, dwelling on the fact that mostly women were in attendance and criticizing it for its lack of sensualism that would appeal to "sexless women and pussycat men" (quoted in par. 57); *The Bystander* thundered that Wilde's Salomé was "not a twentieth-century suffragette attempting an entrance into the House of Commons or asking for Mr. Winston Churchill's head on a charge sheet," as apparently the New Stage Players' production would lead one to believe (quoted in par. 58). Walkowitz comments, "While feminist actresses may have had a number of professional motivations for staging this performance, they brought Salome under the sign of the Militant Woman, rendering her a new icon for the ex-panding militant operations of the Women's Social and Political Union, which had stepped up campaigns of window smashing, arson, and political disruption in the streets of Central London" (par. 60).

Maud Allan herself explicitly tried to disperse these strong cultural asso-ciations of Salomé and suffragism. *My Life and Dancing* includes a chapter entitled "A Word about Women," in which she openly rejects contemporary women's calls for the vote and for full political enfranchisement, attempting to demonstrate that she is no suffragette. In the mentioned chapter, she reproduces a polite letter from a suffragette who is trying to recruit her for the cause by earnestly pleading for the necessity of reform in marriage, divorce, and property laws and flattering Allan for her achievements. Allan then takes the opportunity to explain her own position.

> As regards the question of votes for women, I believe that a woman can do more from an elevated position in the world of art, by bringing all that makes home beautiful into her husband's and children's lives, than she could by casting a dozen votes before the time is ready. . . . Even the above letter, with its praise at the end, has not convinced me that the vote is at present necessary. (110)

Allan reasons that women are overly emotional and thus unsuited to the rationality of the political sphere: "Careful weighing of evidence, exhaustive analysis free from bias, is antagonistic to our nature" (116). Echoing popular nineteenth-century views of women's place within marriage, family, and society, she finds that "the rightful destiny of every woman is to be the wife and mother, to make that inner sanctuary known by the sweet name of 'Home.'" The vote would be granted to woman eventually, maintained Allan, "when she is ready to receive it" (110). In the same chapter, Allan also argues for better educational and employment opportunities for women, to benefit society as a whole—a social reformist stance that had, in fact, been an important tenet of the feminist movement since Mary Wollstonecraft and John Stuart Mill. Allan concludes it "[n]eedless to add, perhaps, that even if I thought the franchise for women desirable, I do not view the tactics adopted by some of its advocates with approval. . . . with woman swaying man to nobler and loftier ideals, the world will move to higher things, and humanity progress nearer divinity" (119).

One reason for Allan's need to profess her disapproval may have been that the association with the suffragettes threatened Allan's popular success among conservative middle-class mainstream audiences, who were still mostly opposed to women's suffrage. Amy Koritz points out that Allan's public orthodoxy in gender matters "was perhaps essential to Allan's success in society, if not in art" (*Gendering Bodies* 43). Calls for women's advancement in this well-known humanist vein were most likely more acceptable to Allan's influential social beneficiaries than was the suffragettes' cause, which was perceived as too radical by many (Koritz, "Salomé: Exotic Woman" 266). A dancer and music hall performer and an unmarried, self-supporting young woman, Allan needed to appear conservative and guard her reputation and career. It is no wonder, then, that Allan tried to "influence the public construction of her persona" and "explicitly used the rhetoric of 'good' femininity to define herself and her dances within the terms of the separate spheres ideology," despite the fact that "Allan's lifestyle violated the dominant ideal of woman as mother and homemaker"; to survive as an artist, "Allan attempted to underplay her transgressions and to locate herself inside that ideology" (Koritz, "Dancing the Orient" 74). To keep the goodwill of important friends like the Asquiths, it was crucially important for Allan to align herself with her financial beneficiaries' views.

Overall, Allan's political statements against women's suffrage in *My Life and Dancing* look more like a strategic move calculated to disarm and appease her critics than like a genuinely felt sentiment against women's independence and changes in gender roles: "She wrote one thing, but she performed another" (Bentley 61). Allan did contribute to the legitimization of women in the performing arts and the further broadening of opportunities for middle-class women, wittingly or not. She increased the visibility and economic opportunities for females on stage who were not just performers of others' works but their own *auteurs*. She also modeled women's general physical self-confidence and self-expression in the public sphere (Walkowitz, par. 7).

When, in 1917, Maud Allan accepted the lead role in J. T. Grein's *Salomé* production for the Independent Theatre Society in London (which specialized in a repertoire of controversial modern plays, especially Ibsen), she was not a random choice for the role. Allan had already adapted, adopted, and inhabited Salomé in a strong interpretation all her own, with overt sexual overtones but an emphasis on artistic invention. Director J. T. Grein, also a well-known drama critic, was keenly interested in innovating London's theater, similar to Germany's Max Reinhardt and France's Aurélien Lugné-Poë. Allan was an obvious choice for the title role: she was the best-known modern Salome dancer, sure to draw a large crowd for this private theater. Wilde's *Salomé* was still banned from public performance in Britain and remained so until 1931, but this was a private production before an invited audience and, as such, exempt from the official censor's supervision.

Neither Allan nor Grein seem to have expected trouble, although demands for moral censorship of public discourse were strong during wartime, so that putting on a work as transgressive as *Salomé* was risky. The print version of Wilde's play had sold steadily since its first publication despite the 1892 theatrical ban, and Allan's *The Vision of Salomé* had also been successful. Nevertheless, "the decision to produce *Salome* in the spring of

1918 was politically unwise" in the prevailing cultural climate of wartime paranoia (Cherniavsky, *Salome Dancer* 240). Calls for a morally righteous, unified home front were strong at a time when the Allies' defeat in France was feared to be imminent. In March 1918, the right-wing newspaper *The Vigilante* and its powerful lobby of conservative conspiracy theorists launched a vicious media attack against Allan and Grein, which led to the fateful events of the Pemberton-Billing Trial.

The Pemberton-Billing Trial

In Britain toward the end of World War I, in a cultural climate of paranoia and xenophobia, Independent member of Parliament Noel Pemberton-Billing authorized the publication in his right-wing newspaper, *The Vigilante,* of a libelous paragraph about J. T. Grein's planned production of Wilde's *Salomé.* Sensationally entitled "The Cult of the Clitoris," the piece effectively insinuated that with *Salomé,* Maud Allan and Grein sought to spread homosexual and moral corruption in Britain in order to aid the German enemy from within. Initial judicial hearings on Allan and Grein's proposed legal action against Billing started in April 1918, although the actual trial did not begin until May 29. Meanwhile, two performances of Grein's production actually took place at the Royal Court Theatre, on April 7 and 14, 1917: Allan played Salomé, renowned actor George Relph appeared as Herod, and British composer Granville Bantock's music accompanied the Salomé dances. Cautiously, however, "before the performance an actress recited a 'Tribute to Britain' by Jack Grein, in which he stated firmly that *Salomé* 'was not an impure work,'" reports Michael Kettle, who wrote the seminal scholarly monograph on the trial (25). During April and May 1918, Maud Allan and J. T. Grein brought legal action against Noel Pemberton-Billing for defamatory criminal and obscene libel, a serious charge that carried the heavy penalty of "imprisonment for an unspecified number of years" (Kettle 19–20).[19] In the ensuing trial, which came to be known by his name, Billing branded Maud Allan and Wilde's *Salomé* as agents for a dangerous moral degeneration of the British public, participants in a vast moral conspiracy in the very heart of Britain, allegedly orchestrated by the Germans and their sympathizers, to weaken British stamina and morale from within. In a strange parallel to Wilde's 1895 trial, the sensational Pemberton-Billing Trial, which lasted only five days, vindicated the defendant and turned against the plaintiff. Billing was found not guilty, even declared a folk hero by many, and succeeded in destroying Allan's and J. T. Grein's careers. Under his direction and through skillful insinuations, medical experts publicly labeled Allan a lesbian and a sadist and suggested that Grein might be a homosexual spy for the Germans. Furthermore, Oscar Wilde's transgressive *Salomé* was once again branded and condemned as a vehicle of moral perversion for the British citizenry, especially vulnerable in wartime.

In the course of the trial, Wilde's *Salomé* and its author were not only the main vehicles for Billing's legal defense but functioned as crucial focal points for his invocation and defense of larger cultural hostility toward art and especially against homosexuality. *Salomé*'s central role during the trial illustrates some of the larger, complex history of interactions and tensions between transgressive aesthetics, erotic affect, ethical norms, censorship, and the national-political project in wartime Britain. It also illustrated and furthered an emerging legal and cultural awareness of lesbianism, around which fears of male homosexual "perversity," feminism, suffragism, xenophobia, and lesbianism coalesced: during the trial, "female homosexuality was variously described as hyperfemininity, as masculinity, as perversion like sadism, and as a symptom of sedition. . . . [It] illuminat[ed] the dramatic flexibility of this emergent identity of 'the lesbian' in 1918" (Cohler 86). The root cause for Allan's downfall, however, was a central problematic assumption at the heart of the trial: the conflation of art with life and of artistic transgression with moral and sexual perversity—the old problem of mimesis. The net of innuendo and intrigue in which Maud Allan would be so tragically caught hinged on the identification of her personal life with her art as well as with Wilde's, and their combined transgressions were branded as threats to morality and the nation.

Among the spectators and reporters in the courtroom at the Pemberton-Billing Trial was a young female artist and journalist who intimately understood that those unquestioned assumptions were the root causes of Allan's legal troubles (as of Wilde's). Claude Cahun (née Lucy Schwob) was a budding French modernist-surrealist photographer and writer on assignment in London for the *Mercure de France,* a preeminent literary and cultural journal. Cahun sat in on the entire trial and wrote a detailed report about it for the journal's readers, "La 'Salomé' d'Oscar Wilde, Le procès Billing et les 47 000 pervertis du livre noir." As Lizzie Thynne has shown, Cahun herself happened to have intimate connections to Wilde and *Salomé:* she was the niece of Marcel Schwob, the Anglophile writer, critic, and founder of the *Mercure de France.* Schwob had been part of Wilde's entourage in Paris, had translated Wilde's "The Selfish Giant" into French, and had helped Wilde with the final corrections to the French text of *Salomé.* As she was listening to the terrible accusations, insinuations, and slander that Allan had to endure in court, Cahun, herself a lesbian, must have realized the public and legal dangers of the kind of sexual and gender transgression that she was already practicing herself. Not only did she disapprove of the assault on Wilde's (and Allan's) sexuality, but she clearly recognized that the freedom of nonconformist art itself was at stake. In her article, Cahun writes:

> Without a doubt [*The Vigilante's* libel] takes aim at all of Wilde's passions, too, and even at the least of his admirers. . . . Moreover, one will find there the thesis of those Puritans who wish to snatch, under the guise of moral reform and invoking the state of the war, all freedom from the artistic expression of thought. (451, my translation)

J. T. Grein's *Salomé* production starring Allan, with her own controversial sexual and artistic ties to the role, was indeed a mere vehicle for a larger moral-political purity campaign launched by the ultraconservative Vigilante Society. Spinning an intricate web of ideology and fear at a time of national duress and war hysteria, Billing and his associates were able to convince jury, judge, and the public that morally and sexually "perverse" art and the persons performing or promoting it were immanent threats to the British body politic. All persons affiliated with this *Salomé* production were allegedly determined to undermine British morality and morale in the war effort against the Germans; they had to be stopped if England was not going to lose the war.

The defendant, Billing, was an archconservative British member of Parliament who had made it his personal mission to warn the public of a supposed vast moral conspiracy in their midst, secretly launched by the German enemy. He was convinced that undercover agents were infiltrating Britain with the task to undermine public morals and spread corruption, disease, and cultural decadence to weaken the United Kingdom. To warn the public of the surmised dangers, Billing, together with a handful of likeminded friends, had founded the so-called Vigilante Society in March 1917, with the declared purpose "to fight for purity in public life." Their private subscription paper *The Vigilante* (formerly *The Imperialist*) functioned as the main public organ for their conspiracy theories, "[t]he only newspaper that does not accept advertisements and therefore is free to speak the truth" (Gagnier, *Idylls* 199). Billing's friends at the Vigilante Society were of the sinister sort. Among his colleagues were H. H. Beamish, an anti-Semite who published hateful tirades against Jews and foreigners in England; Dr. J. H. Clarke, who assisted the same cause with pseudoscientific medical explanations; and Arnold White, editor of *The English Review*, whose pathologizing homophobic and xenophobic rants Billing gladly reprinted in *Imperialist:* "[A] great cancer, made in Germany, is eating at the heart of England and civilization. . . . The tendency in Germany is to abolish civilisation as we know it, to substitute Sodom or Gomorrah for the New Jerusalem, and to infect clean nations with Hunnish erotomania" (quoted in Kettle 5–6).

In court, Billing freely admitted that he and the Vigilante Society systematically tried to provoke such individuals as Allan and Grein to sue them for libel, hoping to draw attention to moral and sexual corruption in spectacular courtroom cases. To this end, alerted by Vigilante Society member Marie Corelli about Grein's planned production of *Salomé, The Vigilante* ran a piece by staff writer Captain Harold Sherwood Spencer:

> The Cult of the Clitoris
> To be a member of Maud Allan's private performances in Oscar Wilde's 'Salome,' one has to apply to a Miss Valetta, of 9, Duke Street, Adelphi W.C. If Scotland Yard were to seize the list of these members I have no doubt they would secure the names of several of the first 47,000. (Quoted in Kettle 18–19)

The article's sensational headline was deemed unprintable in mainstream publications like the *Times* or the *Mercure de France,* because of the signaling function of the word *clitoris* as a code for lesbianism and degeneracy. Lucy Bland explains,

> From late eighteenth-century through into the early twentieth century, one of the most consistent medical characterizations of the anatomy of the lesbian was the claim of an unusually large clitoris. Not only was the clitoris associated with female sexual pleasure separate from reproductive potential, but lesbians were also assumed to be masculinized, and the[ir] supposed enlarged clitoris was one signifier of this masculinity. In presenting lesbians' bodies as less sexually differentiated than the norm—more masculine—it was inferred that they were atavists—throwbacks to an earlier evolutionary stage and thereby "degenerates." (184)

Even though lesbianism was not mentioned in the 1885 Labouchère Amendment and thus still invisible in the eyes of the law and much of the British public, the rise of sexology and psychoanalysis introduced a vague cultural association of lesbianism with sodomy and other "perversions."[20] Preceding Radclyffe Hall's landmark obscenity trial by a few years, the Pemberton-Billing Trial "is significant in lesbian history because of its sensationally negative representation of lesbianism, its attempt to prove that sex-

ual knowledge—knowledge of the word *clitoris*—is an indicator of lesbianism, and its use of [the German sexologist] Krafft-Ebing's [congenital inversion theory in] *Psychopathia Sexualis* as evidence for the defense" (Wachman
14). Both trials "signal the beginning of an important shift in the visibility
of lesbianism in English legal discourse and in the public arena" surrounding World War 1 (Doan 32).[21]

The Vigilante's piece thus effectively linked Allan to a secret "cult" of homosexuality that Wilde allegedly promoted in his works, which Allan promoted in the highest ranks of British society. *Salomé's* fantastic role in the alleged homosexual conspiracy plot was to spread the "cult" further by
providing a secret meeting place for its members, cryptically designated as
belonging to the "first 47,000." This phrase referred to a central touchstone
for the Vigilante Society's vast conspiracy theories, names of British persons
under German influence, many of them in high positions in the arts, society, and politics. These names allegedly appeared in a secret "Black Book"
kept by the Germans, which the defendant and his friends frequently mentioned during the trial. (A long article detailing these accusations had appeared in *The Imperialist* on January 26, 1918, a few months before the trial;
see Kettle 8–9.) With special alarm, *The Vigilante* warned that the Germans
had singled out for sexual corruption the military—especially Britain's all-
important war machine, the Royal Navy—and that undercover German
pederasts frequented public parks to homosexually entangle and blackmail
British peers and even their wives so that "[i]n lesbian ecstasy the most sacred secrets of State were betrayed." One important reason for such fear of
national contamination through homosexuality is often the political and
erotic disenfranchisement of the straight male body, as shown by Klaus
Theweleit and Eve Sedgwick (in *Between Men*). Billing clearly regarded homoeroticism not only as morally corrupt and abominable but as antipatri-
otic because it threatened the heteronormativity of the British military and
leadership, a charge all the more serious during a time when patriotic fer-
vor generally ran high.[22] With homosexual "corruption" identified as an important weapon of the German enemy, it constituted nothing less than treason. As Allan's counsel explained in court, lesbianism was the most serious
libel to bring against a woman's reputation, and "the most horrible suggestion that you can make against any man is that he is addicted to sodomitic
practices. The next more horrible suggestion is that he is a traitor to his
country, and is in the pay of the Germans" (Kettle 245).

In light of these observations, it becomes clear that *The Vigilante's* accusations were very serious indeed. In May 1918, the British public was increasingly concerned and worried that Germany was winning the war and

that Britain was not striking back as forcefully and effectively as it should. On June 5, the *Times* commented: "no lawsuit of modern times has attracted such universal and painful interest. . . . Not only in London, but even more in the provincial towns and countryside, the daily reports have been read and discussed with almost as deep anxiety as the news of the war itself" (quoted in Kettle 271). The trial against Allan, *Salomé,* and the ghost of *Salomé's* "perverse" author assumed national importance under these circumstances. For a while, it even dominated newspaper headlines side by side with the latest grueling news from the front.

Although Billing was technically the defendant, his defense "resulted, in effect, not in Billing being on trial, but Allan and *Salome*" (Bland 186), as well as the memory of the play's author. In 1918 Wilde's name still signified disgrace to most Britons; during the trial, even the presiding Justice Darling openly voiced what seemed like a commonsensical opinion to many: it was "possible to regard [Oscar Wilde] as a great artist, but he certainly was a great beast; there is no doubt about that" (quoted in 263). Billing focused his defense on Wilde's infamous sexual reputation, the scientific sexological causes and effects of perversity, its evidence in *Salomé,* and the supposed impact of its aesthetic representation on the British public. From the start, parallels between Wilde's trials and Billing's case were on everyone's mind. Not only was the location for both trials the same, the Old Bailey in London, but the later trial also involved one of Oscar Wilde's own attorneys: Sir Travers Humphreys, one of Allan's counsels, had been a junior during the 1895 trial. In this symbolically charged courtroom, even the charges were similar: one person had libeled another for homosexual affiliations. Hence not only were the material and symbolic connections between the two trials strong, but Maud Allan had also been attacked on moral grounds for her performance in *The Vision of Salomé,* adapted from Wilde's play. Billing's goal was to show that Wilde had written *Salomé* for "sexual perverts, Sodomites and Lesbians" and that by virtue of her affiliation with the play, Maud Allan ranked among these herself. If he could prove his allegations were true, the court would regard *The Vigilante's* paragraph as justified, and Billing could win the trial. As the editor and publisher of a paper that openly invited and provoked libel action, Billing had taken a considerable legal and personal risk: in 1918 British law, a public libel conviction carried an unspecified number of years in prison.

The medical discourse that dominated the trial helped cement the assumption that perverse art mirrored perverse minds and bodies and vice versa. Dr. Serrell Cooke, a doctor in charge of mentally ill patients at Paddington Hospital, was Billing's medical expert. Cooke testified that, scientifically speaking, Wilde was "a well-known monster" with a diseased mind (quoted in Kettle 152). Billing skillfully enlisted both voices of authority—the medical expert and the presiding judge—to condemn such "mental perverts" and agree that they would best be "locked up" for the public good (quoted in ibid. 151). The failure to elaborate or reflect on the alleged social menace is typical of the Pemberton-Billing Trial, which was based on a set of tacit assumptions about art and society, about the role of the legitimate artist as a moralist, and about erotic affect and excess.

To prove Wilde's dangerous perversion in life and art, Billing cleverly solicited the help of an even more effective star witness, Lord Alfred Douglas, Wilde's former lover. Just a few years after Wilde's death, Douglas had renounced Wilde and homosexuality and become one of the most vicious homophobes and hypocrites of his generation. He was waging a homophobic literary campaign of his own at the time, which aligned him perfectly with Billing's cause. In 1915 and 1916, his two intensely homophobic and xenophobic satirical poems appeared, "All's Well with England" and "The Rossiad," which blamed the British defeat at Flanders on homosexuals and their powerful political friends in Britain, particularly on Robert Ross (Wilde's former friend and literary executor) and on the Asquiths. Douglas had fought a bitter battle with Ross about Wilde's *De Profundis*. Ross was also friends with the Asquiths, who reportedly supported Ross's efforts to rehabilitate Wilde's works. In "The Rossiad" (alluding to Pope's "The Dunciad"), Douglas drew satirical connections between Ross and the Germans, sounding a lot like a conspiracy theorist from the Vigilante Society: "Oh England, in thine hour of need, / . . . Raise up the best, hack down the worst, / Tear from thy heart the thing accurst. / Two foes thou hast, one there one here, / One far, one intimately near, / Two filthy fogs blot out thy light: / The German, and the Sodomite" (quoted in Kettle 15).[23] Asked in court if he regretted ever having met Wilde, Douglas answered without hesitation:

> I do most intensely . . . I think [Wilde] had a diabolical influence on everyone he met. I think he is the greatest force of evil that has appeared in Europe during the last 350 years . . . He was the agent of the devil in every possible way. He was a man whose whole object in life was to attack and to sneer at virtue, and to undermine it in every way by every possible means, sexually and otherwise. (Quoted in Kettle 173)

In her report for the *Mercure de France,* Claude Cahun showed pity rather than anger and frustration toward Douglas, despite his homophobic rants against Wilde and her own previous, youthful admiration of him as one of her gay literary heroes (Thynne 190). Cahun indirectly acknowledged the heavy toll that the fallout from Wilde's scandal had evidently taken on Douglas, describing him as "an aging and discouraged man" who seemed very much "at the mercy of the first person who has arrived armed with the name of Wilde" ("La 'Salomé' d'Oscar Wilde" 455, my trans.). Cahun may have realized that Douglas's connection to Wilde and *Salomé* was no less tragic than Maud Allan's—both were forever marked and tainted by the whiff of Wilde's homosexual scandal.

During testimony, Maud Allan tried hard to defend the play and Salomé's character as pure and innocent, in order to redeem the play, her art, and her moral reputation in the eyes of the judge, the jury, and the British public. Pressed by Billing to explain Salomé's desire for Jokanaan, Allan declared it to be spiritual, expressed in orientalist terms. Realizing that many regarded Salomé's behavior as offensive, she blamed the habits of "the Eastern world" for the excesses of the play.

> I wish the Jury to understand that Salome lived in the Eastern world at a time when our rules were not in vogue, and when to see his head in front of her was nothing. I wish the Gentlemen of the Jury to know that Salome was not a perverse young woman: therefore Mr. Billing has no right to talk about sadism. I am not the first woman to play the role of Salome; I am not the first in town to play that role. (Quoted in Kettle 74)

To counter Billing's suggestion of impurity and impropriety, Allan portrayed Salomé as the opposite: namely, a lover of beauty and purity.

> Salome loathes and despises everything that is ugly and uncouth, and makes it plain in open speech, but the beautiful and the pure appeal to her. . . . [S]he admires what is beautiful and . . . hates everything that is coarse and vulgar. . . . Salome fell in love with the holiness and beauty of this man . . . And she feels the insult of this man who treats her as a wanton and a harlot, which she was not. (Quoted in ibid. 71–74)

In her statement, Allan tried hard to stay within women's social, cultural, and political limits—hence her frequent recourse during the trial to the discourse of high art and to Salomé's innocence and purity. But Wilde's *Salomé* is, of course, excessive and transgressive, and Allan's protestations rightly appeared questionable to many. Allan's line of defense blatantly contradicted the public's memory of her own notoriously sensual *The Vision of Salomé* dance, as well as her unwelcome feminist-suffragist association.

With her testimony, Allan unwittingly set the scene for one of the trial's most surprising lines of argument: Billing's theory that the most dangerous perversion comes in the disguise of beauty and art. In the hands of perverts, works of art could be enlisted as dangerous, clandestine propaganda for sexual and moral corruption. For individuals like Wilde, art functioned as a screen on which they projected their desires, fantasies, and diseased personality. *Salomé* was but a mask for the perversions of its author. Its true danger lay in the encryption of its vice: corruption deceptively cloaked in beauty so that it could infiltrate the unsuspecting society at its will.

In his examination of witnesses, Billing thus focused strongly on the play's style and language and tried to forge a connection between sexual perversion and the ideas of "beauty" and "spirituality" in the play, between immorality and aesthetics.

> Billing: Is it customary for sex perverts to describe as beautiful and glorious all their perversions? . . . And is it customary for them to read into the distinctly physical acts of sex something spiritual?
> Cooke: Spiritual, poetic, beautiful, pure love; those are their expressions.
> (Quoted in Kettle 150)

Lord Alfred Douglas's testimony further helped to drive home the point. Asked specifically about the relation between Wilde's homosexuality and his aesthetic tools and repertoire, Douglas replied that surely, "whenever [Wilde] was going to do anything particularly horrible, it was always disguised in the most flowery language, and always referred back to Art. That was his idea of Art" (ibid. 175). Douglas called such a relationship to language endemic to "Sodomites": "Those sort of people always refer to revolting things under pretty names. They try to disguise the horribleness of the action by giving it such names; they say beautiful, classic, and so on. They will not speak of it by the outspoken English name; they disguise it" (quoted in Kettle 177).

Allan had always presented her art as "classical dance"; hence, Douglas's reference to "classic" as a suspect description before this court reflected not only on Wilde but on Allan herself, tightening the net around her. He went on, "With those sort of people evil is their good; everything is topsy turvy; physical is spiritual; spiritual is physical, and so on; it is a perversion, an inversion, of everything" (quoted in Kettle 178). Douglas's use of the term *inversion* alluded to medical discourse, but its target was the role of art. According to Douglas, Sodomites "disguise[d]" their horrible actions through aesthetic and cognitive means; they simply called what everyone else calls vice in "outspoken English" by other "pretty names." This new naming implies that their inverted use of language directly reflects the sexual condition of sodomites—which can, in turn, be inferred from it. Not only tropo-logical but also moral chaos results: good becomes evil, physical becomes spiritual, "and so on"—"everything" is infected. Sexual and aesthetic "in-version" were supposed to mirror each other.

Douglas and Billing argued that with their deliberate confusion of lan-guage and their disguise of the very process, sodomites threaten the very possibility of clear moral standards and norms—the very pillars of society and patria. The argument implies that the functioning of the body politic depends on a *contrat social* assembled by and through a language shared and appreciated by all its members—a reliable, consistent language, trans-ferred across generations. The deconstruction of this language makes mean-ing and signification dangerously unreliable and confusing. If vice comes along in aesthetic disguise, how will one be able to tell the real beauty, spir-ituality, or truth from its evil twin? How will one be safe from infection; how can one inoculate oneself against the contagious disease of perverse art? Af-ter all, as medical expert Dr. Cooke argued, Oscar Wilde himself had only "bec[o]me a monster (from all the records that we have) after reading about and taking an aesthetic interest in sexual perverts" (quoted in Kettle 152).

Dr. Cooke helped explain the perverse nature of Wilde's work and the threat it posed to the public. Asked why "a play like that should have been written by such a man," Cooke asserted that the Wilde would have written it out of pleasure, for himself and "other perverted individuals," in whom it would cause "sexual lust" to see perversion enacted: "They would take ex-treme delight in the whole play; it would appeal to them immensely, they would probably have sexual excitation, and even orgasm, watching the play." According to Cooke, *Salomé* was "an open display by physical means of several forms of sexual perversion. . . . The probability is that [Wilde] had von Krafft-Ebing's book *Psychopathia Sexualis* in front of him all the time" (quoted in Kettle 152). Douglas confirmed that he "kn[e]w of [his] own knowledge that this book [*Salomé*] was written after a study of Krafft-Ebing" (quoted in ibid. 173). Wilde's reading and aesthetic translation of a sexologist who was also—ironically—a German again invoked the alleged German homosexual conspiracy. Dr. Clarke, another medical witness, stated that the play was such "a perfect museum of sexual pathology" that it "might be produced in a medical theater," if one did not have to fear the moral well-being of the medical students (quoted in ibid. 194). The circle seemed complete: as Lucy Bland points out, the "selective and opportunis-tic" deployment of sexology during the trial condemned Wilde and *Salomé* and gave Billing the means to orchestrate Maud Allan's downfall through guilt by association (192).

On the first day, Billing grilled Maud Allan about her personal life and moral views, her interpretation of Wilde's play, and the role of Salomé, suggesting that through her performance, Maud Allan was implicated in the grand scenario of perversion. In his plea of justification, Billing called her "a lewd, unchaste, and immoral woman" about "to give private performances of an obscene and indecent character, so designed as to foster and encourage obscene and unnatural practices among women." He maintained "that said Maud Allan associated herself with persons addicted to obscene and unnatural practices" (quoted in Kettle 313). Medical expert Dr. Cooke testified that it was "very, very difficult . . . to imagine any woman acting such a part. If any woman did so, in order to reproduce what Oscar Wilde actually wanted to be produced, she would have to be a sadist herself" (quoted in ibid. 159). Indeed, Cooke had professed that "[he] should think that anybody of average intelligence who was connected with the play as Oscar Wilde put it must probably have a perverted mind" (quoted in ibid. 163).

To establish the connection between Wilde's and Allan's alleged perversion, Billing tried to show that Maud Allan possessed secret knowledge of an indecent sort. When asked if she knew what the word *clitoris* in *The Vigilante*'s headline meant, Allan freely admitted that she was generally familiar with it; she understood it well enough to make her want to "have [her] name cleared" in a British court and "not to let a man like [Billing] run [her] down" (quoted in Kettle 82). Billing, however, brilliantly reversed positions, arguing that Allan's knowledge of the word *clitoris* gave her away. He claimed that only those who were familiar with lesbianism or other "sadist" perversions knew the term. If Allan and her manager J. T. Grein knew what the word *clitoris* in the *Vigilante* headline meant, they surely must be part of circles that entertained such coded terminology for the corresponding immoral thoughts and actions (ibid. 229).[24] Dr. Cooke agreed that "nobody but a medical man, or people interested in that kind of thing, would understand the term" (quoted in ibid. 159). Medical terminology was an accepted exclusive code, understood and designed to guard sexual knowledge that would have threatened gendered norms of social and moral propriety: "to know about the clitoris implied knowledge of women's sexuality autonomous from men. Non-experts such as Allan would only have such knowledge . . . if they were compelled by their perverse proclivities to seek it out" (Bland 189). The defense pathologized Wilde's Salomé along the same lines. Captain Spencer described her as "a child suffering from an enlarged and diseased clitoris," thus suggesting that Salomé was a lesbian— an entirely nonsensical conclusion, considering that Salomé clearly desires a male character in Wilde's play (quoted in Kettle 117). It is important to re-member here that in 1918, as Bland explains, "[i]n relation to male homo-sexuality there was . . . an identified sexual type—above all personified by the figure of Oscar Wilde," but there was "no equivalent sexual type in re-lation to the lesbian" and "no common understanding of what constituted lesbianism." Billing had to "subsume lesbianism's specificity and to imply that it was an aspect of the sexual perversions which were more easily identifiable in *Salomé*—sadism, masochism, fetishism, namely the other perversions listed by Krafft-Ebing. The fact that the clitoris also carried the inference of wider sexual deviancy—nymphomania, 'primitive' sexuality, hypersexuality—facilitated this reduction" (Bland 193; see also Travis 151).

In one of the most climactic and personally devastating moments of the trial, on the very first day, Billing called Maud Allan to the witness stand and publicly revealed that she was, in fact, the sister of convicted murderer Theo Durrant. Allan's family secret had been exposed by the U.S. press when she toured the United States in 1910, but "[i]n London, where she re-turned in 1911, it was still not public knowledge, nor did it shadow her on her tour of Asia in 1913 and 1914" (Walkowitz, par. 13). Billing's merciless revelation made international headlines and dealt a devastating blow to Al-lan's personal and professional life. With Billing's goading, medical experts related Theo's crime to Allan's personal aesthetic preferences. Dr. Cooke dwelled on Theo's "sadism" and affirmed its hereditary transfer, maintain-ing that given Allan's family history, it was likely that she showed such ten-dencies herself (Kettle 151). Was it a wonder, then, Billing argued, that Al-lan would be eager to perform in such plays as *Salomé*—whose author was a convicted sexual pervert and whose female protagonist was also described by the medical experts as sadistic? To make matters worse, Wilde's play had also been a great success in Germany. In fact, the "Wilde cult" itself was sup-posed to have originated in Germany: "Like Allan and *Salome,* sexology was deemed to be essentially German. Krafft-Ebing was wrongly assumed to be German and the writings of non-German sexologists were ignored" (Bland 190). It was not surprising to anyone that "sexual perverts, including les-bians, were also traitorous lovers of all things German" (ibid. 195). Sodomists and lesbian perverts stood in ideological opposition to straight British patriotism and allied themselves with the German enemy. Allan had studied music in Berlin and associated intimately with Margot Asquith, who was well known to have personal affinities for all things German—as well as for all things female. Like the famous Mata Hari who was executed just a year earlier for German espionage, Maud Allan was also an orientalist dancer as well as "an independent, sexually knowledgeable woman"

(Wachman 18). Billing's carefully prepared rhetorical circle thus neatly closed around Wilde, sexual perversions, lesbianism, the Germans, and scantily clad dancers.

In the war hysteria that accompanied the trial, his outrageous innuendo worked. In five days of sensational testimony, Billing had finally offered enough circumstantial evidence to refute Allan's libel claim. He convinced the jury that Wilde's *Salomé* was "an open representation of degenerated sexual lust, sexual crime, and unnatural passions and an evil and mischievous travesty of a biblical story" that "would particularly attract many of the people whose names appeared in the German list [the Black Book]" (quoted in Kettle 219). Addressing the jury in his final plea, Billing sounded an aggressively homophobic and patriotic note, portraying himself as the prophet in the wilderness, only following his conscience: "The best of the blood in this country is already spilled; and do you think that I am going to keep quiet in my position as a public man while nine men die in a minute to make a sodomite's holiday?" (quoted in ibid. 222). Launching one final attack on Wilde and *Salomé,* Billing summarized the dangerous conspiracy he saw between sexual perversion, art, science, moral disease, the law, and the urgent interests of the state to shore up all its powers against the enemy on the inside. Wilde's art became a contagious disease hiding underneath a dangerously deceptive poetic mask, intended to infiltrate and infect an unsuspecting public at its weakest and most vulnerable point, the mind.

> [T]his social leper, Oscar Wilde, had founded a cult of sodomy in this country, and traveled from end to end of it perverting youth wherever he could. He was not satisfied even that his evil influence should die with him; he left behind his works, so that his crimes may be perpetrated even after he was dead. And I tried to stop that [. . .] Have I convinced you that this is a beastly play? I trust I have . . . On one side it is poetry, art, solace to a nation in sorrow; on the other side, it is calculated scientific filth; and also calculated to spread disease—disease of the mind, which is the most difficult disease of all to cure. (Quoted in ibid. 233)

From Billing's final plea on until the end of the trial, "Maud Allan was observed to be in tears" (Kettle 234). In his final words to the jury, the judge once again condemned *Salomé* as an immoral play, reminding everyone "that Oscar Wilde wrote filthy works, as you know: he was convicted in this Court and suffered imprisonment, and social extinction, and death in due course" (quoted in ibid. 261). Not surprisingly at this point, the jury returned a "not guilty" verdict for Billing on all counts of libel. After the verdict was read, the judge advised the audience that he hoped the trial would bring about reform of indecent costumes on stage; when women finally got the vote, they should "make it their business to see that much more purity is introduced into public representations than this is the case at present" (quoted in ibid. 267–68). This was an attack aimed at Allan's supposed ties with the suffragists and at the cultural dangers associated with her scanty costume in *The Vision of Salomé* just ten years earlier, and it reveals lingering anxieties about feminism, "immorality," and gender rebellion as a central thread of the trial's fabric, along with its condemnations of homosexuality and transgressive art. An outrageous trial thus ended with an outrageous verdict that not only indicted Maud Allan, J. T. Grein, and once again the ghost of Oscar Wilde but put art itself on trial.

The Pemberton-Billing Trial was the result of a unique constellation of circumstances, players, and social and political fears, "an hysterical configuration of art, politics, military strategy, medicine, and sex" (Gagnier, *Idylls* 203). For Billing, the trial was an opportune tool to advance his own political interests. It was rumored that the prime minister, Lloyd George, was preparing secret peace talks with the Germans; implicating him in the vast conspiracy plot could turn public opinion against him, force him out of office, and thereby change the course of the disastrous war (Kettle 22, 46). While Billing savored his victory with the exultant crowd outside the courthouse, Maud Allan slipped out by a side door and, soon afterward, left England to live abroad, not to return until 1928. Her career and reputation never recovered: "She spoke of Billing as 'the worst man there ever was,' and the ignominious memory of the trial hung next to the other skeleton in her cupboard, Theo's murderous crimes, both to haunt the rest of her days. She was shunned by theatre managements after the trial, and advised not to appear on stage" (Hoare 218). Although Allan continued to perform and tour after a while, reviewers treated her coolly. Despite her once spectacular fame, Maud Allan died in obscurity in a Los Angeles convalescent home in 1956. Independent theater manager and producer J. T. Grein was financially ruined by the legal costs of the Pemberton-Billing Trial, lost his job as a dramatic critic for the *Sunday Times,* and suffered a nervous breakdown. It is unclear if either Maud Allan or Jack Grein ever suspected or knew that "they had simply become political pawns in a much bigger game" (Kettle 63). In a powerful story of moral conspiracy that linked the star power of a famous dancer to the deaths at Flanders, Allan and Grein fell victim to a game of power—a case in point to cite, reinforce, and newly inscribe the materiality of aesthetics as an ethical force that needed to be reined in tightly. Among the most important results of the Pemberton-Billing Trial was its reminder to the British public that aesthetics was dangerous territory—frequented, inhabited, and patrolled by monsters, perverts, and the state.

Claude Cahun, who had correctly diagnosed the mimetic problem as the crux of Allan's trial and was personally invested in it, went on to write a short story that indirectly reflected her experiences and thoughts on the case. "Salomé the Skeptic" (published in 1925 in *Heroines,* a collection of fifteen feminist rewritings of mythological, religious, and popular heroines) indirectly comments on the dilemma that fazed Maud Allan: the nearly impossible balancing act between old models of domestic, moral, conservative femininity and pioneering, avant-garde art. During the Pemberton-Billing Trial, Billing constantly tried to get Allan to identify herself with her role, even though Allan insisted, "Does that make me the part because I act it? Of course not" (quoted in Kettle 81). Maud Allan desperately tried to defend Salomé's supposed purity, innocence, and spirituality by downplaying Wilde and emphasizing the biblical dimension of the story, in order to whitewash her own assaulted and damaged reputation; she did not vigorously deny or question Billing's and the judge's thinking about the relationship of art to life itself. Referencing Mallarmé, Wilde, and Freud's theories of the relationship of dreams and art to life, Cahun's story picks up the mimetic problem and gives it a uniquely feminist—and, as Dean (83) and Thynne (198) argue, possibly lesbian—twist. While Allan sought to reinterpret and purify Salomé's transgressive identity in an effort to save her own reputation, Cahun's heroine—also an actress, like Allan—does the opposite. She does act Salomé for the pleasure of others, who mistake her expert professional display of lurid sensuality as her own nature, but in the story, Cahun gives her actress a rebellious, transgressive voice of her own. The actress only dances for Herod because she feels gratitude for his interest in her dreams (a common symbolist and surrealist theme) and because she thinks he might be a possible ally who understands her more deeply than others do (an interesting twist on Herod's incestuous desire), but she performs for him without any pleasure of her own. She even forgets the name of John the Baptist, whose head she is to order as a reward: "Once I, erotic sleepwalker, have shed my skin seven times for his pleasure, I will demand that they bring me on a silver plate the head of the prophet Whatshisname (I forget his name; it's not important! my stepfather understands)." She is disgusted by those who want her to kiss the head, revealing the legend's core to be a (male) fantasy that has no grounds in (female) reality and smacks of unwanted sexual solicitation: "My repulsion is completely esthetic.—Touch it? yes, they always want that: admire it since it's so realistic!—But to kiss it? why? . . . Ah! . . . Yes! They imagine I'm in love with it. *My God! if it amuses them.* I did not know they had so much imagination.— Kiss it? Do they want me to do more?" (Cahun, *Heroines* 78). Personally, the head of the Baptist "leaves her cold" (ibid. 79).

"Salomé the Skeptic" brilliantly diagnoses and rejects the confusion of the artist's mask/persona with his or her own personal life, the blurring of the artwork with the producing or performing artist's soul and body. The last statement of "Salomé the Skeptic" is a thought-provoking question to the reader rather than a key to the mystery of Salomé's identity. Cahun's actress cautions the reader against mistaking her otherness and her emotional noncompliance with her assigned role for lack of humanity: "If I vibrate with vibrations other than yours, must you conclude that my flesh is insensitive?" (Cahun, *Heroines* 79). The unfortunate Maud Allan, still closeted as a sexually active, lesbian or bisexual woman, never had the opportunity to ask this question of her tormentor Billing, the judge, or the newspaper-reading British public. In her tale, Claude Cahun brilliantly gave Allan a voice. She also added her own razor-sharp analysis of why Allan could have never won a trial that was built around the assumption that artists' transgressive artworks imitated their personal lives. Fittingly, Cahun dedicated "Salomé the Skeptic" to Oscar Wilde.

4

Alla Nazimova's *Salomé: An Historical Phantasy by Oscar Wilde*

Four years after Maud Allan's public disgrace in the Pemberton-Billing Trial, Russian-born actress and Hollywood movie star Alla Nazimova (1879–1945) decided to adapt Wilde's drama in her striking art film *Salomé: An Historical Phantasy by Oscar Wilde*.[1] Aided by Natacha Rambova's extraordinary, Beardsleyesque set designs and costumes, *Salomé* invoked both the symbolist-decadent fin de siècle context of Wilde's play and its reputation as an avant-garde work, courtesy of Reinhardt's and Strauss's censorship scandals and successes. Although Wilde's play had never caused as much controversy in the United States as it did in England, Strauss's opera remained banned in Chicago, New York, and several major U.S. cities. Similar to Maud Allan's work and its interpretation in the Pemberton-Billing Trial, Nazimova's *Salomé*, the first faithful movie adaptation of Wilde's play, is characterized by avant-garde aspirations, pioneering feminist agency, and daring gender transgression. Unlike Allan's *The Vision of Salomé*, Nazimova's film quite openly embraced and stressed the homoerotic and transgressive elements of Wilde's play, provoking it to be read as an homage to Wilde with a queer aesthetic. It also continued her personal commitment—as a star actress in Ibsen's plays on Broadway—to serious modern drama and its complex modern heroines.

Nazimova's *Salomé* has much interested film scholars, modernist studies scholars, and gay and lesbian literary and historical scholars in recent years. Previous studies of the film have emphasized Nazimova's pioneering role as one of the most popular and highly paid stars of silent cinema as well as one of the first female filmmakers and producers; the modernist visual and technical elements of the film; and its homoerotic and camp elements, which explain the film's enduring cult status and popularity at queer film festivals. As much as it aspires to avant-garde status, Nazimova's *Salomé* is also characterized by the film's bows to popular taste. Its style is best described as popular avant-gardism, the combination of highbrow theatrical aesthetics with fashionable themes and styles of the times, such as the continuing art nouveau vogue (settings and costumes allude to Aubrey Beardsley's designs) and the emerging jazz age flapper. As Patricia White shows, the film is positioned at the fertile intersections of modernist consumerism, queer visibility, and avant-garde experimentation.

One crucial aspect of Nazimova's adaptation that has received very little attention, however, is the continuity between Nazimova's stage and film production careers, specifically her well-documented preference for and personal investment in Ibsen's complex modern dramatic heroines, in relation to Wilde's *Salomé*. Such strong, psychologically complex and morally ambiguous female heroines as Nora Helmer, Hedda Gabler, and Hilda Wangel were welcome challenges to her own art of acting, but Nazimova's interpretations also endorsed and expanded their transgressive feminist value. Whereas Maud Allan had unsuccessfully fought public perceptions of her alliance with the suffragists and officially upheld orthodox gender doctrine, Nazimova courted the feminist association in *A Doll's House* and *Salomé,* the two films she made with her own independent production company, Nazimova Productions. Before Nazimova got to Wilde's *Salomé*, she had poured all her energy into Ibsen, and his feminist themes also influenced her striking 1922 cinematic adaptation, a milestone for female-authored cinematic modernism and the first surviving feature film of Wilde's play.

The Broadway Years: Nazimova's Stage Career

Alla Nazimova was a huge star in Ibsen's plays on Broadway in the mid-1900s, a legacy that she later tried to bring to the movies. Even though her theater career is almost forgotten today, Nazimova's stage success lasted at least three decades; she was routinely compared to such star actresses as Eleanora Duse and Sarah Bernhardt. Born Maria Ede Adelaide Leeton on June 4, 1879, in Yalta, Russia, to Jewish parents and a troubled family life, Nazimova originally trained as a violinist before she enrolled in the Academy of Acting in Moscow, where she soon established herself as one of the best students and got a chance to apprentice at Stanislavsky's esteemed

Moscow Art Theater. She started her professional acting career in czarist Kostrome and St. Petersburg and married a penniless drama student, Sergej Golovin, before joining Paul Orlenev's St. Petersburg Players, who soon took her on tour to Europe, including Berlin and London. Here, in late 1904 or early 1905, the troupe was discovered by none other than avant-garde theater producer J. T. Grein, who booked their play *The Chosen People* to open at his Avenue Theatre on January 21, 1905. Grein admired every actor in the troupe, "but above the crowd towered the figure of Nazimova. . . . The moment she spoke, the audience hung on her lips . . . and when she delivered a speech which in its accents of denunciation equalled Zola's 'J' Accuse' in the Dreyfus case, the audience rose in a frenzy." Even during their first interview, Grein had found himself powerfully "carried away" when Nazimova acted one of her monologues for him: "Never will I forget the impression she made . . . She had a voice that sounded like harps in the air, and she had eyes—so lustrous, so wondrous, so expressive, full of tenderness, depth, and passion—that for a long time afterward they haunted me" (quoted in Lambert 110). Transferring their enormously popular *The Chosen People* from the Avenue Theatre to the Pavilion, Grein then arranged for it to be played alongside Ibsen's *Ghosts* and *Hedda Gabler.*

Their London success gave the company director hope that the troupe could be even more successful in the United States, which had a large Russian immigrant population. The St. Petersburg Players arrived in New York City later in 1905, first performing in borrowed theaters, then moving into a leased space on the Lower East Side, naming it the Orlenev Lyceum. Beset by serious financial difficulties, the troupe nevertheless quickly gained an enthusiastic following among the Russian immigrant population and attracted critics, who soon wrote glowing reviews, especially about the company's presentation of Ibsen's *The Master Builder,* often singling out Nazimova for special praise. This was all the more notable since hardly any of the critics understood a word of the actors' Russian. Just as for J. T. Grein in London, the language barrier did not seem to matter—Nazimova's great acting skill transcended it. The critics' enthusiasm resulted in such headlines as "Ibsen by Russian Actors Draws Crowds to the Bowery: New Tragedy Queen Is Found On East Side." The *Century Magazine* reviewer wrote a letter to the *New York Times:* "Those who care for acting as an art should take a trolley car to Orlenev's Lyceum. There may be enjoyed some of the best acting ever seen in New York" (quoted in Lambert 126). Nazimova was recognized for her "charm and grace, and subtle intelligence of interpretation" as Regina and for her "feeling and intelligence" and "high pitch of emotional power" as Leah, and Orlenev and his company were praised as genuine artists and

"really excellent players."[2] In early February 1906, Nazimova was interviewed by and featured in *The World* as "one of the most interesting personalities on the New York stage," "a type of the intellectual Russian," "a talented, versatile actress" who also arranged the interlude music and designed
and sewed costumes for Orlenev's troupe (De Foe). When, despite their impressive critical successes, the St. Petersburg Players could not overcome
their financial and personal difficulties and decided, in the end, to leave for
Russia, Nazimova had to make a choice. Would she return with them and
relive her old life in Russia, or stay in the New World and strike out on her
own? Courageously, she decided to do the latter.

Luckily, theater impresario Lee Shubert offered the now famous Nazimova a contract, with the stipulation that she learn English as quickly as
possible, so she could perform Ibsen for English-speaking audiences. Nazimova personally chose Hedda Gabler as her debut role in an English-lan-
guage production. In her unpublished diary, she wrote about the affinities
she felt with Hedda's idea of actively molding, rather than passively accepting, destiny: "Hedda Gabler! Yes, that's it. Hedda Gabler, not in the sense of
being possessed with the idea of controlling someone else's destiny, but to
mold my own destiny in the most wonderful way, into something worth-
while and unexpected, even to myself!" (quoted in Lambert 133). She was
able to learn enough English in six months to appear as Hedda in an En-
glish-language production at the Princess Theater on November 12, 1906,
to enthusiastic response. (Henrik Ibsen had recently died, on May 23,
1906, so productions of his plays garnered special attention from that fact.)
Nazimova played Hedda "as a subversive character of almost mythic proportions," clad "in a severe dark gown, hair drawn back starkly, high heels
adding to her stature, a glare of scarlet lipstick enlarging her mouth" (Lambert 137–38). She also added important interpretive touches, such as
putting Hedda on a footstool in a crucial scene to make her appear majesti-
cally tall and dominant. In another scene, Hedda was "[l]eft alone on stage,
backed against a wall, and as she extended her arms, her black robe fell
slowly open to reveal a blood-red lining" (ibid. 137). A tribute poem published in *Theatre Magazine* in August 1907 highlighted the femme fatale appeal of Hedda/Nazimova that accounted for Nazimova's success (Untermeyer 219). The *New York Times* also praised Nazimova's art: "Great creative
acting . . . One of the most illuminating and varied performances which our
stage has seen in years" (quoted in Lambert 137).

Although the play was officially directed by Henry Miller, he recognized
that Nazimova knew more about Ibsen than he did, and he actually let her
take over rehearsals and practically direct the play herself, a very unusual

honor: "In 1906, there were no women directors in the New York theatre, and it was equally unheard of for a producer to allow an unknown foreign actress to direct her own debut" (Lambert 135). Nazimova surprised her fellow actors with innovative techniques, such as ensemble acting and more simple, less pathos-infused techniques of enunciation and movement on stage, which she had learned as Stanislavsky's apprentice in Moscow. The nineteen-year-old budding playwright Eugene O'Neill saw Nazimova in *Hedda Gabler,* his first experience of an Ibsen play. He went back to see the production ten times and later recalled, "That experience discovered an entire new world of drama for me . . . [and] gave me my first conception of a modern theatre where truth might live" (quoted in Lambert 138).

Next, Nazimova debuted for Shubert as Nora in *A Doll's House,* first at the Princess Theater on January 14, 1907, and then at the Bijou Theater from March 1907. She would later reprise the role in a production opening at the Plymouth Theater on April 29, 1918, three years before tackling her own screen adaptation. As Ibsen's Nora, she turned in another sensational performance that showed her complete versatility as an actress. *Harper's Weekly* described the astonishing contrast between her Hedda and her Nora: "It is Madame Nazimova's command of expression—her eyes, perhaps—which contributes so much to her characterizations. Her face is as variable as the sky. As Hedda it is all cloudiness, threatening, and sinister, with never a ray of sunlight. As Nora she is as radiant as an April day and as serenely unwarning of the clouds which swing up in startled flight across the sky. The feline in Hedda is the playfulness of the kitten in Nora" ("Acting and English of Nazimova"). *Theatre Magazine,* which devoted several articles and interviews to Nazimova in various 1907 issues, also marveled at the astonishing contrast: "Her Hedda had all the brilliancy, viciousness, and alluring charm associated with that somewhat abnormal character, her Nora has all the youthful spontaneity, feverish unrest and introspective self-assertion that goes with Torvald, [*sic*] Helmer's child-wife." As Nora, Nazimova sported "a fluffy halo of hair, frilly white blouse, and skirt, stature diminished by low heels, mouth by absence of rouge" (Lambert 138). Nazimova's interpretation revealed Nora's character like no other American actress had been able to do: "It is a creation not intermittently inspiring, but a sustained and soul-revealing study of the ingenious side as well as the profound depths of Nora's misunderstood character" ("Mme. Alla Nazimova as Ibsen's Nora").

Nazimova declared in an interview that "she profoundly admire[d] Ibsen. To portray his characters one must think, think, think" (Peterson 220). Think she did, in particular about Nora's famous final scenes and provocative exit from her bourgeois home life. According to Lambert, "[d]iscarding frills and froufrou for Nora's last scene, Nazimova chose to walk out the door in a plain winter coat and head scarf. Before leaving, she took out a hand mirror, glanced at her reflected face, and, to emphasize the moment of self-illumination, had a spotlight trained on the mirror" (138). *Theatre Magazine* commented, "it was in the final act that Mme. Nazimova revealed the full sweep and depth of her natural art. Her repose is marvelous in its expressiveness, and when the true weakness of her husband's character was revealed her instant appreciation of the wide gulf that separates their souls was delivered with a wild outburst of righteous indignation that was electrifying in its effect" ("Mme. Alla Nazimova as Ibsen's Nora").

In the audience at the *Doll's House* performances was Halvdan Koht, a critic who would later write a major biography of Ibsen. He described Nazimova's "electrifying effect" on audiences, who took the finale as a politicized call to action. "Koht recalls his horror when members of the audience, mistaking 'the work of art' for 'a collection of ideas,' began to applaud Nora's every line as if it were a political harangue.' . . . Displaying what the modern theatre condemns as bad manners, the 1908 audience was responding to Ibsen's powerful feminist poetry, the exhilarating promise that on the other side of the doll house, women, no less than men, could learn to take themselves seriously" (Templeton 142). Audiences read Nazimova's performance as explicitly feminist, even though Ibsen's own feminist sympathies were ambiguous and ultimately did not satisfy admirers like the actress Elizabeth Robins, who recognized Ibsen's political shortcomings and went on to revise Ibsen's female characters in her own pro-suffrage play, *Votes for Women* (1907).[3] (The critical controversy about Ibsen's feminism still lingers today; see Templeton 110–45.)

Hedda and Nora made Nazimova a true star. *Harper's Weekly* wrote, "It is not to be gainsaid that Madame Alla Nazimova is the dramatic sensation of this season in New York" ("Acting and English of Nazimova"). Reviewers for the *New York Times* and *Century Magazine* praised her artistry; *Cosmopolitan* ran a special illustrated feature on Nazimova; she appeared in *Theatre Magazine* on the cover (June 1907), in articles, and in photographs, as Nora, Hedda, and Comtesse Coquette. Together with Untermeyer's poem dedicated to Nazimova's Hedda Gabler, *Theatre Magazine* also ran a poem entitled "To Mme. Nazimova as Nora (After seeing the Actress' Portrayal of the Heroine in Ibsen's 'Doll's House')" by LeRoy Arnold, underneath a large-scale photograph of Nazimova in tarantella costume and pose (August 1907). The two poems accompanied a long interview with Nazimova that touched on gender issues, her love of Ibsen, and her wish to be artistically independent and an inspiration to others (Arnold; Peterson 219).

On September 23, 1907, Nazimova left the femme fatale Hedda and the child-wife Nora behind and appeared as the utopian dreamer Hilda Wangel in the American premiere of *The Master Builder* at the Bijou Theater in New York, where the play ran for the phenomenal number of sixty-five performances. In the previously mentioned August 1907 interview with *Theatre Magazine,* Nazimova explained that Ibsen's Hilda was her favorite Ibsen role and inspiration: "My ideal woman is Hilda in 'The Master Builder.' She was to the architect what a woman should be to a man, the man she has chosen, his inspiration. Most women do not want to be a man's inspiration. They want to be his wife, the mother of his children, in one word, his comfort. Women of the type of Hilda are a man's ever-inspiring companions" (quoted in Peterson 220). To Nazimova, Hilda was "the most interesting of Ibsen's women. She is young, a woman of ideas, a woman of brains, a woman who does something. She lifts up the man she loves. She is greater than love. A woman should be bigger than her love, particularly a young woman" (quoted in Darnton). Following *The Master Builder,* in February 1908, Nazimova went on a national tour with all three Ibsen plays—*A Doll's House, Hedda Gabler,* and *The Master Builder*—selling out theaters across the country.

The complexity, variable temperament, and impressive strength of Ibsen's heroines were a perfect fit for Nazimova's aspirations as an actress, as they had been for the famous American actress and Wilde protégée Elizabeth Robins. Ibsen's huge importance to modern actresses "had everything to do with our particular business—the art of acting. . . . [N]o [other] dramatist [had] ever meant so much to the women of the stage" (Robins 32–33, 55). For Alla Nazimova, too, playing Ibsen's women roles provided a lifeline: they pushed and expanded her own boundaries as an artist. Nazimova had established herself as America's prime Ibsen actress (along with Minnie Maddern Fiske), as evidenced by the Yale Drama Department's invitation for her to lecture on Ibsen. Later published in *Independent Magazine,* Nazimova's speech focused on "Ibsen's women" and highlighted their contrast to Shakespeare's fictitious historical heroines: "[Ibsen's] modern woman is more complex. She knows more; her nerves are exaggerated." Nazimova also defended Nora's decision to leave her husband and family: "She had to go away to grow up . . . Her children were better off without her. She saw that. What could she do with them except spoil them as she had been spoiled?" (quoted in Lambert 146–47).

Even as she brought in spectacular revenues as an Ibsen actress, the Shubert brothers (Lee, Sam, and Jacob, theatrical managers and producers of a vast theater organization in New York and other U.S. cities) saw their chance to further capitalize on Nazimova's audience draw. They started to assign her she roles in more shallow, mediocre, crowd-pleasing plays, though they promised her could also continue acting Ibsen. Nazimova played along because she was on a five-year contract and was making real money for the first time in her life, but she hated the new plays. These included *Comtess Coquette* (a high-society comedy that had been a great success in Paris and London and opened on Broadway on April 12, 1907); *The Comet,* a stereotypical vamp play by the American playwright Owen Johnson (one of Nazimova's early supporters), in which the *Times* wrote that Nazimova "look[ed] like the Whistler portrait of a human vampire" (quoted in Lambert 145); and the forgettable *The Passion Flower.* Another stereotypical vamp role she had to play later was the lead role in *Bella Donna* in 1911 (under a different contract, with Charles Frohman, after her contract with the Shuberts had run out).

In a June 1930 *Theatre Guild Magazine* interview with the modernist writer and journalist Djuna Barnes, Alla Nazimova confessed her loathing of such roles, which demanded nothing of her art and cheapened her own, more serious ambitions. The sympathetic Barnes portrays Nazimova as a "thinking person who had felt too long and too little valued her own certitude," an actress with a passion for modern theater, especially Ibsen (357): "She was discussed and acclaimed. Her series of matinees gave way to regular evening performances at the Princess. One after another, Ibsen's women came to life before the eyes of astonished thousands. . . . Then came the fall" (356). Although she understood herself to be an actress of highbrow modern drama, her five-year contract with the Shuberts (and, later, commercial need) forced Nazimova to "feed her great talents to a public which had appetite for nothing more than the conventional stage vampire" (Barnes 354). Barnes comments that "[h]er artistry was so extraordinarily flexible and persuasive that she could make a common vampire of melodrama seem, for the moment, as great a creation as Hedda" (356). Nazimova appeared in many of those "sorry plays that besmirched, rather than dimmed, her genius. She made huge sums of money, she was the darling of every tea, she was feted and cried over, complimented and kissed! [But] [o]ne can see her longing in her every fiber to play parts that called for overtones and underacting. (She has the intelligence to know that quietly the world was made, and quietly it turns its sterner cheek.) One can see her valuing that sort of thing, the kind of thing she had once portrayed in Ibsen" (Barnes 356). But "she had been thrown into the abyss" of bad art (ibid. 358). She despised sensationalism, predictable plots, and overt stereotyping. Like Maud Allan, who turned Greek art into deliberately poised movements that channeled overt passion into artistic refinement, Nazimova favored an aesthetics of sophistication and indirection: "I wanted to do thoughtful things, things subtle and only hinted at. When anything is very great it is like that, is it not? . . . So it is that I wanted to play. One fails when one is asked to give less than one has, though the public may think it is success" (quoted in Barnes 358).

In hindsight, Nazimova probably realized that "in satisfying cultural pre-conceptions, in embodying a cultural archetype, she had temporarily lost sight of her own artistic vision" (Bockting 193). According to Laurence Senelick, Nazimova "made a successful career in America by compromising her artistic ideals with a necessary quantum of commercialism. . . . Her popularity came in part from her willingness to assimilate. . . . Throughout her long career in American stage and film, Nazimova precariously juggled her ideals of a sophisticated, socially engaged, literary theatre with conces-sions to popular taste" ("American Tour" 11–12). This is also evidenced by Nazimova's role as a fashion idol and celebrity endorser of popular con-sumer goods, such as cigarettes and beauty products, throughout the 1910s and 1920s.[4]

In 1909, Nazimova had brought "the total of her earnings for the Shu-bert organization to more than $4 million, a notable amount" for that time (Lambert 150). Nazimova was so good at her interpretations of Ibsen's com-plex women and so fascinating even in her stereotypical vamp roles that the Shuberts decided to honor her in 1910 by naming one of their theaters for her. The remodeled Thirty-Ninth Street Theatre, which belonged to the Shubert brothers, was renamed Nazimova's 39th Street Theatre. On its opening night, on April 18, 1910, Nazimova starred as Rita Allmers in Ib-sen's *Little Eyolf,* which garnered forty-eight performances. Nazimova com-mented, "I do not think there is any other writer who understands the soul of women as he does, [and] there is a mighty purpose in every one of his dramas" (quoted in Lambert 150).

Nazimova, Ibsen's Women, and Wilde's *Salomé*

From the beginning of her theatrical career, Nazimova had been extremely interested in and passionate about Henrik Ibsen's complex, modern women characters. Therefore, Nazimova's twin choice of Ibsen and Wilde as her first projects for her own film production company was no coincidence. Nora Helmer had been one of Nazimova's famous roles on Broadway, so it was reasonable to think that a film adaptation of the play would be a great success with the moviegoing public. Salomé was an unrealized dream role of Nazimova's, one she had long desired to play. In 1906, Orlenev had put Wilde's *Salomé* on the St. Petersburg Players' schedule and asked Nazimova to star as Salomé, but he changed his mind at the last minute and produced a different play (Lambert 253–54). In choosing *A Doll's House* and *Salomé,* Nazimova simultaneously sought to regain her previous status as an expert actress of modern drama and to capture on film her own version of two of modern drama's most impressive, interesting female enfants terribles—one she had played many times and one she was itching to play.

The transition from Ibsen to Wilde was a smooth one for Nazimova, as Wilde's Salomé has much in common with Ibsen's Nora Helmer, Hedda Gabler, and Hilda Wangel. The decadence and boredom of Hedda, the courageous resolve of the childlike and underestimated Nora, and the utopian dreaming of the New Woman Hilda Wangel compare directly to certain character aspects of Wilde's heroine, who sums up many of their traits and takes their rebellion to outrageous heights. Oscar Wilde himself hinted that he would have liked to see himself compared to Ibsen, and such scholars as Kerry Powell have traced some remarkable parallels and points of contact between Wilde's and Ibsen's works. Powell suggests that Wilde's daring Salomé was indirectly enabled by Ibsen's transgressive women and by the enormous success of Wilde's actress friend Elizabeth Robins in those roles on stage: "Wilde saw Robins' performance [as Hedda] at about the same time he set out to create what was, in one sense, the same kind of role for Sarah Bernhardt in *Salomé*" ("Wilde and Ibsen" 229).

The influential critic William Archer, Wilde's contemporary and also Ibsen's prime champion in England, was the first to note an affinity between Wilde's *Salomé* and Ibsen's *Hedda Gabler.* In his favorable review of Wilde's French book edition of *Salomé* ("Mr. Oscar Wilde's New Play," *Black and White,* May 11, 1893), Archer pointedly compared Salomé to Hedda via a complex metaphor of orientalism and pathology: "The atmosphere of the play is certainly none of the healthiest; but if an artist sets forth to paint a fever jungle, we can scarcely complain if his picture be not altogether breezy and exhilarating. . . . Salomé is an *oriental Hedda Gabler;* and who could portray such a character in the hues of radiant health?" (in *Oscar Wilde: The Critical Heritage,* ed. Beckson, 142). Hedda and Salomé both have a markedly decadent or perverse streak, deriving from their existential boredom and sense of being stuck in a world not of their own choosing.

Like Jokanaan for Salomé, Eilert Lovborg seems like a breath of fresh air at first, a welcome diversion in Hedda's hopelessly dull, disappointed existence as the wife of Tesman, a naive homebody she mistakenly had expected to offer her an exciting intellectual and social life. Lovborg, the psychologically volatile intellectual genius whom Hedda craves to control and usurp, initially seems to offer her the opportunity of controlling someone's destiny, as the muse and enabler of a great man, since in her strongly gendered and classed society she cannot be great and influential herself. Like Jokanaan in Wilde's play, Lovborg is not up to the task or interested enough, however, and like Salomé, Hedda falls into the mode of a terrible destroyer goddess, wielding her power of death where she cannot control and dominate a life. Jane Marcus, who offered the first scholarly feminist reading of Wilde's *Salomé* in the 1970s, writes, "Both women, condemned to spiritual death as sex objects and thwarted in artistic expression by their culture, kill the men they love. The men, who are also punished by society for breaking the stereotypes, are condemned to suffer their own humiliations. Salomé and Hedda destroy not their masters but their brothers" (12).

Hedda's "beautiful" suicide and Salomé's murder are presented as paradoxically tragic yet triumphant. These modern heroines effectively leave behind a world they utterly despise, while engaged in an action of extreme individualism of their own choice. In each shocking finale, the heroine's demise functions more as a positive transfiguration and attainment of her own vision than as the convincing punishment of a notorious femme fatale. Both female protagonists represent a perverse but extremely satisfying shaming of the mediocrity, pettiness, and existential angst of inferior male adversaries who represent patriarchal authority (Tesman and Herod). In dramatic terms, Hedda's and Salomé's spectacular deaths paradoxically affirm that radical individualism and the pursuit of beauty are not only feasible but worth dying for.

Ibsen's Nora Helmer in *A Doll's House* compares to another aspect of Wilde's Salomé: the mixture of childlike innocence with courageous resolve. Both Hedda and Nora offer female rebellion against a stifling, male-dominated environment that subjects them to the incessant gaze of sexual objectification (or, in Hedda's case, the expectation of motherhood). But whereas Hedda is like a femme fatale and is gender-transgressive in her associations with male instruments of power (General Gabler's pistols, horses, Eilert Lovborg's manuscript), Nora and Salomé carry cultural associations of the child-woman and the *femme fragile* (evident in other characters' obsession with Salomé's delicate feet and hands, for example, or in Helmer's addressing Nora as a songbird, a playful squirrel, and a doll). The contrast between their looks and their inner power gradually emerges, deriving from inner sources the other characters did not even suspect they had.

Finally, Hilda Wangel in *The Master Builder*, Nazimova's favorite role, sheds light on the utopian aspect of forceful femininity that characterizes Salomé and also relates well to Nazimova's own feminist leanings. In a personal dedication to her niece Lucy Olga Lewton in an autograph album in 1914, Nazimova quoted Hilda's central utopian speech from act 3 (with slight variations due to her recitation from memory): "Hilda: 'and then we will build the loveliest—the very loveliest thing in all the world . . . Castles in the air . . . they are so easy to build—and so easy to take refuge in!' (*Master Builder*, Act 3, Ibsen) Your auntie Alla."[5] Following Solness's suicide at the end of *The Master Builder*, Hilda Wangel still believes that it is possible to build castles in the air to dream about and for exceptional human beings, such as the master builder Solness, to achieve true greatness and visionary heroism, unimpeded by death or irony. Exploited as sexual or domestic fantasy objects, Hedda, Nora, and Salomé have nothing productive to do. Hilda, by contrast, finds relief and hope in the creative alliance with a like-minded equal, Solness, even though that alliance is ultimately doomed as well. Solness and Hilda resemble Wilde's constellation of Jokanaan and Salomé: she adores him and hopes for an expansion of her lifeworld though this charismatic, visionary male, but she actually dares to transgress and dream yet further. Hilda is, in fact, a more truly Nietzschean free spirit than Solness. To Nazimova, she was the true survivor and winner of the play. Nazimova wrote that Hilda "triumphs even though he fails," discovering her strength beyond being "man's ever-inspiring companion," as his wanes (quoted in Lambert 144). Hilda Wangel embodies what Salomé could have been, had Jokanaan only looked at her.

Nazimova's feminist understanding of and interest in Ibsen's women characters are further solidified when one looks at another starring role of hers during this time, Hedwig in Marion Craig Wentworth's very popular one-act, feminist antiwar play *War Brides*, which was also made into a movie (now lost) starring Nazimova. Both the play and the film have strong overtones of Ibsen, including an obvious allusion to *Hedda Gabler* in the final scene, in which the female heroine kills herself (and her unborn child) with her father's pistol in the bedroom next door to his, to protest against women's oppression and male warfare. *War Brides* was strongly supported by such women's organizations as the New York Association of Suffragists and went on tour to several American cities, such as Pittsburgh and Boston. Wentworth was a socialist and a suffragist who used her writing as a platform for political agitation. Nazimova felt a sense of mission: "I am not merely doing something as an actress, but for the womanhood of the world," she told the *New York American* (Lambert 172). To the *Brooklyn Eagle,* she said, "Those women who don't believe in suffrage, they're not awake, that's all" (ibid. 173). Nazimova was a success in the play, and its following screen adaptation (released in 1917 by Lewis J. Selznick Enterprises) provided Nazimova's entry into the movie business. The director of the film *War Brides,* Herbert Brenon, taught Nazimova much about the art of moviemaking and acting for the camera (Lambert 180–81). This training laid the basis for her own foray into directing and producing just a few years later, when she launched Nazimova Productions and decided to adapt *A Doll's House* and *Salomé* for the movies.

From Stage to Screen: Nazimova Productions and *Salomé*

In the early 1920s, Alla Nazimova wanted to transform the cinema into a serious artistic medium that would mirror and equal the prestige of the theatrical stage. She had high hopes for her literary screen adaptations, literally staking her reputation, her fortune, and her artistic vision on her two chosen projects, *A Doll's House* and *Salomé.* With Nazimova Productions, she effectively became one of the first female auteurs of silent cinema. At a time when many still perceived the movies as a cheap, slightly seedy form of lowbrow entertainment and when women were rarely seen in executive or other influential positions in Hollywood, Nazimova also wanted to show the world that the person developing, producing, and embodying movies as highbrow art could be a woman.

When one looks at her theatrical career in the 1910s, one notices Alla Nazimova's continuing struggle to leave the vamp roles behind and return to highbrow modern drama and feminist-inflected roles. Even before the germination of Nazimova's production company and her choices of *A Doll's House* and *Salomé,* feminist themes were already clearly present in Nazimova's work. There runs a crucial common thread through the strong women roles in which Nazimova excelled for one and a half decades before taking Nora and Salomé to the silver screen. Nora, Hedda, Mrs. Alving, Hilda Wangel, and Hedwig in *War Brides* were not only complex but deeply ambiguous, nonstereotypical contemporary heroines, caught between their own utopian longings for escape from oppressive patriarchal authority and social institutions (such as marriage or motherhood), on the one hand, and their own delusions, mistakes, lack of agency, or neurotic madness (as in the case of Hedda or Hedwig), on the other.

Taking these heroines to the movies was a shrewd move for an actress with an interest in advancing the movies as a serious art form while popularizing modern complex women characters who had already advanced and influenced the cultural conversation about feminist issues. As early as 1912, Nazimova realized that the still relatively new medium of film offered her a fantastic chance to commit her own star persona and acting method to the screen and thereby preserve them for future generations. The feature film was still in its early infancy (most films were no longer than one reel, about twenty minutes), but Nazimova understood herself as a pioneer and leader. *Motion Picture Story Magazine* reported that she

> is "crazy" about the "film plays," visits the picture houses whenever possi-
> ble, and, with all fervor and conviction, declares that it will be a proud day
> for her when she can present before the machines, Nora, Hedda, Hilda,
> and the other rôles that have made her famous. "I shall be doing it soon,"
> she declares, "and while I may be the first in a prominent position, in
> America, to do it, I surely will not be the last. All the others will follow."
> (Giffen 168)

When she first started starring in silent films in 1916 (in *War Brides*) on a spectacularly lucrative contract with the Metro film company, Nazimova already hoped she could bring modern theater to the screen. But although Nazimova, who was at the height of her career (she earned thirteen thousand dollars a week, three thousand more than the highest-grossing female star thus far, Mary Pickford), won a crucial say in picking her directors, scripts, and male costars, her work for Metro disappointingly continued the previous vamp typecasting trend, necessitated by the rising movie industry's search for popularity and maximum profit formulas during the early years.[6] Her early films for Metro included *Revelation, Toys of Fate,* and *Eye for Eye* (1918); *Out of the Fog, Red Lantern,* and *The Brat* (1919); and *Stronger than Death, The Heart of a Child,* and *Madame Peacock* (1920). Welcome reprieves were the rather unusual *Billions* (1920) and *Camille* (1921, with a screenplay adapted from Alexandre Dumas's melodramatic novel and costarring an as yet unknown Rudolph Valentino), two films that constituted Nazimova's first collaboration with designer Natacha Rambova, who would go on to design the *Salomé* sets and costumes for her.[7] In *Billions* and *Camille,* Nazimova and Rambova united forces to realize their vision of the European art film, developing striking art deco designs and costumes and a famously stylish fantasy sequence in *Billions* that anticipate the visual sumptiousness of *Salomé*. Despite their artistic look and stylish designs, however, neither *Billions* nor *Camille* satisfied Nazimova's desire for artistic freedom. According to Lambert's biography, Nazimova thought that Metro had started "a campaign against a woman who the Hollywood male establishment decided had grown too powerful" (Lambert 248–49).[8] As early as 1907, Nazimova proclaimed that she would very much like to be artistically independent and free of financial considerations in picking her roles: "I have my dreams, like all actresses. I should like to have a theatre of my own, where I should play what I liked, and where I need not think about the box office, because the people would like me well enough to come see me no matter what I played" (Peterson 221). In 1921, then, Nazimova finally grasped at her chance to produce "thoughtful things" that would marry her interest in avant-garde modern drama's strong and complex heroines with her well-established, iconic star power. She ended her relationship with Metro and founded Nazimova Productions, according to her belief that "[a] woman living a creative life is bound, necessarily, to do things sometimes defiant to convention. In order to fulfill herself, she should live freely" (quoted in Abrams 77).[9]

Financed entirely by herself, Nazimova Productions gave her the longed-for chance to oversee "virtually every phase of production: scripting, titling, editing, casting and acting," taking control of the complete artistic process from beginning to end (Druesne 323). Under the pseudonym Peter M. Winters, Nazimova herself wrote the screenplays for *A Doll's House* and *Salomé*. The influential fan magazine *Photoplay* had accused her of trying to "do too much," which may have been one reason why Nazimova chose to write under a pseudonym instead of taking credit for the screenplay herself (Lambert 251). She also gave her common-law husband, Charles Bryant, official director's credit for both films, even though Alla Nazimova effectively directed the film herself: Bryant did little more than shout, "Lights! Camera! Action!" (ibid.). Bryant had been Nazimova's leading man in nine previous movies; she had first met him during the filming of *War Brides*. From 1918 to 1925, Nazimova, who had not been able to divorce her obscure Russian husband, conducted a lavender marriage with Bryant, who was either bisexual or gay. Although there was initially much affection and some sex between them, the relationship soon cooled and was kept up for convenience's sake.[10] Nazimova, who was bisexual and unable to obtain a divorce from her husband back in Russia, needed to shield her many affairs with both men and women from public scrutiny and willingly kept up the public impression that she and Bryant were actually married.

"Protected by her bogus marriage to Charles Bryant, Nazimova quickly became the doyenne of the lesbian community" (Schanke 137), throwing lavish house parties and surrounding herself with young protégées and lovers, including Mercedes de Acosta, Eva Le Gallienne, Dorothy Arzner, and even Dolly Wilde, Oscar Wilde's niece.

The first of Nazimova Production's two projects, *A Doll's House*, received strong critical acclaim and at least partly restored Nazimova's reputation as a serious actress of modern drama. Like many films of the period, *A Doll's House* apparently did not survive the fatal corrosion of the early film stock, but some film stills and contemporary reviews still exist. It appears that Nazimova added her own touches to Ibsen's play, such as a final scene, after the famous slamming of the door, in which Nora is shown briskly walking off with determination into a cold winter night, emphasizing her independent drive and the beginning of her life outside the home. Nazimova liked her film adaptation even better than the stage version of Nora that had meant so much to her career. In a telegram sent to Eva Le Gallienne during the last week of shooting, Nazimova exclaimed, "Very happy doing Doll's House Am Sure you will like it better than on the stage Never felt so enthusiastic" (quoted in Lambert 253). Still, the mass public she had hoped for never turned out to see the film, and box office returns were disappointing.

Undeterred, Nazimova embarked on her second project, *Salomé*, investing $250,000 more of her own money into it, thereby seriously endangering her personal finances. "The cameramen photographed each scene at least six times, accumulating 300,000 feet of film," and the total cost of the film would amount to $350,000 at the end, "for that time an exorbitant amount for a movie made on such a small scale" (Morris 89). *A Doll's House* had been a realist film, but in *Salomé*, Nazimova tried out a daringly different visual style of artificial, nonrealistic set and costume design. Hailed as an art film, *Salomé* was a stylized, highly creative theater production with deliberately artificial-looking sets and costumes that showed unmistakable camp elements. Nevertheless, it offered a surprisingly faithful adaptation of Wilde's play. Nazimova took Oscar Wilde's aesthetic vision for *Salomé* just as seriously as she had taken Ibsen, employing central cinematic techniques like camera work, mise-en-scène, and the process of visual narration through editing, to extend and interpret some of Wilde's main themes, such as fatality, synesthesia, veiling, and the dangerous gaze.

In interpreting and extending Wilde's play, Nazimova also adapted a 1890s text to a 1920s Hollywood context: the film clearly builds on recent cinematic traditions and tastes to attract and impress contemporary audiences. Her *Salomé* employs current cinematic fashions, tropes, and techniques that include, among others, the iconography of the flapper, the film vamp, and an extended use of the close-up (an important vehicle of star power in early cinema). As Gaylyn Studlar points out, the cultural vogue of orientalism in U.S. culture at this time (with fan magazines, films like the 1921 Rudolph Valentino blockbuster *The Sheik,* and the effective use of orientalist designs in marketing and consumer culture) may have played an important role in Nazimova's choice of subject (105–6). The film's visual aesthetics also seem influenced by the popular Ballets Russes (with which designer Natacha Rambova had had contact via her former lover Theodore Koslov, a dancer in Diaghilev's troupe in their first season), specifically by "the ur-camp staging of *La Tragédie de Salomé* by the Ballets Russes in 1913–14, choreographed by Boris Romanov, with Tamara Karsavina in the title role. . . . Designed to be a vehicle for Karsavina, . . . it turned out to be an exercise in too-studied exotica, with outlandish, nouveau-Beardsley costumes and décor by Serge Soudeikine" (Bizot 83). The actors' exaggerated and slow gestural and facial acting style may also have been influenced by what Nazimova knew of Alexander Tairov's 1917 *Salomé* production in Moscow, "with its emphasis on ritualized movement and mime" (Lambert 260).

The striking modernity of Nazimova's adaptation and its difference from popular cinematic orientalism becomes clear when one compares it with the only major previous feature film about the topic, Theda Bara's 1919 *Salome* (another lost film), and with a popular literary Salome-themed novel of the time, Anzia Yezierska's *Salome of the Tenements* (1923). Directed by J. Gordon Edwards for William Fox, Theda Bara's *Salome* was a pseudobiblical spectacle starring Bara in one of the many orientalist, evil vamp roles for which Bara was famous.[11] The *Bioscope* reviewer describes the film as "an ambitious and elaborate spectacle," "a gorgeous and sensational pageant-drama mounted with the utmost splendour" with "many striking exteriors, planned on a vast and elaborate scale, in which hundreds of players figure, not to mention camels, horses, and other beasts." The film borrowed from both the Bible and Oscar Wilde but altered their plots freely to portray Salome's/Bara's seductive wickedness to maximum effect, tagging on to the box office successes of Cecil B. DeMille. According to the *Bioscope* review, Theda Bara's film included a whole fictional prehistory of the core story of Salome and John the Baptist that was unrelated to the main plot and evidently meant to amplify Salome's vile aspects. Before the Baptist even appears on the scene, Bara's Salome is already responsible for a murder; a jealous stepfather, Herod; a fatal family intrigue between cousins; an attempt at poisoning Herod's wife, Maria (the renamed Herodias character);

an intrigue to seize the power from Herod; and Maria's subsequent execution, which finally makes Salome the First Lady of Jerusalem and Judea. Salome is "pictured as an inhuman fiend, with an insatiable passion for wickedness for its own sake" ("Salome: Gorgeously Mounted" 74).

In the 1923 novel *Salome of the Tenements* (1923) by the Russian American and Jewish writer Anzia Yezierska, the Salome figure—called Sonya Vrunsky—is also recognizably orientalist, although Yezierska's use of the Salome theme takes a slightly different turn to depict the Jewish immigrant experience as well as female struggles for agency in the early twentieth-century New York City tenements, a similar immigrant environment to the one Alla Nazimova herself experienced. Through the struggles of her protagonist, a second-generation Eastern European immigrant like herself, Yezierska plays out the tensions between Jewish tradition and the complex challenges and promises of the modern New World for young Jewish women in the tenements. Sketching Sonya's desire to climb the social ladder by all means, Yezierska turns to the problematic stereotype of the sexually driven, orientalist Jewess, portraying Sonya as Salome, "this primitive woman," "feminine mystery" (Yezierska 35), "a flame—a longing" (ibid. 37), a "Ghetto princess" (25) with "wild love-madness" (58). Sonya cleverly engineers her own rise above the deprivation of her immigrant community, by sexually enticing her "John the Baptist," the millionaire philanthropist John Manning, to marry her. The novel hence capitalizes on cultural connections between the stereotype of the Jewish temptress and Wilde's and Strauss's versions of Salome's rebellious individualism, amalgamating orientalist stereotyping and feminist potential. At the end, Yezierska's allegorical tale of Jewish womanhood between orientalist tradition and feminist modernity turns into a sentimentalist moral and cultural warning to assimilate and embrace the American Dream.

In comparison to Bara's scenario of sex, sin, and spectacle or Yezierska's focus on Sonya's orientalist hypersexuality and cultural assimilation, Alla Nazimova presents Salome distinctly differently, as a mixture of the modern woman, the femme fatale stereotype, and, finally, a homoerotic and aesthetic stand-in for Wilde. In cinematic terms, its faithfulness to Wilde's story of Salomé (rather than the biblical version) marked, as one reviewer commented, "a distinct departure from the conventional pictures which pour so multitudinously from American studios." It achieved its artistic effect "by the simplest means. There are no armies with banners; no vast chambers of Oriental palaces . . . [and] the screen is all the while filled with vivid beauty, animated by costumes outre [*sic*] and bizarre, in conformity with no period, yet sprung richly endowed from a keen and splendid imagination. . . . Intelligence of the keenest sort has gone into the making of the picture. . . . Compared to the former production of the same story, in which Theda Bara figured, it is 'Hyperion to a satyr'" (Bonte). Interviewed about her new film, Nazimova commented on its risky artistic ambition: "People have shaken their heads sadly as if to say, 'It's too bad you've made an artistic picture. The public doesn't like art.'. . . I am sure that if the story, as seen on the screen, truly reveals itself, it will be liked. I am not afraid that the people will not understand it" (ibid.).

Reviewers uniformly praised the artistic nature of the work, although the picture later flopped at the general box office. Reviewer Robert E. Sherwood commented in *Life:* "The persons responsible for SALOME deserve the whole-souled gratitude of everyone who believes in the possibilities of the movies as an art" (quoted in Pratt 495). The *Variety* reviewer marveled at this "highly fantastic 'Salome,'" calling it "extraordinarily beautiful to look at" (Reviewer signing the name "Fred"). Shot entirely on a studio stage and featuring stunning sets and costumes, the film had a deliberately stylized feel and look that imitated the theatrical environment. In its deliberate staginess, *Salomé* invited a direct comparison of cinema and theater and thus indirectly participated in the contemporary debate, led by Hugo Münsterberg and others, about the increasing sophistication and cultural value of the "photoplay."[12] Building on and expanding theatrical conventions by cinematic means in *Salomé,* Nazimova, like Münsterberg, sought to prove that the cinema could be the theater's privileged artistic equal and heir.

The most striking aspects of Nazimova's version, however, are its unmistakable homoeroticism and queer aesthetics. Whereas Maud Allan and J. T. Grein had struggled in vain to dissociate themselves from the inevitable association of *Salomé* with decadence and sexual perversity, Nazimova's film overtly embraced them. There is enough basic material in Wilde to encourage a homoerotic reading of the play, of course, and in the wake of Wilde's 1895 trials, the controversy surrounding Strauss's opera, and the Pemberton-Billing Trial (which had been widely publicized in the United States), parallels between Wilde's scandal and the transgressive *Salomé* were commonly taken for granted. In Wilde's play, one male protagonist, the Page, woos another, the Syrian captain Narraboth; Salomé also promises to drop Narraboth a "little green flower" (*CCW* 588). This has often been interpreted as Wilde's allusion to the green carnation he was fond of wearing, reportedly a nineteenth-century code signaling homoeroticism among young gay men in Paris (although interpretations of the green carnation as a sign of homosexuality also differ widely).[13] Although the homoerotically themed evidence in Wilde's play itself is subtle and, by some accounts, perhaps even slight, there can be no question that forbidden desire, homo-eroticism, and gender ambiguity pervade Nazimova's version, "a film full of flagrant homosexuality" and camp, which was easily read as a tribute to Wilde's life as well as to *Salomé* as a highbrow work of art (Slide 128). The *Variety Movie Reviews* critic stressed the "effeminacy" of the entire male cast, noting that they moved and posed in stylized, artificial poses as if inviting the contemplation of their beauty ("Salome"). Natacha Rambova and Alla Nazimova chose to put many of the male actors in drag, elaborate wigs, headdresses, and heavy makeup and to place them in lavish orientalist ban-quet scenes complete with basins of incense and enormous, rhythmically moving peacock feathers (another visual allusion to fin de siècle deca-dence). Some soldiers in the film wear giant beaded necklaces and black leotards, and the Young Syrian sports a tight-fitting top with exaggerated, painted nipples. Three male actors in drag play the Ladies of the Court, in bizarre wigs and exaggerated makeup; they tend to their makeup and hair in handheld mirrors and flirt with the male Roman soldiers. These cos-tumes and mannerisms are so overdone that they sometimes acquire an ironic camp quality, which adds to the gender playfulness of Nazimova's otherwise artistically straight-faced adaptation of Wilde's text. Anthony Slide finds "[t]he gay and lesbian undertones to the film . . . so strong that one is tempted to describe it as a 'limp-wristed production'" (128).

In Nazimova's film, Beardsley's prominent visual presence deliberately invokes and recalls the original 1890s cultural context of Wilde's play (his name is also mentioned in the opening titles of the film). Natacha Ram-bova's art nouveau set design and costumes, in black and white with occa-sional silver and gold accents, invoked the florid lines and perverse sexual-ity of Aubrey Beardsley's 1894 popular illustrations of Wilde's *Salomé*, providing further associations with decadent homoeroticism and with Wilde (whose face Beardsley famously incorporated in such illustrations as "The Woman in the Moon"; see Navarre). The film's Beardsley allusions are particularly evident in the design of the cistern area, with its gigantic flower trellis cage; in one fantasy sequence in which Nazimova's head appears in the midst of an art nouveau tableau of clouds and peacocks; and in a strik-ing femme fatale robe with matching turban into which Nazimova changes in her final scenes.

Nazimova's interpretation of the Salome figure likewise feeds into the film's homoeroticism, as her gender identity and sexual appeal are ambigu-ous. Because of Nazimova's slim figure and androgynous costumes, the movie was able to extend the homoerotic elements of Wilde's play further. An androgynous Salomé—subtly suggested in Wilde's play but clearly elaborated in Nazimova's film—"undermines the heterosexual significance" of the traditional context of the legend, as Tydeman and Price point out, while highlighting the play's transgressive qualities: "Nazimova, reputedly a lesbian and surely familiar with the Billing case, would have found in Wilde's play a transgressive sexuality all the more powerful for its inscription within roles all too easily reduced to heterosexual stereotypes" (159, 161). Thomas Craven of *The New Republic,* who evidently expected a smoldering femme fatale, lamented Nazimova's boyishness and lack of erotic femininity: "She flits hither and thither with the mincing step of a toe-dancer; she has the figure of a boy. . . . Try as she will she cannot be seductive" (quoted in Pratt 496). Natacha Rambova's costume design for Nazimova further emphasized Nazimova's boyish body and alluded to Beardsley's androgynously themed depictions of Salomé. Rambova spectacularly attired Nazimova in a series of costumes and wigs that contribute to the camp quality of the film. Throughout most of the film, Nazimova sports a very peculiar, surreal-looking, short black wig with white pearls bobbing on short antennae and wears a dark, close-fitting body slip that leaves her slim legs and arms bare. For the dance scene, Nazimova changes into an identical short white gown and a bobbed wig bleached blonde, accompanied only by a white chiffon veil. This was a remarkably minimalist, nonorientalist costume for the famously sexy, feminine, lurid Dance of the Seven Veils that American audiences had come to expect from "Salomania" dancers and performers in previous years. According to Michael Morris, Rambova's biographer, Nazimova rejected Rambova's original design, "a white, multilayered, diaphanous gown trimmed with pearls . . . an enormous train, an accompanying face veil, or yashzmak, and a headdress from which two wirelike antennas radiated, holding an additional veil," in favor of a more flapperlike costume that "show[ed] off to greater advantage the trim figure of which she was very proud" (Morris 87). The dance itself was stylized and subdued, although Nazimova did interesting things with the veil in front of the camera (described later in this discussion).

Nazimova's gender ambiguity supports homoerotic overtones in the sexual attraction that other characters feel for her and hence suggests a double reading. In falling for Salomé, the Young Syrian, Narraboth, prefers boyish androgyny (Salomé) over fully developed masculinity (the Page), rather than simply a woman to a man. Salomé's androgyny also introduces a certain gender ambiguity into her wooing of Jokanaan. In one striking scene, Salomé comes very close to and almost kisses Jokanaan (Nigel de Brulier). The scene shows Jokanaan almost giving in to Salomé's ever more urgent physical approaches. When they finally almost touch and she asks to kiss him ("Suffer me to kiss thy mouth, Jokanaan"), he hesitates and slowly moves his hands toward Salomé's uplifted face as if to kiss her, before abruptly breaking away in angry revolt: "Never! Daughter of Herodias! Never!" Jokanaan's slender, white body looks similar to Salomé's androgynous one, and the almost-kiss has homoerotic overtones. In both the play and movie versions, the three relationships of erotic longing (Narraboth/ Page, Narraboth/Salomé, Salomé/Jokanaan) thus amplify and supplement one another and support their respective homoerotic readings.

In addition to the costume styles and acting, well-known rumors at the time of the movie had it that the entire cast of the picture was gay. According to Kenneth Anger, Nazimova reportedly "employed only homosexual actors," in open tribute and "as 'homage' to Wilde." Hollywood gossip also added that Natacha Rambova and Alla Nazimova, who shared Nazimova's Los Angeles home (called the "Garden of Alla") for a while, were lovers; Anger writes that Rambova was one of the protégées of "the equally lesbian" Nazimova, who then functioned as a matchmaker between Rambova and Rudolph Valentino, Nazimova's costar in *Camille* (113). At the time of *Salomé*, Nazimova was also said to have been involved with Paul Ivano, cameraman Van Enger's assistant (Lambert 255). Ken Russell's biopic *Valentino* (1977) refers to these homosexual rumors, as a reporter asks Nazimova (Leslie Caron) if it is true that Valentino "refused to be in your all-homosexual production of *Salome*" (Parish 333). Scholars and biographers of Nazimova provide conflicting accounts. But whether or not Nazimova's fascination with the Salome theme and Wilde's play stemmed from a personal agenda to infuse a homoerotic subtext into the overwhelmingly heterosexual culture of cinema does not seem that important for an analysis of the movie on its own terms. Even unsubstantiated scandalous rumors of an all-gay cast undoubtedly impacted the movie's reception—by an audience already sensitive to issues of immorality and censorship in contemporary Hollywood cinema (fueled by the recent Fatty Arbuckle rape scandal and the establishment of the Hays Office)—and provided fodder for moralists or curious audiences interested in movies of the more lurid sort (see Maltby 83; Kuhn 30–31). Either way, Nazimova's rumored lesbianism encouraged contemporaries to read the artist's interest in Wilde's play as a sexual as well as aesthetic alliance with Wilde and as a coded means of self-expression, just as it had already been assumed to be the case for Maud Allan in London just a few years earlier. In such a charged atmosphere, Nazimova's decision to adapt a notoriously scandalous play by a known homosexual author was risky at best. Her highly idiosyncratic film stressed the homoerotic elements of Wilde's play and treated them playfully and affirmatively, so that the film was easily read as a tribute to Wilde's sexuality.

The foregrounding of the homoerotic subtext of Wilde's play later became a distinguishing trope for other twentieth-century film versions, such as Ken Russell's *Salome's Last Dance* and Suri Krishnamma's *A Man of No Importance* (see chap. 5). Russell's movie openly alludes to Nazimova's *Salomé* in some of its sets and costumes as well as in the prominent use of human dwarfs, who feature in Nazimova's film around the Dance of the Seven Veils. Following Nazimova's version, other examples of twentieth-century readings that emphasize the homoerotic and camp elements of Wilde's play are Lindsay Kemp's 1977 transvestite staging of the play in London's Round House, which Neil Sammels describes as follows:

> Kemp saw [Wilde's play] as a score for his own luridly androgynous production-style which "aimed to restore to the theatre the glamour of the Folies Bergères, the danger of the circus, the sexuality of rock'n roll and the ritual of Death." . . . . Kemp himself played a transvestite Salome in his bravura, all-male "variation on" Wilde's play in which only about a third of the original text survived: the production has been characterized as "an assault on the senses, with deafening drumming, green and blood-red lighting, joss sticks in the hair of the slaves, incense burning in braziers, a live snake and a live dove, smoke, feathers, snatches of Wagner and Mozart and more besides." (73–74)

In 1974, a combined screening in New York of Nazimova's *Salome* and Peter Dallas's twenty-four-minute silent *Broken Goddess* (starring Holly Woodlawn, "the prophetic-bizarre transvestite of Warhol superstardom" [Geng]) also suggested a reading of Nazimova's *Salomé* as a cult camp film, and it has been a favorite at gay film festivals for many years.

Just as much as Nazimova's androgyny supports a homoerotic and camp reading of the film, her portrayal of *Salomé* also alludes to the jazz age flapper figure so popular at the time, mixing homoeroticism with the appeal of feminism and modern consumerism. Nazimova, then forty-three years old, decided to play Salomé as a petulant, strong-willed, twelve-year-old teenager with childish gestures, light on her feet, sensuous, and independently minded. As she expressed in one interview, she clearly had recent fashions in mind.

> [Salome] was usually played as a vamp. I did not believe she was like that. According to history, she was a child of 12. I tried to play her as a sophis-

ticated kid. Then came the post-war rage for sophisticated girls with slender boyish figures, and frank outspoken manners. She was a far cry from the snaky vampire, and the baby doll of Mary Pickford. (Quoted in Frank)

Nazimova's stylized, revealing costumes and facial expressions in the movie emphasize her fashionably slender body and flat chest and the frequently pouting mouth of the flapper. The petulance, independence, and willfulness of her Salome easily fit the flapper's figurative leanings toward modern consumer culture and feminism. Her Salomé exhibits a noticeably vulnerable, almost innocent quality, while all the while making sure that she gets exactly what she wants. In *Salomé*, Nazimova combined her faithful tribute to Wilde with the current movie fashions concerning the female body: visualizing Wilde's innocent, fragile, white princess of the moon as a flapper styled Nazimova's body in correspondence to movie audiences' current tastes. Nazimova thus married avant-garde art and transgressive gender themes with current visual fashions and subtle feminist appeal.

Nazimova's interpretation of Salomé's strong agency and will further emphasizes her sense of a feminist potential in Wilde's Salomé figure, as two slight but significant changes to the original in Nazimova's script illustrate. The first change manipulates the sequence of events, inserting one of Jokanaan's earlier speeches into Salomé's later haggling with Herod, to suggest Salomé's anger at Jokanaan's misogyny as a reason for killing him. After the tetrarch has promised her the world's largest emerald, white peacocks, and most extraordinary jewels, the movie script has Jokanaan utter a line that occurs much earlier in the play: "It is thus that I will wipe out all wickedness from the earth and that all women shall learn not to imitate her abominations!" In Wilde's play, Jokanaan actually directs this speech against Herodias; but in the film's new context, it comes across as a direct insult to Salomé as well as to womanhood in general. Salomé's immediately following, final demand, "GIVE ME THE HEAD OF JOKANAAN!" ("'Salomé' Part 5," reel 5) seems like a direct reaction to Jokanaan's proclamation (see n. 1 in the present chapter). During two previous fantasy sequences, it had seemed somewhat possible that Salomé might still change her mind, but hearing Jokanaan spew hateful prophesies against women's wickedness and abomination irrevocably makes up her mind and strengthens her resolve.[14] With a furious look on her face and a menacingly balled fist, glowering at Herod, she angrily demands her due.

The second significant script change is Nazimova's reinterpretation of the femme fatale stereotype associated with Salomé to give it some feminist overtones, as Nazimova's interpretation of the next scene illustrates. The impatient Salomé, waiting for the delivery of the head, exclaims, "I tell thee there are not dead men enough!" ("'Salomé' Part 6," reel 6). Then she grabs a sword from one of Herod's guards and triumphantly wields it over her head as if she was threatening to single-handedly kill Jokanaan herself. While these actions also fit the profile of the lethal film vamp, the context in which they appear—right after Jokanaan's final misogynist prophesy and Salomé's angry reaction against it—suggests a feminist reading, as Salomé's indictment of male misogyny and oppression.

Both of these changes strengthen the subversive, daring nature of Nazimova's Salomé. Nazimova's citation of the flapper's independence and the young woman's anger at misogynist objectification openly evokes the period's cultural and political changes regarding the perception of women's gender and gender roles. To many, the flapper expressed women's increasing economic, political, and sexual independence in the early 1920s (when women in the United States had only just been granted suffrage), even though the stereotype itself was a fully commercialized figure, elaborately styled and designed to sell. Nazimova's homoerotic, androgynous Salomé carried overtones of women's emancipation as well, channeled subtly through the flapper and the vamp. This was a potentially explosive, transgressive mixture.

Perhaps to counter criticism and censorship of her film, Nazimova, like Allan, publicly defended Salomé's supposed purity, innate innocence, and spiritual search. According to Nazimova, Salomé has a kind of childlike innocence despite her savagery.

> She was the one pure creature in a court in which sin was abundant. Yet she remained uncontaminated, like a flower in an unfriendly soil. The first time she loved, she asked all, since she was willing and eager to give all. Her capacity for self-sacrifice was rebuked and her love was repudiated scornfully. . . . Nowhere about her in the court life of Herod was there any parallel to her encounter with a spiritual influence. (Quoted in Morris 9)

Salomé here appears tragically trapped and reduced to much less agency than she is capable of, her aggression and malice arising directly from her frustration and deprivation, her murderous instinct the direct result of patriarchal oppression. Nazimova's Salomé echoes Hedda Gabler's quest to control another's destiny: "Since she could not rule, she was impelled to ruin the life that might have saved her" (ibid.). The original 1922 version's opening titles stress Salomé's initial innocence in the corrupting world of Herod's court, too.

Profound was the moral darkness that enveloped the World on which the
Star of Bethlehem arose. . . . In a chaos of crime and wickedness, Herod
ruled Judea but was himself ruled by Passion. He had murdered his
brother, usurped his throne, he had stolen his wife, Herodias, and now
covets his brother's daughter, Salomé. . . . It is at this point that the drama
opens, revealing Salomé who yet remains an uncontaminated blossom in a
wilderness of evil. Though still innocent, Salome is a true daughter of her
day, heiress to its passions and its cruelties. ("'Salomé' Part 1," reel 1)

At the same time as it highlights Salomé's innocence, this introductory sum-
mary also develops Salomé's potential as a glamorous melodrama heroine,
using the last line of her final monologue as the overarching "moral" of her
story that the film is about to set before the viewer: "She kills the thing she
loves; she loves the thing she kills, yet in her soul there shines the glimmer
of the Light and she sets forth gladly into the Unknown to solve the puzzle
of her own words—The Mystery of Love is greater than the Mystery of
Death" (ibid.). Thus we know from the start that this Salomé is a "soul" in
search of love, a curious and eager seeker for a "Light" in the "Unknown,"
and that her story is one of universal human proportions—of "Love" overcoming "Death."[15] In an interview, Nazimova expressed confidence that
"[i]f people see the character of Salome as I do, her environment, the glamour of the court of Herod and its emotional grossness, the spell of the spiritual appeal of St. John the Baptist—as I see them—I have no fear [that they
will not understand her]" (Bonte).

The film's faithfulness to Wilde's original in other respects is visible in
Nazimova's attempts to capture the overall atmosphere of the play as well as
central themes, which are often creatively enhanced through the medium of
cinema. Salomé's extreme stylization and synesthetic effects would be hard
to capture on film, one might think; but with her use of costumes and set
design, mise-en-scène, camera work, and editing techniques, Nazimova effectively transposed the play's main themes and moods to the screen. For
example, the film captures well Salomé's overall mood of fatality and deadly
doom, which merges with the theme of superstitious fear expressed in the
recurring phrase "Something terrible may happen." There is literal fatality
and death caused by Salomé's deadly sexuality, of course, with the Young
Syrian and Jokanaan as victims. When Narraboth kills himself and Herod
slips in his blood, Herod immediately associates the Syrian's death with Salomé: "It is strange that the Young Syrian has killed himself. . . . I remember
that I saw he looked languorously at Salomé. Truly, I thought he looked too
much at her" (CCW 592). Nazimova's film actually adds another suicide
(not included in Wilde's play) in the scene preceding Narraboth's death, to

really emphasize Salomé's femme fatale qualities. The slave whom Herod dispatches to bring Salomé inside finds himself literally trapped, like a wild animal, between Salomé's and Herod's threatening gazes: Herod keeps him under check from within the banquet hall, while Salomé, outside, stares at him hatefully and declines to enter (a refusal for which the slave knows Herod will sternly punish him). In his despair, he jumps off the high palace walls into the sea rather than face their wrath. After Narraboth's death, the fatal chain of events thus continues, rapidly building up to the climax of Salomé's dance, then Jokanaan's and eventually Salomé's deaths.

Wilde develops fatality throughout his play by the advancing moon color scheme (white, red, black) and Jokanaan's sinister prophesies of an impending Judgment Day. Specifically, Wilde introduces and develops the Angel of Death theme to characterize Herod's inner torment and paranoia. Jokanaan prophesies the appearance of a sword-wielding, horrific avenger of sin, whose giant beating wings cause a stirring wind that announces his coming. While none of the characters really heed Jokanaan's warnings, Herod thinks the doomsday prophesies are directly geared at him. Herod repeatedly hears and feels the angel's giant wings about him and feels persecuted: "I tell you there is a wind that blows . . . And I hear in the air something that is like the beating of wings, like the beating of vast wings" (*CCW* 589). Herod is also afraid of Jokanaan's menacing prophesies and particularly fears the prospect, raised by some Nazarenes, that Jesus could raise the dead and thus bring them back: "It would be terrible if the dead came back" (ibid. 596). Presumably Herod thinks of his brother Philip, whom he killed to marry Philip's wife, Herodias; if Philip came back, he might take revenge on the living. The Angel of Death theme and Herod's superstitious paranoia work together in Wilde's play to portray a man haunted by his own guilt and fearful of the future.

In her cinematic version, Alla Nazimova develops and unfolds this theme very interestingly via lighting effects and editing. Frequent crosscuts between Jokanaan's figure in the cistern and Herod's fearful face suggest the effects the prophecies have on Herod. For the Angel of Death, Nazimova invented a visual metaphor, created through lighting effects, which she called "the Shadow of Death." Assistant cameraman Paul Ivano (another of Nazimova's lovers) recalls its function as visual symbolic commentary: "One of the most difficult lighting effects for the photographer was the so-called 'Shadow of Death,' which hovered over Saint John the Baptist, and Salome in their most important scene on the terrace of Herod's Palace, and likewise it was raised over John's body in the cistern in which he was held" (quoted in Morris 89).

A further aspect of Nazimova's faithfulness to Wilde's text is her visual translation of some of its figurative oppositions and contrasts, especially concerning Salomé and Jokanaan. Amy Koritz suggests that Wilde's play presents an interesting structure of opposition between the worlds of the audible (Jokanaan, who is mainly present as a voice) and the visible or viewed (Salomé). They represent a mind-body dichotomy: Jokanaan's voice stands for the inner workings of the mind, while Salomé operates in the realm of physical spectacle. To highlight the central relationship between Salomé and Jokanaan, Nazimova also chose to visually emphasize their incompatibility by creating a stark contrast between the prophet's and Salomé's white bodies against a dark background. This contrast complements the black-and-white effects of the set, so that, at times, the set itself evokes this opposition at the story's heart. Through her visual interpretation of such irreconcilability, Nazimova's version further underscores the theme of fatality and stasis. To indicate the sense of an ending world in paralysis, Wilde's play uses symbolist style, repetitive phrases evoking circular contemplation and stillness in time and space, and the imprisonment of the central characters in a world with no material or mental future. We may recall here Mallarmé's symbolic entombment of his Hérodiade in a tower, where she contemplates her split self in front of a mirror—a picture of stasis, frozen in time yet circling around herself in words, uttering sparkling, poetic, mysterious invocations of inhuman Beauty.

Nazimova's film makes interesting use of real time precisely to capture Wilde's atmosphere of contemplative stasis, mainly through the unusually long duration of its close-ups and lingering shots. The camera's extreme long takes produce a dreamlike, atemporal, extremely stylized atmosphere. In cinematic terms, they evoke the symbolist style of Wilde's play by inviting the audience to muse, linger, adore, revel, and tremble while looking at the rich pictures presented. Like Wilde's play, Nazimova's film thus seems to strive to create an extension of artistic space beyond time, a visual and narrative flow that mirrors Wilde's intent of a synesthetic staging for *Salomé* (described in chap. 2).[16]

Wilde actually develops two different meanings of the fatal gaze throughout the play, contrasting the other characters' desirous and sometimes desperate looks at Salomé with Salomé's much larger, bold determination to see and possess. The others' looks at Salomé pursue a certain unrealistic vision of her, a vision that always remains a projection of their own desires; while they are infatuated with her, none of the characters really "know" her. On the contrary, when they glimpse the truth about her, they cannot bear it. The power of her look is Salomé's weapon, but Jokanaan is the only character who refuses to lay eyes on her and who thus remains untouched by the circle of desire in which the other characters are caught. Nazimova's film makes a point of showing Jokanaan in an unusual close-up with his eyes closed (in two equally impressive shots, he is shown with his head bent back and upward, toward the light that illuminates his head and shoulders from above). The only point in the movie that actually shows his eyes happens in the scene of his final confrontation with Salomé, when he looks at her for the first and last time (Salomé's wooing of Jokanaan is shown in close-up). He returns her devouring gaze only to shout at her, "Back, daughter of Babylon! I listen but to the voice of the Lord God" ("'Salomé' Part 3," reel 3). In Wilde's play, Jokanaan rejects her aggressive wooing with a refusal to return her erotic gaze: "I do not wish to look at thee. I will not look at thee, thou art accursed, Salomé, thou art accursed" (*CCW* 591).

In Wilde's play, Jokanaan seems autonomous and strangely untouched by Salomé even in death, his closed eyes "refusing" her the look she has craved from him: "But wherefore dost thou not look at me, Jokanaan? Thine eyes that were so terrible, so full of rage and scorn, are shut now. Wherefore are they shut? Open thine eyes! Lift up thine eyelids, Jokanaan! . . . Art thou afraid of me, Jokanaan, that thou wilt not look at me . . . ?" (ibid. 604). Gazing at Jokanaan alive, Salomé explores the aesthetic of beauty; looking at him dead, she ponders the aesthetic of love and death, without fear or apparent regard for morality or convention. At the same time, Herod is becoming aware that the object of his desire is not identical with the ferocious agent of desire he now sees in front of him. His earlier invocation of gendered standards of modesty now seems a travesty, proof of Herod's ignorance of his stepdaughter: "The head of a man that is cut from his body is ill to look upon, is it now? It is not meet that the eyes of a virgin should look upon such a thing" (ibid. 601). Salomé is not an innocent virgin; on the contrary, she is determined to look and immodestly to claim what is withheld from her against her will.

In preparing for the ending, Wilde has already introduced the theme of masks and mirrors, to indicate Herod's inability to deal with terrible truth and knowledge: "Your beauty has grievously troubled me, and I have looked at you too much. But I will look at you no more. Neither at things, nor at people should one look. Only in mirrors should one look, for mirrors do but show us masks" (*CCW* 601). Mallarmé's Hérodiade was frozen in time before and in the surface of the mirror, which she longed to traverse (see chap. 1). Wilde, by contrast, portrays Herod as quite the opposite, wishing for mirrors and masks in order to deceive himself, to blot out the terrible truth. At the end of the play, Herod expresses his existential need to hide from the sight of Salomé, to be safe from the awful truth of people and things without their masks on. Refusing the terrible visibility of the spectacle of Salomé's truth unfolding in front of him, Herod orders all torches put out in order to prohibit all looking and being looked at, then fearfully retreats to hide in his palace: "I will not look at things, I will not suffer things to look at me. . . . Let us hide ourselves in our palace, Herodias. I begin to be afraid" (*CCW* 604–5).

In hindsight, it seems rather ironic that Wilde's and Nazimova's Herod reacts in a similar fashion as did the later censors of Maud Allan's and Alla Nazimova's performances—with fear, repugnance, and rejection of female transgression. In Wilde's play, Herod is fearful that he does not know the meaning of appearances and events; not knowing how to interpret them, he retreats into fear and superstitious interpretation, noting signs of a fateful conspiracy everywhere. In Allan's trial, Billing argued that appearances could not be trusted; the very metaphoricity of the language and style of Wilde's play was a dangerous entrapment that could lead to moral chaos. Not being able to decipher the "true" meaning of signs meant losing intuitive control over one's fate. One unsettling lesson of Wilde's play is that if things look the same on the surface but cannot be pinned down—if the moon looks like a beautiful princess one minute, like a dead woman looking for lovers the next—one cannot trust one's eyes any longer. Perhaps this is one reason why Billing, many state authorities, and censors in these cases insisted that art speak the truth—that words remain firmly attached to their concepts. Like the fearless realist Herodias in Wilde's play, many in a modern world in uncertain flux surely wished that one should be able to trust that "the moon is like the moon, that is all" (*CCW* 592).

Finally, another striking feature of the film is Nazimova's visualization of the theme of dangerous looking itself, which she expresses and develops through the effective use of the camera, especially the close-up. As discussed in chapter 1, in Wilde's play, the isolated look or gaze displays the powerful allure of desire as well as its frustration, of desperate but futile longing for something or someone. Nazimova's movie effectively uses camera and editing techniques to emphasize this Wildean thematic of the dangerous gaze. One filmic sequence perfectly encapsulates and illustrates Nazimova's approach. When Salomé tries to persuade Narraboth, who is in charge of guarding John the Baptist's prison, to hand over the key to the cage and have the prophet brought up for her ("I will but look at this strange prophet," "'Salomé' Part 2," reel 2), the camera focuses on her eyes in a gigantic close-up and also employs an iris-in frame to isolate the eyes from the rest of her face. Looking intently at the spectator, who imagines oneself in Narraboth's position, Nazimova's Salomé displays what could be called a typical femme fatale look (narrow eyes, not twitching, closely watching the object from a slightly upward-tilted angle). The film thus also widens the tropological circle of Wilde's theme of looking and being looked at, to include the audience. The countershot back to Narraboth shows him heavily breathing, transfixed by her gaze as if hypnotized. This sequence of shot and countershot visually establishes for the spectator the experience and effect of Salomé's eyes. It suggests the audience's identification with Narraboth's reaction, since we are looking into his face as a mirror of Salomé's powerful gaze at him. The Page fearfully lets go of Narraboth's arm and retreats into the background, leaving the ground clear for Salomé, who charges toward the bewitched victim of her powerful look like a female torero in an arena built for killing. Defeated, Narraboth slowly draws an enormous key out of his waistband (in a scene with quite comical phallic overtones) and sinks on his knees in utter devotion. Salomé stands above him, chin raised in triumph, then carelessly steps over him, to await the fulfillment of her demand, the arrival of Jokanaan. Salomé's determined gaze is irresistible; she must be obeyed even at the cost of death (Narraboth's suicide immediately follows in the next scene). Although the screen characters must inevitably suffer as a consequence of their desire of Salomé, the actual movie audience can experience their voyeuristic pleasure without physical danger or fear of punishment: the cinematic gaze at Salomé is virtual, mediated, distanced, and safe, enabling unrestrained voyeurism.

Here again, Nazimova's faithfulness to Wilde's play intermingles with her skillful appeal to modern fashion and audiences' expectations, in particular her own status as a celebrity of the stage and screen. Most close-ups in this film showcase the main protagonist and star Nazimova. As the *Variety* reviewer sarcastically remarked, "'Nazimova in Facial Expressions,' with Salome as the background, would have been a much better billing for the picture" (Reviewer signing the name "Fred"). The striking focus on the female star's eyes in gigantic close-up in the scene just described invokes Nazimova's star power and invites the contemplation of her beauty, advertising her to the audience. Feminist film critic Mary Ann Doane explains that "with the formation of a star system heavily dependent upon the maintenance of the aura, the close-up became an important means of establishing the recognizability of each star"; the framed face is "entrapped" by the close-up for the audience's pleasurable gaze, making it momentarily possible to possess the star's face (46–47).

Nazimova's Dance of the Seven Veils is a good illustration of the voyeuristic aspect. It is appropriately abstract for the stylized nature of the picture, avoiding outright nudity and instead playing extensively with close-ups, camera movement, and Salomé's veils to create an extended erotic dance scene. After her four assistants have veiled Salomé for the first time, shielding her from Herod's and the audience's view behind their geometric art nouveau cloaks, Salomé emerges from her onstage dressing chamber clothed in white, completely veiled from the waist upward. She thus presents a striking phallic image: her arms are stretched upward and veiled together with her head and face so that the line from her naked legs upward is continuous, and she seems much taller. In the ensuing dance, accompanied by a bizarre band of dwarfs in orientalist costumes and huge headdresses, Nazimova uses the veils playfully to veil and unveil herself again and again, while the camera captures her face in close-ups. The action of repeated veiling and unveiling of the object of desire seems like a metaphor for the allure of the femme fatale/fragile, who seems to call out to her spectators in one moment, "Come and get me—here I am, look at me," and in the next, "You can't get me anyway—now I'm gone again." In her analysis of the filmic femme fatale, Doane points to the important function of the screen itself as an erotic mediator and enhancer of the femme fatale's eroticism: "In the cinema, the magnification of the erotic becomes simultaneous with the activation of objects, veils, nets, streamers, etc., which intercept the space between the camera and the woman, forming a *second screen*" (49). Salomé's veil and the function of the camera as a second screen run parallel: they literally screen out or select certain parts of the body and hide others. Together with the theme of the desirous look—especially important during the dance scene, in which the editing intercuts the dance itself with close-ups on spectators' transfixed eyes—Wilde's original veiling trope thus undergoes interesting further complication and amplification through the medium of film. Like the partition that designates the sanctuary, the veil in the cinema often acts as a trope to suggest, as Doane explains, "a depth which lurks behind the surface of things. . . . The function of the veil here is to transform the surface of the face into a depth, an end in itself" (54, 55).

Unlike in the theater, the characters' and the audience's "look" can indeed be emphasized and directed through the artificial eye of the camera itself, a hidden process of selecting and directing the gaze. Theorizing cinema's traditional objectification of the female figure, feminist film critics have designated this process as a gendered one, pointing to its tendency to fragment and construct the female body as an object of fantasy and desire. Laura Mulvey's still useful concept "to-be-looked-at-ness" (from her 1977 landmark article "Visual Pleasure and Narrative Cinema") indicates the inherent purpose in such representation.[17] As Lucy Fischer has shown in *Shot/Countershot,* it is this habitual use of cinematic techniques, plots, and processes of representation that later feminist filmmakers have frequently attempted to criticize, resist, or counteract. Nazimova's *Salome* was still a mixed film with regard to this trajectory: it combined stereotypical techniques, like the close-up and editing, to produce and reproduce current scopophilic trends that could be found in much of early cinema; yet it was also a project that established practical artistic agency and independence for Nazimova, an achievement that has its own significance in the context of feminist cultural agitation.

Any discussion of the possible feminist significance of Nazimova's *Salomé* has to take into account the "space between" in which female auteurism and feminist agency in the arts inevitably operated at this time and in which female artists consciously and often successfully operated in order to advance their interests. Nazimova's recourse to the established tropological system of the cinema star and her paradoxical combination of the fashions of the film vamp and the flapper must be understood in relation not only to cinema's history and figurative preferences but also to what it took to be (or at least attempt to be) a successful pioneering female filmmaker, producer, financier, and visionary artist in the male-dominated Hollywood film industry. The inevitable mingling of her portrayal of Salomé with Nazimova's star status and her iconic status for female consumerism, fashion, and fan culture was itself a hybrid feminist strategy at a time when consumerism and political liberation converged and when lines and oppositions between the two were not yet clearly drawn. Nazimova realized the feminist as well as the artistically and sexually transgressive potential of Wilde's *Salomé* within these contexts. She portrayed the young princess as an independent, assertive, yet psychologically and morally complex heroine who defies gender expectations and sets an astonishing, daring example of female individualism against male power, a gesture that parallels Nazimova's own.

Unfortunately, like Wilde's Salomé, Nazimova ultimately suffered the consequences of her own daring. According to James R. Parish, censors succeeded in their demand that several scenes be cut, including one that showed a homoerotic relationship between two soldiers (333). Nazimova's attempt to promote the artistic nature of the film to enhance its understanding and acceptability to censors and reviewers was at least partly successful, and the National Board of Review finally approved the film.[18] This hurdle mastered, Nazimova encountered another one: the distributor, United Artists, delayed its distribution several times and failed to market the film widely enough—deliberately so, as Nazimova complained. Michael Morris argues that "[s]ome publications taunted movie industry executives who had seemingly conspired to suppress Nazimova's film" and that quite possibly "the attempt to keep *Salome* from reaching public theaters was a plot against independent filmmakers like Nazimova" (91–92). The delays and the misleading advertising campaign—United Artists advertised the movie as "an orgy of sex and sin" (quoted in Schanke 141), which it clearly was not—led to the film's failure to make enough money at the box office to recoup Nazimova's personal investment. As an art film putting itself forward as an heir of the theater, *Salomé* was too new and idiosyncratic a project to have real impact beyond the curiosity it aroused; as a rendering of the story of a famous biblical femme fatale, it disappointed audiences used to more familiarly raunchy fare à la Theda Bara. After an interesting and enthusiastic attempt at "doing thoughtful things" her own way, Nazimova was forced, a short time later, to close her young production company. In a letter to her sister Nina Lewton, Nazimova writes about various money worries and laments the decision to sell her much-beloved country house "Who-Torok" to settle her accounts after the failure of Nazimova Productions: "You see, not making a cent for 2½ years has got so on my nerves that now every cent that comes in I look upon as a find, and *keep it*" (September 11, 1923).

Although Nazimova's career, like Maud Allan's, was severely hurt by her decision to adapt and act in Wilde's *Salomé,* the failure of her project still left Nazimova's name and reputation largely intact. Even though censorship issues clearly impacted Nazimova's film at the time, the film itself actually helped Strauss's opera and even Wilde's play in America.

> When the press reported that [Nazimova's] *Salome* had received the Board's approval, the strictures that had long been in place against the performance of Strauss's opera in Chicago and New York suddenly collapsed. Nazimova's film was given credit as the catalyst that legitimated the controversial artistry of Wilde's play. (Morris 91)

To make a living, Nazimova continued to act in minor roles in the movies and took on some of her former vamp roles, which she continued to despise. She fared better in her return to the theater, where she delivered a few more critically acclaimed performances of Ibsen's plays—for example, in *Ghosts* (1935) and *Hedda Gabler* (1936). Sadly, however, she never got another chance to play Salomé.

Like Maud Allan's, Nazimova's creative appropriation and adaptation of Wilde's *Salomé* had been caught in a double bind. On the one hand, it afforded her an alignment with a play that was recognized as belonging to the

European avant-garde. On the other hand, the play was inevitably also associated with transgression and perversity, the whiff of scandal and outrageous daring, even obscenity—both because of its subject matter and because of its author, Oscar Wilde, whose sexual transgressions were read into and through *Salomé* and vice versa. In the case of a prominent female performer and producer in the 1910s and 1920s, such associations also produced an intertextual nexus mingling with the cause of women's cultural and political emancipation, provided by Allan's unwanted identification with the suffragettes and Nazimova's open championing of complex New Woman characters on stage and in film. Contemporaries regarded with fascination as well as suspicion the public eroticization of the two women's bodies and their various cultural associations. Allan's and Nazimova's choice to adapt Wilde's transgressive *Salomé* was easily understood as a secret code of gender rebellion and as an effort to overthrow contemporary standards, norms, and values not only in art but in society. Nazimova's and Allan's cases intersect not only with the censorship of aesthetic and homoerotic transgression but also with the history of attitudes toward, controls on, and representation of women's bodies.

Added to the feminist overtones was the public's budding awareness of lesbianism as another category of sexual and social transgression, cloaked in "art." The reception of Maud Allan's and Alla Nazimova's work in terms of female homosexuality thus marks an important new step in the history of the Salome theme. In each instance, the public not only read their work with and through their own sexual personae as independently minded female stars but also interpreted it as a dangerous statement of affiliation with Wilde's homosexuality. The rather counterintuitive association between male homosexuality, on the one hand, and assertive female sexuality as well as lesbianism, on the other, seems to have looked so commonsensical to Allan's and Nazimova's contemporaries that they did not question it. One of the most striking aspects of my research into Allan's trial, Nazimova's film, and contemporary cultural debates surrounding these texts has indeed been the apparent naturalness of such a conflation, the inferences drawn by contemporaries of Allan and Nazimova not only about the immoral aspirations or personalities of the artists themselves but about the perceived threat their art seemed to pose to English and American culture. Allan's and Nazimova's examples enable us to see the subtle cultural forces at work that first developed and made plausible a connection between male homosexuality, feminist themes, lesbianism, and transgressive art as supposedly dangerous agents of moral and national "perversion" that could be consumed for pleasure but ultimately had to be reined in. As the remaining chapters of *Salome's Modernity* will show, precisely such a dialectic of transgression and normalization came to be characteristic for versions of the Salome theme from the late twentieth and twenty-first centuries, in the wake of Oscar Wilde.

As far as Nazimova's *Salomé* is concerned, Patricia White has argued convincingly that Nazimova's lesbianism (or, more precisely, her bisexuality) is inextricably linked with her feminist and artistic agency as a creator and catalyst of female cinematic modernism. Nazimova's film is "too easily assimilated to the more defined gay male aesthetic in this case, and Wilde as a presence overwhelms the precarious authorial position of a powerful female performer-turned-producer in the Hollywood of the 1910s and early 1920s" (White 67). Hence Nazimova's true artistic agency is unfortunately "veiled by her gender. As a woman, she is a spectacle, or at best she is seen as paying homage to Wilde rather than as making her own contribution" in *Salomé* (ibid. 69). In fact, however, "a cross-gender identification with Wilde lent Nazimova the discourse of aestheticism through which to make her originality and agency visible . . . Nazimova borrowed more than an artistic signature from Wilde; she borrowed a queer one" (ibid. 79–80).

Maud Allan desperately fought off the associations with feminism and homosexual "perversity" by stressing Salomé's (and her own) innocence and purity, only to be done in by Noel Pemberton-Billing's ruthlessness. Allan lost her case because she could not convince the jury that art lived in a different realm and did not have to follow the same ethical standards as society. Alla Nazimova, by contrast, openly embraced the feminist and queer aesthetic in her work, but she, too, hid its transgressive nature behind discourses of highbrow art. She was initially much more successful in defending her adaptation of Wilde's play, however; and her willing cooperation with censors (the cutting of several scenes that were seen as too offensive, the orchestrated special previews for the National Board of Review, and Nazimova's public statements about the movie) seems to have alleviated much of the criticism. Nevertheless, in imitating theatrical avant-garde aesthetics of the 1890s with its art nouveau designs, on the one hand, and provoking the censors with her outright evocations of Wilde's homoerotic transgressions on the other, Nazimova's film walked a very thin line. In the end, I would argue, Nazimova's *Salomé* failed not because of its queerness or its innovative aesthetic that sought to set new directions for the cinema as art but, rather, because its tangled contradictions as a popular avant-gardist work (with conflicting agendas of high art, mass appeal, queer aesthetic elements, and feminist overtones) could not easily be consumed by the public or a movie industry thriving on stereotypical depictions of gender and commonplace orientalist spectacle.

5

Portraits of the Artist as a Gay Man and Salomé as a Feminist Icon: Wilde and Salomé in Popular Culture since the 1980s

In this final chapter, I turn to recent adaptations of Wilde's Salome figure in film and popular literature and culture since the 1980s. There was a decades-long lull since the 1950s, after Billy Wilder's classic *Sunset Boulevard* (1950, now also a Broadway musical by Andrew Lloyd Webber), in which an aging film actress (Gloria Swanson) imagines and acts out her comeback as Salome, and Wilhelm Dieterle's technicolor spectacle *Salome* (1953), starring Rita Hayworth. Neither film was a direct adaptation of Wilde's play, but both probably benefited from *Salomé*'s notoriety. *Sunset Boulevard* builds some elements of Wilde's symbolism into its plot, as Daniel Brown has shown,[1] while Dieterle's film is a loose interpretation of the Salome story based on biblical sources as well as on the quasi-Flaubertian story line of Massenet's opera *Hérodiade*.[2] Since the 1980s, however, interest in Wilde's version and the Salome theme in general has revived. While contemporary interpretations of Wilde's *Salomé* obviously differ in their approach, scope, and intent, two recent larger trends are observable. One is to enlist Wilde in contemporary antihomophobic projects via a sentimentalization and allegorization of his personal struggles; the other is to present Salomé as a feminist icon by focusing on the liberating force of her excessive sexuality. As the following analysis shows, there are important reasons to critique these interpretations, however—especially from a queer-positive and third wave feminist perspective. In this chapter, I first analyze two major film adaptations of the 1980s and 1990s, by Ken Russell and Suri Krishnamma, before turning to a focused discussion of the two mentioned dominant trends, which I have termed, somewhat polemically, "homosexual humanism" and "regressive feminism."

Ken Russell's *Salomé's Last Dance:*
Irony and Tragedy

Ken Russell's sexually explicit independent film *Salomé's Last Dance,* set in 1892 London—very roughly at the time of Wilde's original conception of *Salomé* and its ban from the English public stage—constructs a gleefully ironic historical fable of Wilde's participation in a thriving Victorian sexual counterculture. *Salomé's Last Dance* offers a full-fledged interpretation of Salomé as Wilde's aesthetic and sexual mask, presenting *Salomé* as an overtly sexual and homoerotic drama. In many respects, the film is an honest homage to Wilde as a misunderstood genius and to *Salomé* as a serious artwork. It takes the form of a raucously funny, creative literary-biographical tribute in the manner of Russell's previous irreverent, politically provocative, sexually explicit independent biopics of iconic cultural figures, among them Richard Strauss in a suppressed 1970 film from the British Broadcasting Corporation fittingly entitled *The Dance of the Seven Veils.*[3] *Salomé's Last Dance* politicizes *Salomé* by presenting it to the contemporary film audience as a testament to Wilde's rebellion against Victorian sexual prudery and moral hypocrisy, and it politicizes Wilde by making him a sexual and aesthetic martyr.

Ken Russell twists the historical chronology of *Salomé's* censorship and Wilde's arrest so as to suggest a direct relation between Wilde's art and Wilde's life. The film stages almost the entire text of *Salomé,* and Russell manipulates the date of the lord chamberlain's ban of *Salomé* and the (fictional) premiere of Wilde's play (the "first performance on English soil") to coincide with Guy Fawkes Day, November 5, 1892, the yearly commemoration of Fawkes's daring but failed insurgent Gunpowder Plot (1605). According to Taylor, who has planned the illicit brothel premiere of the banned *Salomé* as a tribute to his good friend and customer Wilde, "the date [of this performance] is not without significance. Guy Fawkes wanted to strike a spark for freedom and bring down a parliament he considered oppressive. You have done the same with your play, *Salome.*" Another chronological manipulation appears in the clever arrangement of the opening credits, inscribed on loose leaves of the printed *Salomé,* interspersed with Aubrey Beardsley's notorious illustrations, which increase *Salomé's* recognition value for contemporary audiences.

The fictional historical setting and frame narrative that Russell chose for his staging of Wilde's text further direct our reading of Salomé and Wilde as playful, courageous rebels. The mise-en-scène is in a colorful and bawdy luxury brothel in London, where the brothel keeper, Alfred Taylor (a real-

life acquaintance of Wilde's who testified in the 1895 trials, played by Stratford Jones), organizes a surprise performance of the freshly banned *Salomé*.
The audience for this colorful play-within-a-play is Oscar Wilde (played by
Nicholas Grace), a wisecracking, handsome gentleman dandy who turns up
at the brothel for an evening of exquisite sexual entertainment together
with Lord Alfred Douglas/Bosie (played by Douglas Hodge). In the lawless
space of the brothel, reminiscent of Arthur Schnitzler's brothel/pub in *The
Green Cockatoo* and Jean Genet's whorehouse in *The Balcony,* Wilde's mask
comes off to reveal a serious rebel underneath, whose interests in cutting-
edge art and kinky sex go hand in hand. As a theatrical as well as a cinematic spectacle, it deliberately blurs certain boundaries: those between
stage and screen and those between art and sex. Since the whores, pimps,
and other personnel of Taylor's establishment team up to form the theatrical cast of *Salomé,* with Taylor himself playing Herod and Wilde's lover
Bosie taking on the role of John the Baptist, *Salomé* becomes sophisticated
sexual innuendo. The ensuing underground production of the forbidden
play has sexual overtones from the start. Wilde implies as much to Taylor
before the curtain opens: "Are you going to *perform* yourself? . . . They say
that sex is the theater of the poor."

With Wilde's arrival at the brothel, the mise-en-scène instantly suggests
that the viewer is about to enter an intriguing, secret space. A dense fog cov-
ers Westminster; it is dark and empty when Wilde's carriage pulls up, but
for a few children playing with fireworks and their echoing laughter in the
streets. Contrasting with the drab street scene outside, the richly colored
and expensively furnished brothel interior steeps the viewer in an attractive
fantasy world. The movie set, mostly stationary with a few props added and
removed in different scenes, features a blue gauze curtain studded with
golden stars marking the makeshift stage, plush red carpet, a fireplace, a
tiger fur divan in the auditorium, and quirkily stylized and expensive-look-
ing costumes for the *Salomé* production. Sensual and sexual pleasures
merge as the brothel cast presents a creative and visually sumptuous interpretation of *Salomé* to a surprised and delighted Oscar Wilde, who settles in
on the luxurious divan to watch the performance.

Stylized as the quintessential dandy and stereotypical queer wit, Oscar
Wilde's persona is central. The elegantly attired Wilde amuses his friends
with his constant flow of paradoxes and witticisms (most of them famous
Wildean quotations or creative variations thereon): "There is only one thing
worse than to be talked about, and that is not to be talked about," "No line
is ever stale that leads directly to the box office," "I can resist anything but
temptation," "'I wish I had said that.'—'You will, Bosie, you will'" (the latter

an allusion to a rumored exchange between Wilde and James McNeill Whistler). To these more or less historical quotations, however, Russell adds his own translation of Wilde's persona into an overtly bawdy randy dandy, who replies to the butler's "Good evening, gentlemen. How are we this evening?" with "As close as two testicles" and admonishes Bosie, "No sermons, please. . . . I am not in the mood for the missionary position just now."

In the ensuing performance, sexual acts not only take place within the play-within-a-play on stage but also cross over into the framing narrative, where the spectator Wilde courts and then has sex with the Page of Herodias and where Salome comes to sit beside Wilde, caresses him, and gazes into his eyes while speaking her lines. At some point, the whole cast crosses over into the auditorium to join Wilde in the audience, rowdily cheering Salome on as she insists on receiving the head of John the Baptist as a reward. The film's ironic interpretation of *Salomé* includes various nude scenes and a whole carnival of sexual practices (including sadomasochism, group orgies, suggestions of oral sex, anal penetration), but because of its presentation of *Salomé* as an aesthetic mask for Wilde's own sexuality, there is a strong focus on homoerotic and transgressive moments. When the theater curtain rises, bare-breasted soldier dominatrices in black leather and face masks harass a helpless, half-naked John the Baptist through the bars of a cage, kicking and lashing out at him with their whips. They eventually sodomize him with an oversized dildo on a spear—a scene Wilde watches with apparent nonchalance and amusement, as an immediately following close-up reveals. In a later scene, they violently whip a fettered Jokanaan as he rejects Salome three times, continuing the sadomasochistic and misogynistic themes. Phallic symbols dominate the stage setting and come into play at crucial moments: Salome entices Herod by suggestively peeling and slowly eating a banana while she is looking at him intently; the executioner Naaman wears a loincloth with long metal spikes and carries an overdimensional sword; when Salome receives the platter, she places it on a very tall slim pedestal before she herself gets pierced by a spear (rather than crushed by soldiers' shields, as Wilde's stage direction advises). In the closing scene of Wilde's arrest at the end of the evening, Glenda Jackson's character Lady Alice/Herodias ironically remarks that Salome's murder was merely "a death by misadventure. . . . She slipped on a *banana* skin."

Salomé, we recall, is actually a tragedy—yet Russell chose to present it within a frame, as well as in a manner of style, that mixes it with comedy. From the start, *Salomé's Last Dance* ironizes its own aesthetic grounds, the theater and the cinema. The bordello stage on which *Salomé* is performed for its fictional and real audience repeatedly draws attention to itself as an improvised set and humorously highlights its own artificiality. The film also ironizes itself as a voyeuristic medium, revealing the inherent illusionary quality of the discourses of theater and film. By including himself as a photographer within the plot, Ken Russell thematizes his own act of looking so important in Wilde's play: the look through the camera is already an instance of voyeurism. Russell's photographer constantly scurries about, climbing clumsily around the stage, the auditorium, and even down into the Baptist's prison (a dumbwaiter), in search of the best angles and lighting. During the Dance of the Seven Veils and its corresponding orgies off-scene, he hilariously scrambles from scene to scene to capture each sexual climax (at which, fittingly, his flash goes off).

Russell's choice to include Wilde and his lover in the framing narrative and to have Douglas take on the role of John the Baptist in the play dominates the film's homoerotic reading of *Salomé*. We are not allowed to forget that Wilde and Bosie/John the Baptist are lovers: Bosie establishes eye contact and flirts with Wilde from the stage, and Wilde emotionally identifies with Salome's suffering when Bosie/John the Baptist rejects her. In addition, Russell frequently employs camera crosscuts between actions on stage and Wilde's reactions to them, revealing the hidden homoerotic potential of lines that—read "straight"—would be unsuspicious. One example involves John the Baptist's line "It is through woman that evil entered the world": the speaker of the line pointedly glances at Wilde from the stage, and the camera countershot reveals an amused Wilde who smiles to indicate his understanding. Russell's editing and acting choices thus deliberately introduce a double reading of the prophet's misogynistic line as a secret joke between two gay lovers. In another homoerotic scene, Wilde is seen holding the Page of Herodias (played by Russell Lee Page) in his arms on his divan, comforting the page as he mourns the suicide of Narraboth ("He was my brother. Closer even than a brother. I gave him a little box of perfumes, and a ring of agate, which he always wore on his hand. In the evenings we would stroll by the side of the river, under the almond trees. And he would tell me stories about his country"). Later, Wilde is shown making out with the page in a corner, passionately kissing him and eventually disappearing with him behind a curtain; he then reemerges with traces of the page's gold body makeup on his face, which he daintily dabs away so as to hide his betrayal before the Baptist's/Bosie's suspicious glances from the stage.

Through this intricate intertwining of onstage and offstage people and events, *Salome's Last Dance* hence establishes a strong allegorical association between the dramatic plot of *Salomé* and Wilde's own life and suggests that *Salomé* provides a direct window into the author's homosexuality. Even before the play-within-a-play begins, the framing narrative of Russell's screen-play prepares this cross-gendered association between Salome and Wilde. Taylor jokes that the attractive incense Wilde notices is "a blending of green carnations and the pubic hair of virgins," linking for the audience the themes of Wilde's homoeroticism (identified through Wilde's trademark green car-nation), the virginal princess, and sexual transgression (how else would one harvest "the pubic hair of virgins"?). The play-within-a-play reaffirms this symbolic connection several times, as Salome joins the cigar-smoking Wilde on the divan ("How fresh the air is here. . . . At last one can breathe"), sips from Wilde's glass of champagne, and accepts a green carnation from him. Later she seduces Narraboth (played by Warren Saire) with the same green carnation, casually caressing him with it and then fastening it on his chest as she promises to drop him "a little green flower" by the gate.

Alla Nazimova's modernist *Salome* provides the most obvious cinematic and intertextual reference for Russell's emphasis on cross-dressing and ho-moeroticism. Probably alluding to Nazimova's previous homoerotic inter-pretation of the lead character, Ken Russell chose an actress for Salome (Imogen Millais-Scott) whose androgynous physique supports a homo-erotic reading of the play. Millais-Scott's idiosyncratic, tight-fitting cos-tume—mixing a punk style with that of a science-fictional warrior princess, with phallic strings of beads between her bare legs—further emphasizes the actress's slim, petite, boyish figure.[4] The Ladies of the Court are played by male actors in drag who are fanning themselves and fixing their makeup, another visual and conceptual allusion to Nazimova's 1922 film.

This androgynous and homoerotic reading of Salome's body emerges most strongly in Russell's staging of the Dance of the Seven Veils. In flashes of rapid crosscuts between Salome and what turns out to be a male dancer in identical costume, Russell creates the illusion that Salome's body looks male and female at the same time. (The illusion works because of the ac-tress's own slim figure, the veiling of both dancers' faces, the feverish pace of the dancers' movements, and the rapid camera editing.) Dancing to Edvard Grieg's "In the Hall of the Mountain King" from *Peer Gynt,* a piece that works up to a furious frenzy, Salome removes the last veil from his/her loins to re-veal first male and then (in a crosscut back to the actress's body) female sex organs. In the dance's dizzying climax (an editing masterpiece), Salome unites both male and female traits, and crosscuts to other sex scenes (be-tween Wilde and the Page of Herodias and between Herodias and two sol-diers) increase in pace. Then Salome's body visually splits into two separate bodies, so that the two dancers whirl about synchronously side by side for a few moments, before they are channeled back into one androgynous body.

One cannot help but wonder if the enthusiastic Herod is so enraptured by Salome's performance because she unexpectedly reveals a hidden phallus.

In what is probably the most sincere, serious scene of the film, her love soliloquy to John the Baptist's severed head, Salome finally fully assumes her tragic dimension as Wilde's alter ego. Her address to the unresponsive Baptist/Bosie seems to echo Wilde's own painful relationship with Lord Alfred Douglas, whose selfishness and lack of love he later mourned in *De Profundis*. An intimate interplay of crossover close-ups of Salome on stage ("If you had looked at me, you would have loved me . . . Why did you not look at me, John the Baptist?") and Oscar Wilde's deeply moved and disturbed face suggests that Salome's pain in this scene expresses Wilde's: tears are running down his cheeks. The scene turns genuinely moving for the movie's audience as well, suggesting a biographical reading of Wilde's play as an expression of his tragic struggle with Lord Alfred Douglas. The image of Wilde's rapture and grief in looking at Bosie/John the Baptist emphasizes Wilde's heartfelt humanity underneath the dandy's mask and queer wit.

At first sight, such sincere dramatic moments contrast strongly with the film's overall ironic, exuberant, tongue-in-cheek tone. The entertainment effect does not wipe out the dark, unsettling elements that increasingly enter the plot as the film progresses, however. In a second deliberate alteration of historical chronology, *Salome's Last Dance* has Wilde's arrest immediately following the performance of the banned *Salomé*. In fact, Wilde was never arrested in a brothel, and his trial did not take place until almost three years later, in 1895. This anachronism is significant because it helps the film draw a direct line from Wilde's transgressive art to his sexuality and to Victorian society's punitive apparatus: "We're here to run you in. . . . You're under arrest, charged with gross sexual indecency, and the corruption of minors." Climbing into the police carriage casually carrying his glass of champagne as if he was going to another party, Wilde only momentarily betrays his pose and sourly complains, "I think Bosie was miscast. He really should play Salome, and I should play the prophet."[5] When Taylor asks, "With your head served up on a silver platter?" Wilde delivers his final bawdy repartee, "Or my balls," laughing the matter away. Not taking his arrest seriously, Wilde drives off with Taylor and Lady Alice, laughing and toasting. But as the camera pans out and down behind a forbidding-looking iron fence, the visual metaphor of imprisonment suggests Wilde's following downfall and shame.

The film audience's knowledge that Wilde's arrest and ensuing trials actually led to his professional and personal ruin thus chains the film's ironic mode to an overall tragic framework that forbids its unproblematic interpretation as camp and that colors its exuberance with sadness.[6] The dystopian dismantling of the safe space of the brothel and the theater at the end suggests the real dangers lurking outside of that sexual and aesthetic space: institutional and state violence. Feeding on the audience's knowledge that *Salomé* was censored and that Wilde's free spirit and transgressive body were ultimately crushed by Victorian philistinism, *Salomé's Last Dance* redirects the audience's identification with the historical-fictional Wilde into sentimental empathy and an indirect antihomophobic rejection of social hypocrisy and legal brutality.

Aesthetic Redemption in Suri Krishnamma's
A Man of No Importance

Salomé's Last Dance was a low-budget independent film (it cost only $400,000 dollars to make) by an idiosynratic cult director, a self-proclaimed art film geared at a small theater audience in cinema art houses rather than big movieplexes. By comparison, Suri Krishnamma's *A Man of No Importance* was aimed at a much broader mainstream, middle-class, largely heterosexual audience. Made for television by BBC Northern Ireland, Krishnamma's film strategically invokes audiences' knowledge of Oscar Wilde's tragic fate and includes a host of recognizable quotations from *Salomé*, "The Harlot's House," *De Profundis*, "The Ballad of Reading Gaol," and other works. Relying on Wilde and *Salomé* as cultural signifiers, *A Man of No Importance* is a coming-out film about a closeted gay bus conductor in Dublin, which indirectly criticizes the destructive personal and social impact of homophobia past and present by linking its protagonist to Wilde. It is pro-gay entertainment that aims to create empathy, but as I show, it does so quite problematically through a sentimental and funny narrative that does not ruffle too many feathers.

Alfred Byrne is a sweet, sixty-something bus conductor in 1963 Dublin who still lives with his sister Lily (played by Brenda Fricker) and is well respected in his modest middle-class, strictly Catholic community. He is also an ardent Oscar Wilde fan, who recites from Wilde's works for the regulars on his bus and dreams of directing his own production of *Salomé,* which he calls "Wilde's masterpiece." Skillfully arranging Byrne's verbal and visual quotations from Wilde as coded commentary on his own life and desires (Byrne's room at home is a virtual shrine to Wilde and 1890s dandyism), the film suggests a reading of Byrne's dreams and struggles against the backdrop of Wilde's disastrous trials, as well as *Salomé*'s 1892 ban. The film

also produces a historical déjà vu effect by building in allusions to characters from Wilde's life.

Throughout Krishnamma's film, Alfred Byrne interprets his own experiences by incessantly invoking Wilde's words, most of which he knows by
heart, having lovingly studied them for decades. Wilde is a doubly
significant symbolic figure of sexual and aesthetic identification for Byrne:
not only was Wilde a gay man negotiating the dangerous territory of a
morally and legally policed social and cultural environment, but he was
also a famous Irish writer born in Byrne's own Dublin. Wilde's language is a
powerful indirect means of self-expression for Byrne; Wilde's words express
and aestheticize "the love that dare not speak its name" in a tight-knit, homophobic, bourgeois Catholic environment that leaves no room for Byrne's
sexual orientation. Byrne is in love with Wilde's art as much as he is in love
with the handsome young bus driver Robbie, whom he has nicknamed
"Bosie" and with whom he makes his daily rounds. Robbie, who is straight
and feels a friendly affection for the much older Byrne, dimly suspects that
Byrne's quotes may have a secret meaning, but he only gently teases and
does not pursue the truth: "You're at it again. . . . That stuff you do. Big
words, poetry. I'm going to find out who this Bosie is. Better be a bloke.
Regular young fella, you know what I mean?"

Initially, Oscar Wilde's words provide a safe public mask for Alfred
Byrne and a daily theatrical space in which his private forbidden desires can
dare to go public without too much risk. Besides extensive quotes from *Salomé,* the works from which *A Man of No Importance* cites largely relate to
physical transgression, longing, and punishment. Together with well-
known passages from Wilde's trial transcripts, particularly the crucial exchange between Wilde and Carson about "the love that dare not speak its
name," the famous line from Lord Alfred Douglas's poem "Two Loves,"
these direct quotes have a high recognition value for the film's audience and
drive home the suggested parallels between Wilde's and Byrne's personal
and professional tragedies. The audience understands Byrne's secret as it
learns to read him through the interreferential mask of Wilde and *Salomé,*
but through the juxtaposition of truth versus mask, the film establishes a
knowledge lag between the audience and the film's unsuspecting cast of
characters who listen to Byrne's open riddles. The association is first established in the movie's opening scene. Byrne walks on a bridge while reciting
Wilde's "Ballad of Reading Gaol," then kisses and casually tosses a green
carnation into the water as if in tribute to Wilde. The second scene shows
Byrne reciting "The Harlot's House" to his bus passengers, who eagerly
await the daily reading. Later, the mise-en-scène of Byrne's private, locked

room at the home he shares with his sister Lily shows unmistakable Wildeana, such as the Yellow Book, dandylike clothes and toiletries, and (in the background) an Aubrey Beardsley illustration to *Salomé,* a first visual clue to the play's central importance for Byrne.

Byrne's Dublin is a deeply homophobic society in which homosexuality is a taboo topic, abhorred as a mortal sin and a threat to the Irish culture and Catholic morality. Walking back from church, the butcher Mr. Carney remarks to Byrne's sister Lily (while Byrne listens with a troubled expression) that there is "only one sin that's worse than adultery," "the unspeakable sin" of homosexuality, "the sin committed by that poor benighted creature [over in England], Stephen Ward." The reference is to the notorious 1963 Profumo Affair, a sex scandal that led to the resignation of Secretary of State Profumo and to the suicide of the gay manager of an illegal sex ring, Stephen Ward). Byrne is painfully aware of the unspeakability of his own homosexuality in this community. Still a virgin, he has found an outlet in his almost priestly devotion to Wilde's art. "I am committed to *art,*" Byrne emphasizes time and again to everyone who will listen; for him, Wilde is the high priest of high aestheticism who "lived only for art." Byrne is convinced that Wilde's art was pure, but more important, he needs it to give meaning to his own modest middle-class existence and purify the shame he feels for his own sexual desires. He explains that Wilde's art elevates and transforms the mundane and banal business of life into timeless beauty: "That's Wilde's great achievement, to take the crude clay of real life and to transmute it into art. So though Salome is a belly dancer, she is pure as quicksilver is pure, do you see? Wilde had no life aside from art, remember that. He lived in the realm of the aesthetic. He never descended into the sewer."

Wilde's *Salomé* becomes a pivotal test for Byrne's theory, as he attempts to put on the play with a cast of enthusiastic but thoroughly amateurish actors cobbled together from his passengers and friends and to convince his local priest and bishop that it is a thoroughly artistic, biblical play worthy of the parish hall's stage. Answering the pastor's concern about whether the play contains any "immodest dancing? The archbishop is very strong on immodest dancing" with the deadpan reply "Not immodest, Father Kenny! It's *art,*" Byrne downplays *Salomé's* transgressive side with the same argument. To his friend Baldy, Byrne explains further (modifying a famous paradox from the preface to *The Picture of Dorian Gray*), "There is no such thing as modest or immodest dancing. Dancing is either well done, or badly done. That is all." For the closeted Byrne, yearning for beauty in his humdrum life, the decision to stage *Salomé* signifies an act of defiance and personal justification through art, in Wilde's name and in his own. He quotes *De Profundis:* "If I can produce only one beautiful work of art, I shall be able to rob malice of its venom, cowardice of its sneer, and pluck out the tongue of scorn by the roots." By adopting art as an accepted public representation of forbidden private desire, Byrne attempts to make himself representable and speakable. His effort to bring *Salomé* to his local community constitutes Byrne's attempt at owning and redeeming his way of seeing the world and expressing his closeted homosexuality through aesthetic means. Byrne tells his best friend Baldy that his production of *Salomé* will "be my testament. This'll be my *coup-de-grâce* [the final blow]. This'll be my monument, Baldy."

The historical contexts of *Salomé*'s 1892 censorship and Wilde's 1895 trials provide the intertextual foils for the film's negative portrayal of the community's religious hypocrisy and philistinism. When the church pastor and the ultraconservative religious watchdog group Sodality of the Sacred Heart learn that Wilde's *Salomé* is not a faithful rendition of the biblical story of Saint John's martyrdom, as Byrne had pretended, but an "immoral" play that involves taboo words like "fornication" and "lost virginity" as well as the dreaded "immodest dancing," they bring the enthusiastically re-hearsed production to an abrupt halt. The butcher Mr. Carney, the driving force behind the censorship and the epitome of the petty hypocrite, is im-mediately identified by Byrne as Lord Alfred Douglas's jealous and ill-tem-pered father, "Queensberry! A ghost, a specter . . ." Similar to *Salomé's Last Dance,* the film suggests that the outrageous censorship of *Salomé* inaugu-rates the tragedy of Oscar Wilde.

In support of its empathetic reading of Wilde/Byrne as a misunderstood social and sexual transgressor in search of true love and pure art, *A Man of No Importance* uses Salomé as an alter ego and foil for Wilde by associating Wilde's stand-in, Alfred Byrne, with the young woman playing Salomé, Adele Rice (played by Tara Fitzgerald). From the moment she first steps on his bus, Byrne sees in the young, beautiful Adele the "perfect princess" for his play, the embodiment of ideal purity corresponding to Wilde's descrip-tion of Salomé ("She is perfect. She is like a dove that has strayed, she is like a narcissus in the wind, she is like a silver flower"). Despite Byrne's ideal-ized view of her, however, Adele is also a secret transgressor and a fugitive from Irish Catholic society. Originally a small-town girl, she has come to Dublin to seek out her cold and unresponsive lover, fittingly named John, from whom she is expecting a child out of wedlock. Adele tells Byrne, "I'm far from a princess, far from it. But I know you won't judge me too harsh." The close bond that emerges between Adele and Byrne as they start re-hearsing Wilde's play is one of innocence and true friendship; they harbor for each other the mutual appreciation and understanding of social outcasts, even though each does not know the extent of the other's secret until much later.

Wilde's play marks a transformative encounter for both Adele and Byrne and becomes the unexpected catalyst for their inevitable social ostracism and individual growth. In a climactic scene depicting the dress rehearsal, a crying and shaking Adele unwittingly gives away her carefully guarded secret as she reads her own desperate situation into Salome's love soliloquy to the severed head: "I was a virgin and thou didst take my virginity from me." As the surprised and horrified Byrne picks up her clue and realizes that Adele is not the innocent, pure princess he thought she was, the scene inaugurates Byrne's own personal crisis and sexual denouement. After the concerned Byrne follows her home and inadvertently witnesses a radiantly transformed Adele having sex with her lover, John, he finally realizes that "[t]he only way to get rid of temptation is to yield to it." Dressed up in Wildean dandyesque garb and makeup as if making a dramatic entrance, he bravely attempts to solicit "a cuddle" from a young hustler at a bar, but the long-awaited kiss turns violent as the hustler and his friends instead mug and beat up the helpless Byrne, leaving him lying unconscious in the gutter. The policeman who finds Byrne cruelly sneers, "Dirty queer," and casually hands him over to the scandalized Lily and Mr. Carney: "Take him home. He's not going to press charges, is he? They never do." His homosexuality scandalously exposed, Byrne suffers humiliation and shame as friends and family shun him. Adele is the only friend he can turn to; recognizing a kinship of suffering, she consoles him ("Love is a funny thing, Mr. Byrne. I hope it comes to you some day"). Even though their respective transgressions are different—for one, Adele is sexually active; Byrne isn't—they share the danger and fear of exposure in a society that officially regards homosexuality and extramarital sex as extremely grave moral offenses. This portrayal of the difference between the possibilities for the heterosexual Adele and the gay Byrne to live out their respective taboo desires subtly underscores the film's portrayal of sexual power relations: as Eve K. Sedgwick has shown, even in the respective epistemologies of the closet, heteroerotic desire appears privileged.

The film's immediate ethical recovery of Adele and Byrne after their sexual encounters, which are shockingly transgressive in the eyes of their society, relies heavily on the contrast between public appearance and personal truth. When the film's crisis comes and Byrne and Adele are exposed and shamed, the audience's emotional identification with them is already established. For the policeman, Byrne is just another "dirty queer," but for the audience, he is the epitome of the kind gentleman whose very human dreams of love and self-realization are instantly recognizable. This reversal of the Dublin community's hypocritical moral point of view puts the audience at odds with the harsh moral censorship exhibited by some of the movie's characters (e.g., Lily and Mr. Carney). Seen from an average liberal middle-class, contemporary perspective, neither extramarital sex nor homoerotic desires appear shameful or criminal; on the contrary, the movie makes us root for Byrne and Adele as naturally fallible human beings in search for love who should have never have been prosecuted in the first place.

What the fictional society in *A Man of No Importance* regards as sin appears, when represented with a different aesthetic system and from a different narrative point of view, as innocent and pure—vice redeemed, or, rather, revealed as love. The rhetorical movement of the movie as a whole toward an aesthetic redemption of sexual "perversity" thus repeats, on a larger scale, a main motive of its plot. The film seeks to show the unifying human truth and desire underlying transgression, in order to legitimize and make it intelligible. Emphasizing the beauty of perversity, it seeks to establish the notion that it was never perverse in the first place. Toward the end, Byrne is shown as successfully standing up to his viciously mocking superior, insisting on his aesthetic vision of homoeroticism by once again quoting Wilde: "Mr. Carson, the love that dare not speak its name, do you know what that is? . . . It's fine. It's beautiful. It's the noblest form of affection. There's nothing unnatural about it."[7] Luckily at this point, the movie audience could not agree more.

Within the narrative of *A Man of No Importance,* the theme of love unfulfilled legitimizes and defends Byrne's homoerotic desires. Firmly established in the ancient tradition of tales of love and romance, the trope courts audiences' favorable reading of Byrne's very modest transgressions as human tragedy, which, of course, they are. I would argue, however, that it is also a rather clichéd, normalizing way of creating sympathy with the gay hero. The strategy of reclaiming homoerotic desire through discourses of platonic love or tragic romantic love is a familiar one. Oscar Wilde himself deployed it when asked about "the love that dare not speak its name" in court, insisting that platonic love between an older and a younger man existed frequently and that there was nothing shameful or impure about it, effectively desexualizing and normalizing the relationship to avoid censure: "Gay fin-de-siècle self-definitional discourse did just that. . . . it seized upon readily available if slightly dated discourses that help de-sexualize the male homosexual" (Kopelson 19).

A Man of No Importance is beset by a similarly problematic drive toward normalization of transgressive desire. Initially, the ending seems to suggest antihomophobic social progress. After the initial shock, Byrne's friends actually embrace and defend him against the vicious taunts of the hypocritical authority figures Mr. Carney and Mr. Carson (stand-ins for Wilde's historical antagonists Lord Queensberry and the legal prosecutor), both of whom are quite literally thrown off the bus by Byrne's loyal passengers. Nevertheless, the aesthetic-erotic coming-out narrative in *A Man of No Importance* ultimately rings hollow: Alfred Byrne is reaccepted into the community only after his sexual abstinence and moral rectitude have been established, so that there is really no reason not to forgive him. Family and friends welcome Byrne back into their midst not because they have really changed their mind about the "sin" of homosexuality but because they "know him for a good man." Byrne's moral humanism supersedes his homosexuality. In the preceding scene, Byrne's strict sister Lily absolves Byrne only after he assures her, "My hands are innocent of affection." It is also clear that Byrne will most likely remain a virgin. Within the thematic trajectory of *A Man of No Importance,* a sexually inactive, innocent Byrne is obviously more acceptable than a sexually active one.

In the film's final scenes, platonic love and friendship are thus presented as cheery pseudosolutions to Byrne's stilted desire, and the homosexual threat is safely channeled back into the dominant social and cultural framework of conservative Irish Catholicism. Visiting Byrne in the abandoned theatrical space of the parish hall, Robbie cheerily offers his companionship, but not more: "I don't care what you got up to. I like you. You're my pal." The narrative ends precisely where it began, with a recited excerpt from Wilde's "Ballad of Reading Gaol" that echoes the theme of an impossible meeting of souls and bodies. Byrne quotes, "Like two doomed ships that pass in storm / We had crossed each other's way: / But we made no sign, we said no word, / We had no word to say; / For we did not meet in the holy night, / But in the shameful day." Byrne's genuine enthusiasm for Wilde's art, paired with his gentle and pained persona and tragic romance, offers the audience sentimental humanistic identification and empathy rather than flamboyant spectacle.

Paradoxically, despite its well-meaning antihomophobic intent, Krishnamma's film thus ultimately confirms the very social and cultural power structures against which it is directed: forbidden desire is quickly assimilated and conveniently removes itself from view again. As a result, the tried and tested middle-class Irish Catholic community can regain and newly strengthen its former moral balance, without any true reform or revolution. Similarly, the film's sentimental narrative is very attractive and consumable for contemporary audiences. *A Man of No Importance* was even adapted into a Broadway musical.[8] Although its run was relatively short, the authors and producers evidently believed correctly that this kind of material would find a large audience eventually. This may be read as a positive sign that times have changed for gay representation in mass culture, but it also confirms that such representation still comes most often packaged in recognizable, humanistic forms that do not tolerate the shock of actual transgression.

In both *A Man of No Importance* and *Salome's Last Dance,* the theatrical performance of *Salomé* creates a utopian space in which transgressive eros and art can live for a while but in which, characteristically, violence and normalization ensue. The fates of Salomé and Wilde in each film symbolize the destructive effects of sexual and aesthetic censorship. In *Salome's Last Dance,* the fictional Wilde is allowed to watch his aesthetic-erotic fantasy but then finds himself betrayed by his own lover and led off to prison. In *A Man of No Importance,* Byrne's *Salomé* production is censored before it even reaches the public. Both texts stress the historical impossibility—in the 1890s and the 1960s—of art as a successful utopian haven for transgressive eros. While anything is possible in the isolated space of the theater, it is sanctioned immediately on the streets, as Judith Butler has pointed out ("Performative Acts" 278). Both *Salome's Last Dance* and *A Man of No Importance* dwell on the gap between the theater and the real world that makes painfully evident the dangerous consequences of having one's mask stripped off by others who feel threatened by transgression. The films' endings remain deliberately ambiguous: even though Wilde drives off laughing and toasting in Russell's film and though Byrne smilingly listens to Robbie reciting Wilde's poetry at the end of Krishnamma's film, we already know what awaits Wilde (prison and shame) and what does *not* await Byrne (sex and romance).

Wilde and Homosexual Humanism

Within the historical and theoretical trajectory of *Salome's Modernity,* Ken Russell's *Salome's Last Dance* and Suri Krishnamma's *A Man of No Importance* are powerful examples of an ongoing attraction of the modernist aesthetics of transgression, as well as of the cultural conflation of Wilde and Salomé in late twentieth-century popular culture. Where Nazimova's film indirectly suggested the reading of *Salomé* as a mask for Wilde's homoerotic desires, Russell and Krishnamma directly present *Salomé* as a closet drama par excellence. Arranged around fictional stagings of Wilde's play as a play-within-a-movie, each film retroactively relates Wilde's and *Salomé's* censorship history to an implicitly ethical project that speaks to the films' own time and a reading of one historical frame through the other, developing an allegorical critique of homophobia and the cultural, social, and political vilification of sexual and aesthetic dissidence both past and present.

Salome's Last Dance and *A Man of No Importance* encourage audiences to perceive the homophobic social prison they portray as an outrageous destruction of the human spirit, which in the name of humanity can and must be overcome (a goal with which I wholeheartedly agree). The two films ultimately also present a new danger, by normalizing Wilde and *Salomé's* transgressive potential. They readily offer straight and queer audiences alike nonthreatening ways to understand Salomé and Wilde as admirable embodiments of modern individualism and the human quest for freedom of self-expression and happiness. But can statutory transgression still be transgression in Wilde's, Bataille's, or even Foucault's sense of a paradoxical, oscillating, daring, and utopian challenge to and expansion of the literary, social, and cultural limit? Or is such a reinterpretation not, rather, a more subtle form of suppression that safely channels transgression back into the realm of normativity and mainstream culture?

The direct linkage of *Salomé* and Wilde's sexual persona in Krishnamma's and Russell's films implies the belief that Wilde's work contains identifiable traces of forbidden sex, of homosexual identity or experience, and of the pain of the closet. In these films, Wilde is gay, but more important, he is a tragic gay hero who exemplifies the dangers of the aesthetics and the life of transgression in less enlightened times than our own. Wilde has become the stereotypical gay martyr crushed by Victorian homophobia and a celebrated pop culture icon of modern individualism, and his works are read accordingly. The performance of Wilde's *Salomé* and the inclusion of Wilde's persona in *Salome's Last Dance* and *A Man of No Importance* call for similar identifications with the stylized figure of the male homosexual (Alfred Byrne, Oscar Wilde), even though Russell's ironic-sarcastic tone differs from Krishnamma's sentimental and romantic approach. As we have seen, neither of these films is *about* Oscar Wilde in the sense that it attempts a biographical sketch or reinterpretation of Wilde's life. Nevertheless, Wilde has become a mythic signifier in Barthes's sense: audiences know how to read him in a story, and today more than ever, they are explicitly invited to do so. Almost one century after Oscar Wilde's infamous 1895 London trial and the conviction for acts of "gross indecency," Wilde has become a highly charged symbol of the then that can strategically be employed in the now.

As I have argued elsewhere, in reading or teaching *Salomé* today, we have to reckon with a full century's worth of inherited assumptions about Wilde as a cultural icon (Dierkes-Thrun, "Salomé, C'est Moi?" 171). Many popular and scholarly interpretations of Wilde since the 1980s seem unaware of their own inherited burdens when they approach Wilde as if he was our contemporary or as if he was undoubtedly thinking of himself in terms of a (as yet unnamed, Foucault has shown) homosexual "identity."[9] Anachronistic readings of Wilde as a writer whose closeted homosexuality can clearly be detected through his work often reveal more about today's concerns and preconceptions than about the historical Wilde, however. The belated penetration of Wilde's sexed body seems to be driven by a kind of "paralytic demand for essence" of homosexuality, as writes Eve Kosofsky Sedgwick (whose own work on Wilde has been carefully historical as well as theoretically sophisticated). "Each of these readings traces and affirms the gay possibility in Wilde's writing by identifying it—feature by feature, as from a Most Wanted poster—with the perfect fulfillment of a modernist or postmodernist project of meaning-destabilization and identity-destabilization" ("Tales of the Avunculate" 55). Such readings reflect what is now perceived as "the 'common sense' of twentieth-century sexual tropology— however uneagerly the eros of Wilde himself may answer to such interpretation" (ibid. 56).

Starting in the 1950s, Wilde became one of the historical and theoretical anchorage points for recent psychosexual views of homosexual identity and for biographical interpretations of Wilde's work as a clue to his homosexuality.[10] This trend has included interpretations of Salomé as a transvestite mask, spurred on by a now notorious editorial error in Richard Ellmann's biography. In the first edition of Ellmann's *Oscar Wilde,* a photograph of a person in orientalist costume kneeling before a stage prop of the Baptist's head was identified by the editor as "Wilde in costume as Salome," but it was later revealed to be a female Hungarian soprano, Alice Guszalewicz (who bore a striking resemblance to Wilde), in a 1906 production of Strauss's opera. Elaine Showalter and others jumped to the occasion, citing the picture as evidence that Wilde felt a special affinity to and identified with his protagonist (Showalter, *Sexual Anarchy* 156). Even after the original error was publicized and corrected, Showalter insisted on her transvestite and biographical reading of *Salomé.*[11] Jonathan Dollimore writes generally about such efforts to "out" Wilde, "Retrospective decisions about the 'real' Wilde are revealing of the way essentialist conceptions of sexuality and subjectivity have reinforced ethical notions of sincerity and psychic depth in the formation of modern individuality and modern literature, in a way powerful enough to make of Wilde a legend while effacing

what was most challenging about him" (73). As Wilde's grandson Merlin
Holland points out, however, Wilde's equivocality forbids such exclusive,
monolinear approaches to his work and person, centered around his sexuality: the life of Wilde "is simply not a life which can tolerate an either/or
approach with logical conclusions, but demands the flexibility of a
both/and treatment, often raising questions for which there are no answers"
("Biography" 3–4).

One can observe a similar trend to represent Wilde as a historical ancestor of the gay civil rights movement in several well-known 1990s versions
of Wilde's life in theater and film. Brian Gilbert's Wilde (1997), for example,
takes "a 'gay-friendly' biographical approach," while emphasizing Wilde the
father and family man, Richard Kaye writes. Based on Richard Ellmann's
landmark biography on Wilde, which laudably sought to recover Wilde as
a serious artist after decades of scholarly skepticism, Gilbert's film attempts
to reconcile Wilde's public life as a highly regarded author, loving father,
and good husband (who also held favorable, progressive views on women's
dress reform and gender roles) with the hidden gay Wilde who frequented
Victorian brothels and had sex with men. It exemplifies a humanist approach that makes the "playwright not a contemptible cad but poignantly
foolish, a big, befuddled, cuddly giant—a Disney Oscar Wilde" (Kaye, "Gay
Studies/Queer Theory" 216).[12] A similar but more multifaceted fascination
with Wilde's private life has informed Neil Bartlett's semiautobiography
Who Was That Man? A Present for Mr. Oscar Wilde (1988) and his play In Extremis (2000); Terry Eagleton's Saint Oscar (1989) and Tom Stoppard's The
Invention of Love (1997); and David Hare's The Judas Kiss and Moisés Kaufman's Gross Indecency: The Three Trials of Oscar Wilde (both 1998). All these
texts focus on Wilde's sexual activities and subsequent public condemnation as a secretly gay artist in the 1890s. These historically oriented, sympathetic rewritings of Wilde's life explore the figure of a private Oscar Wilde
for contemporary public purposes, to subtly criticize homophobic structures. As many newspaper reports on Wilde's centenary in 2000 illustrated,
Wilde is often anachronistically linked to the gay civil rights struggle.

As gay-affirmative films targeting mainstream, middle-class, largely heterosexual audiences, both Salome's Last Dance and A Man of No Importance
participate in a larger cultural pattern, the so-called positive image activism.
It has been observable in cinema and popular culture since the late 1980s,
characterized by its typically well-intentioned, but ultimately heteronormative, liberal humanist representation of homosexuals as being "just like us."
In his introduction to The Matter of Images, Richard Dyer points out parallels between lesbian, gay, bisexual, transgender, and queer (LGBTQ) posi-

tive image activism and the African American civil rights struggle, which featured similarly problematic "just like us" discourses of affiliation with dominant society (1). Positive image activism often suffers from the difficulty to project an identifiable, solid group image into mainstream culture while not alienating heterosexual audiences. In the case of gay men, the insistence on a common (cultural and/or biological) identity has been an important political strategy to identify, define, and protect common political and social interests and grievances of homosexuals, at least since the beginnings of the early twentieth-century German gay rights movement and even more so since the 1968 Stonewall riots. As many scholars and activists insist, with good reason, "[i]n homophobic society, the necessary fiction of a cohesive identity must be spoken in order for political communities to maintain any sort of presence," even though "there are obviously problems with the articulation of any sort of fixed identity" (Evans and Gamman 39). Positive image activism (which has drawn both gay and straight filmmakers and cultural agents) caters to gay audiences' deep-seated hunger "for positive, progay, upbeat coming out films for audiences that need to be constantly reassured in a deeply repressive and homophobic culture that it is OK to be gay" (Bronski 23). The genre typically oversimplifies the social and political dangers associated with coming and being out, however. Dealing only in minor plot complications and inevitably adding a happy ending, the coming-out film characterized by popular image activism often "misjudges the harshness of homophobia in the world" by limiting its complications to conflicts with family and friends that are overcome relatively easily in the plot, "with good will and even better intentions" (ibid.). "[A]nother traditional feature of the coming out film" we can observe in *A Man of No Importance* "is that, once its main character comes out and deals with the minor problems this has caused, the film ends"; effectively, this dominant rhetorical strategy "actually prevent[s] gay and lesbian characters from having much of a life after coming out" (ibid. 20).

Many coming-out films of this sort hence encapsulate a contradictory operation of humanist universalism, on the one hand, and humanist esteem for difference, on the other. In *Sexual Dissidence*, Jonathan Dollimore introduced a useful term for such operations, *heterosexual humanism*. Dollimore explains that heterosexual humanism regards people "at once as unique individuals and as instances of a universal human nature: irreducibly different and yet ultimately the same," that is, universally human (78). Dollimore's term works well to describe the "much progressed but still repressive resistance" (ibid.) of heterosexual cultural agents and audiences in the texts I have discussed here. It does not address the relatively new phenomenon of gay-affirmative and gay-genealogical discourses of humanist empathy by gay or gay-friendly directors and cultural agents, however. Borrowing partly from Dollimore's concept, I suggest a term for this parallel phenomenon: *homosexual humanism*. This term designates the specific affirmative cultural narrative of development and assimilation that has been applied to the specific sexual subgroup of male homosexuals in popular culture since the 1990s.[13] The ideal uplifting of this group from underdog status to commercial mainstream acceptability seems progressive, but it is also simply convenient: it fits capital's versatile search for new markets and, at the same time, expands and complements the humanist ideals of self-liberation on a philosophical and cultural scale, naturalizing the social accommodation of otherness. It subsumes homosexuals under universalist humanistic ideals that "produce a heteronormative sanitation of queer life," as Eric Clarke argues in his thought-provoking analysis of gay marriage activism, *Virtuous Vice*. Clarke explains, "In terms of homoerotic representation, publicity's subjunctive mood requires that one act as if equal representation, participation and access are achieved through homogenized proxies—lesbians and gay men who are 'just like everyone else.' . . . [E]xcluded groups are brought into the fold, so to speak" (7). Similarly, the current homosexual humanism seeks to promote normalizing, inoffensive, and entertaining images of homosexuals in popular culture. The danger of homosexual humanism as it applies to representations of Wilde is its obfuscation of complexity in favor of simplistic sentimentalism and humanist universalism, which produce a feel-good effect on audiences that perpetuates stereotypes rather than challenging them.

In the last two decades, Wilde has mainly been enlisted for three pervasive stereotypes of male homosexuality derived from humanistic points of view: the tragic, misunderstood outcast (Krishnamma's film and Moises Kaufman's *Gross Indecency*); the glamorous wit and fearless dandy (Russell's film); and the gentle, caring, and intellectual family man and friend with a secret alternative sex life (Brian Gilbert's *Wilde* and David Hare's *The Judas Kiss*). We do not have to look far to recognize the same stereotypes operating in some popular coming-out films and gay-themed shows of the last ten or fifteen years, from *Love and Death on Long Island* (1997) and *Gods and Monsters* (1998) to *Will and Grace* and *Queer as Folk*, among other examples. Wilde's position within this important social development and also in the formation of a new marketing niche through which such images are now exhibited, normalized, and sold has been remarkable.

In the face of the pitfalls of the new homosexual humanism to which representations of Wilde and Salomé have importantly contributed, it becomes an increasingly urgent critical project to analyze and historicize the rhetorical and ideological structures of such representations. Judith Butler has shown how even politically progressive identity categories "tend to be instruments of regulatory regimes, whether as the normalizing categories of oppressive structures or as the rallying points for a liberatory contestation of that very oppression" ("Imitation and Gender Subordination" 308). Motivated by a well-meaning antihomophobic impulse but normalizing male homosexuality through narratives of sexual quixotism and victimization, such projects as *Salome's Last Dance* and *A Man of No Importance* aim to induce social empathy while they entertain. But despite the intended positive critical forces, the two movies' overall project of creating tolerance and inclusivity has extremely problematic implications for the representation and cultural, social, and political understanding of homosexuality, which are rendered nonthreatening and consumable for the benefit of largely heterosexual mass audiences.

In recent years, some creative artists have begun to innovate the iconic use of Wilde, in projects that seek to transform the trajectories of queer representation.[14] Todd Haynes's 1998 film *Velvet Goldmine* is an excellent example. One of the major directors of the New Queer Cinema, Haynes undermines "conventional narrative structure, a structure he associates with the dominant heterosexual culture and its artifacts" (Bartone). "The experimental, non-linear, and complex narrative designs of his films qualify them all as queer, according to Haynes," even though only three of his films—*Poison, Velvet Goldmine,* and *Far from Heaven*—"deal directly with homosexuality" (ibid.).[15] As a 1980s graduate of Brown University's Semiotics Program, which housed many of the intellectual roots of queer theory, Haynes has been outspoken about the constructivist theories that influenced his work (Kaye, "Gay Studies/Queer Theory," 218). *Velvet Goldmine* presents an intensely ironic, colorful carnival of masks and styles that never pretends to give us the "true" Oscar Wilde. Instead, it opts for a deliberately outrageous, playful recasting of Wilde as a space alien and ancestor of 1970s androgynous glam rock and glitter (embodied in the United Kingdom by Roxy Music and David Bowie and in the United States by Iggy Pop and the Velvet Underground). *Velvet Goldmine* (an allusion to David Bowie's 1971 song of the same title) unfolds as a Citizen Kane–like musical mockumentary that extensively quotes Oscar Wilde. Haynes references Wilde as the patron saint of multigendered mask play and aesthetic flamboyance, whose witty dandyism inspired the 1970s sexual and stylistic excesses. (The connection is made explicit in an early scene at the opening of the movie, when the eight-year-old schoolboy Oscar Wilde announces to his classmates and teacher that he wants to be "a pop idol" when he grows up.) The era is cast as a return of a fabulous queer past originated and embodied by Wilde as the godfather of sexual and aesthetic rebellion. In the film's prologue, a female voice mysteriously announces, "Histories, like ancient ruins, are the fictions of empires. While everything forgotten hangs in dark dreams of the past, ever threatening to return . . ." (*Velvet Goldmine* screenplay 3). In Haynes's movie, Wilde returns—from history, as well as, surprisingly, from queer outer space: a pink-colored space ship drops him off as a baby on a doorstep in Dublin, as if to bring the drab earthlings a bit of queer magic.

According to Haynes, *Velvet Goldmine* portrays and continues "a long tradition of gay reading(s) of the world," and its main vehicle for doing so is the referential network relating to Wilde (quoted in Bartone). Kaye notes, "Giddily in love with stylish excess, *Velvet Goldmine* never lets go of the spirit of Wilde" ("Gay Studies/Queer Theory" 218). In a 1998 interview with Nick James in *Sight and Sound,* Haynes explained that he was "interested in glam rock's flag-waving of artificiality—and there's no more articulate spokesperson for artifice than Oscar Wilde. It's that incongruous relationship . . . between a strong anti-naturalist statement—a pose, a stance, and ironic wit—and an ability to be poetic and beautiful and moving. My goal as a film-maker was to incorporate this duality into a narrative context." Haynes dedicated his film to "Oscar Wilde, posing as a sodomite" and incorporated fictional cameos of Wilde's childhood, a strategically quoted passage from *The Picture of Dorian Gray,* and numerous Wildean paradoxes and bon mots into the main story, which revolves around the closeted gay journalist Arthur Stuart (played by Christian Bale). Arthur is investigating the mysterious death of his former idol, flamboyant glam musician Brian Slade (played by Jonathan Rhys-Meyers as a mixture of the bisexual David Bowie and the transvestite comedian Eddie Izzard), and his relationship with the troubled gay rock star Curt Wild (a namesake of Wilde played by Ewan McGregor as an amalgam of Iggy Pop and Kurt Cobain). The movie's tongue-in-cheek quest for Arthur's investigation into "what happened to Brian Slade" develops as a queer history of outrageous sexual and aesthetic queer brotherhood that connects Arthur's painful coming-out as a teenager with the glam era's sexual freedom, on the one hand, and with Oscar Wilde, on the other.

Visually and symbolically, the genealogical chain from Wilde to 1970s glam and glitter is symbolized in the film by a green-colored brooch, a sparkling emerald with almost magical powers, including the power to comfort and unite. In the opening scene, the alien baby Oscar's swaddling clothes had been adorned with this sparkling emerald brooch, and Haynes uses it as an important symbol for the rest of the movie. It is passed on from the infant Wilde's breast to generation upon generation of queer self-styliz- ers, stars, and misfits. Similar to Krishnamma's use of Alfie Byrne's green carnation as a code for homosexuality, Haynes employs the emerald as a sign for both glamour and gayness, exchanged between various gay lovers as a token of love, trust, and belonging, passed on through time from Oscar Wilde to the circle of queer outcasts around which Haynes's film revolves. The emerald symbolically connects Arthur to his idol Brian Slade, to Slade's lover Curt Wild (with whom the young fan Arthur once had romantic sex on a rooftop after a show), and all the way back to Oscar Wilde himself. As Kaye notes, "[d]ispensing with the literal tropes of biographical film narra- tive and its attendant reductive psychology, *Velvet Goldmine* is a supernat- ural tribute to the ghost of an ever-mutating, 'unnatural' Oscar Wilde" ("Gay Studies/Queer Theory" 219), but it does not reduce Wilde's com- plexity. Haynes's film is passionately antihomophobic, inherently political, and a true homage to sexual and aesthetic transgression past and present.

Developing new, effective, and attractive forms of LGBTQ representation within mainstream culture can happen without recourse to essentialist, hu- manist models of identity, even when they deal with such iconic mainstays of sexual and gender nonconformity as Oscar Wilde and Salomé. Doric Wilson's play *Now She Dances!* (1999) is a good example of an innovative antihomophobic *Salomé* adaptation that values complexity and pastiche over simplistic sentimentalism or predetermined story arcs in pro-gay en- tertainment and that does so through the symbolism of Wilde and *Salomé*. Wilson is a playwright, a former Stonewall participant and Gay Activists Al- liance member, and a pioneer of New York City's gay theater and Off-Off- Broadway movements. He also founded and later revived New York's first acting company devoted to gay and lesbian themes, TOSOS (The Other Side of Silence). Largely ignored by academic scholars and critics thus far but well known in the gay theater community, Doric Wilson has garnered many awards.[16] *Now She Dances!* underwent a series of revisions—from 1961, when it was first performed at the Caffe Cino; to 1976, when it was rewritten for TOSOS; to 2000, when it was performed in Glasgow in a dou- ble bill with Wilde's *Salomé*.

By way of an introduction to his play, Wilson writes,

> *Now She Dances!* began as a response to the hilarious histrionics and fruity language of Lord Douglas' translation of Oscar Wilde's *Salome*. Written with overwhelming earnestness in no-doubt equally florid French, Wilde's play has become a touchstone for decadence, equating lavender eau de

cologne and slavering smears of silver eyeshadow with degeneracy. I decided to rewrite it as *The Importance of Being Salome* (Richard Barr found
the right title in one of the last lines of the play). (*Now She Dances!* 405)

Wilson describes *Now She Dances!* as "an angry, ironic, nightmare metaphor
for the trial of Oscar Wilde," written in an angry state of mind after a night
in which Wilson himself was unjustly arrested in a gay raid in New York City.
"Operating on three main levels, *Now She Dances!* is a metaphor for [Wilde's]
trial, blending characters from Wilde's *Salome* and *Earnest* with a Post-Mod-
ernist America" (ibid.). For instance, the young footman Bill, Wilson's version of the Young Syrian, is a buff, naive young American with evangelical
leanings; there are also references to George Bush the elder, the pro-life
movement, and the first Iraq war. Wilson's stage directions illustrate the
amalgam of *Salomé* and *The Importance of Being Earnest* in the play: Salomé is
supposed to be "an uneasy blend of Gwendolen and the ecdysiast of the New
Testament—on the surface, a diffident daughter of propriety, in her soul, a
carnivorous priestess of Moloch"; Herod is an aged "Algernon well past his
prime" (407); Herodias is "a dowager dreadnought . . . Lady Bracknell de-
ranged," with a hat sporting "a fantastic bird of prey" (416); and the sardonic
butler Lane is endowed with intertextual "references from another play," the
butler Merriman from *The Importance of Being Earnest* (406).

The two acts of *Now She Dances!* are replete with references both to
Wilde and to the gay civil rights struggles in New York, in which Wilson
himself was involved. Wilson reinterprets the character of John the Baptist,
whom Wilson calls the Prisoner, as "a contemporary stand-in for Wilde"
(406), but the Prisoner could equally be a gay everyman or Wilson himself.
The play is Wilson's "most fiercely biographical play": "Painfully private and
highly sensitive details of my youth are shattered, stitched back together
and scattered liberally throughout the play. No, they are not the ones you
think they are," Wilson writes on his personal Web site. The Prisoner is "an
attractive, personable, contemporary gay male, dressed for Saturday night
on West Street" (*Now She Dances!* 445) who has offended Herodias by inadvertently handing her a flier for the "Gay Defensive Front." Hounded by
Herod and coolly castigated by Salomé (a savvy, vicious vixen and femme
fatale who finds the "very existence" of a gay man "a denial of [her] femininity" [452]), the Prisoner is trapped between the straight characters' homophobia, on the one hand, and the lack of gay solidarity, on the other,
personified by the sardonic, closeted butler Lane, who is "smug and
guarded—the quintessential closet queen" (408). Lane often chimes in as
the straight characters parade the most clichéd of gay stereotypes (child

molester, murderer, Judy Garland impersonator, perpetually horny pervert, hairdresser, interior decorator, Bette Midler lover, preferrer of long hair, self-hater, the cause of God's wrath in the form of earthquakes and other natural catastrophes), and he even tells bad gay jokes on demand. In one scene, Lane and the maid Gladys refer to Oscar Wilde to explain to Herodias what or who the Prisoner is, encouraging Herodias to go after the Prisoner.

> Lane: Does milady chance to remember Oscar Wilde?
> Lady H: Mr. Oscar Wilde is not a fit subject for conversation. Certainly not in a family entertainment.
> Gladys: The circular ["Gay Defensive Front" flier] comes from one of them.
> Lady H: One of whom?
> Lane: Mr. Wilde's progeny.
> Lady H: They don't have progeny.
> Gladys: (*still needing Lane*) We'll throw 'em all in jail.
> Lane: We seem to have missed one or two.
>
> (14–15)

The contrast between the out Prisoner and the closeted Lane is central to Wilson's interpretation of *Salomé* as a play about gay suffering, guilt, and hypocrisy. Lane fancies himself immune to society's backlashes ("People only get hurt when they deserve it . . . No one ever clubbed me" [452]), and yet he feels intensely threatened by the out gay Prisoner.

> Lane: He fancies himself better than the rest of us.
> Salome: The rest of whom?
> Lane: Those of us who prefer the cool, clean, dark air of the closet.
> Prisoner: Mothballs and mushrooms.
> Lane: I'd rather be standing here, safe and secure in my Gucci's, than stomping around in your boots on a collision with calamity.
> Salome: Closets? What has this to do with closets?
> Prisoner: Everything.
> Lane: Friend—may I call you a friend? Like it or not, maybe we do have a lot in common. We have even more that is not in common. You're committed. I've never found commitment pays my bill at Bloomingdale's. You're an activist, I go to the Opera. You're involved, I rely on opiates.
>
> (453)

Ironically, yet not surprisingly, it is ultimately the cynical gay Lane himself who voluntarily executes the Prisoner and is literally serving up his head on a platter to the powers that be. As a heartless man playing both worlds (cruising at night and playing homophobe by day), Lane is the true ideological target of Wilson's play and appears more culpable than Salome herself. (Evidently he feels some pangs of remorse but chooses not to heed them when the Prisoner implores his solidarity.) At the beginning of act 2, Lane even appears as the High Priest of Moloch (435–36), the symbolic deity to whom innocent children are sacrificed, here gay men. Consequently, *Now She Dances!* criticizes not only the heterosexual social and cultural closet but the closeted: as a dedicated gay activist, Wilson uses his theatrical craft to argue for a change of heart and mind among those who prefer to enjoy the "benefits" that Lane's smug character enjoys (power and status, however contingent) while others struggle and die.

Other recent innovative queer approaches to Wilde's *Salomé* are equally as mindful of the queer and transgressive genealogy of readings of *Salomé* and Wilde but do not confuse the artist with his mask. Dorian Katz, a contemporary female, queer artist based in San Francisco and currently residing at Stanford University, fashioned an illustration of Salomé's triumphant moment in *Kiss* (see fig. 4), which gives Salomé the face of Sarah Bernhardt and substitutes Katz's own face for John the Baptist's. Katz writes, "My own face is portrayed as the decapitated Iokanaan. By placing a female in this role, I am adding another element of homoeroticism to this version; it is my mouth Bernhardt kisses, whether viewers can tell I am a woman or not. Secondly, this element is a tribute to the Baroque painter Caravaggio." Caravaggio often depicted his own head as John the Baptist's in the dozen or so paintings of severed heads he made, including *Judith Beheading Holofernes* (ca. 1598), *David with the Head of Goliath* (1609), and others. Katz continues, "The blood in the self-portrait is made from my blood mixed with salt, gin and acrylic medium. Caravaggio was not the first artist to paint his decapitated head and I will not be the last; however, I do like being part of a lineage" ("Our Sainte Thérèse of the Moon" 5).

Todd Haynes's *Velvet Goldmine,* Doric Wilson's *Now She Dances!* and Dorian Katz's visual artwork are situated at different places along the spectrum of pro-gay cultural production—queer theory and constructivism in Haynes's case, Stonewall history and gay and lesbian identity activism in Wilson's, and kink and sex-positive, queer feminism and transfeminism in Katz's. But all offer thoughtful, complex, and entertaining contemporary readings of Oscar Wilde and *Salomé* that are closer to the utopian, transgressive spirit of Wilde's play than the positive image activism of *Salome's Last Dance* and *A Man of No Importance.*

Fig. 4. *Kiss* by Dorian Katz (2009)

Salomé and Regressive Feminism

While the historical enlistments of Wilde and Salomé in the current homosexual humanism have sought to argue for an incorporation and assimilation of male homosexuality into the normative social and cultural contin-
uum, recent straight readings of Salomé have continued to emphasize and
set apart Salomé's extraordinary, excessive female sexuality. Continuing the

line first begun by Allan and Nazimova, Salomé figures as a symbolic feminist trailblazer in several popular culture texts since the 1990s, which celebrate or warn against the feminist potential of transgressive female sexuality and sexual agency: Nick Cave's play *Salomé* (1993); Tom Robbins's best-selling novel *Skinny Legs and All* (1990); Robert Altman's film *Cookie's Fortune* (1997); and Sandra Goldbacher's movie *The Governess* (1998). These texts perpetuate the modernist reading of Salomé's excess as a positive, awe-inspiring, lawless state of physical ecstasy or jouissance outside rationality and implicitly present themselves as pro-feminist. Nevertheless, none are ultimately very convincing or progressive-looking. Often reducing the Salome figure to hedonistic impulse and aggressive sexuality, they rob Wilde's original Salomé of her ambiguous complexity and also problematically replicate earlier misogynist, naively dehistoricized notions, such as the femme fatale and the militant feminist. Like the homosexual humanist visions of Wilde and Salomé, they inherit their own problematic attitudes that ultimately defy their own project of blasting open the cage of sexual and social unfreedom. From this feminist's perspective in 2010, these body- and instinct-based versions of women's freedom and agency look too dangerously familiar and regressive. They throw us back several decades to feminist schools in which an accentuated and adaptable utopianism of the female body played a central role. Theirs was a rhetorical mobilization of femininity as jouissance that must itself be historicized as a reaction to the crises of modernity, an attempt "within the master narratives of the West . . . to create a new *space* or *spacing within themselves* for survivals" via "the transformation of woman and the feminine into verbs at the interior of those narratives that are today experiencing a crisis in legitimation" (Jardine 25).

Nick Cave's play *Salomé* from *King Ink*—a 1993 collection of poems, song lyrics, and short plays by the Australian singer, actor, and writer (better known as front man for Nick Cave and the Bad Seeds)—is probably the most provocative of all the feminist-themed interpretations of Wilde's *Salomé* published in recent years.[17] Following Wilde's emphasis on Salomé's physical desire for John the Baptist but altering the premise of Wilde's aestheticism, Cave's Salomé is no yearning, lonely soul in search of ideal beauty but a bored, sadistic, narcissistic, and hypersexual teenager who engages in masturbation on stage, enjoys ruthless verbal and physical power play, and "sulks and sighs and allows her heavenly body to pursue coquettishly the serpentine rhythms of music in a manner of cruel titillation" (Cave 69). Cave may have absorbed the fin de siècle Salome theme's intertwinement of eroticism and metaphysical longing found in Mallarmé, Flaubert, and Huysmans, but he presents it with such absurd hyperbole and irony that it is clear he is making fun of the tradition of investing Salomé's body with quasi-divine power. Instead, he takes Wilde's focus on Salomé's secular aesthetic and erotic ecstasy to the extreme, making sexual pleasure and narcissistic self-gratification her only motivations in the play.

Cave's play consists of five very brief acts ("The Seven Veils," "Dialogue with the Baptist," "Salomé's Reward," "The Chop," and "The Platter," some only a few lines long) and has elements of the theater of the absurd. (In act 1, for example, the stage direction determines that "all props, crown, and throne must look like they were made by children.") Herod asks for and immediately gets a surprisingly listless Dance of the Seven Veils performed by Salomé to the sounds of "Arabic wailing and bells," in which she "remains stock-still, facing Herod," and strips completely without any further ado (69). This pathetic "dance" nevertheless makes Herod exclaim, "What you create with your seven veils God, creaking at the hinges, could never approach with his seven days" (ibid.), a statement poised to incite laughter rather than reverence—it comes across as ridiculous. Thus relegating male voyeurism and the metaphysical elevation of female sexuality to the realm of the absurd, Cave's play then proceeds to reclaim it for Salomé's own pleasure and portrays female power play and transgressive autoeroticism as ends in themselves. In act 2, perhaps echoing the scene in Ken Russell's *Salomé's Last Dance* in which John is imprisoned in a giant cage (whipped by two dominatrices and finally sodomized with a spear), Salomé sits on top of John's wooden cage and listens to his prophetic condemnations while masturbating, "swinging one long bright naked leg in front of the cage. One hand slips beneath her robe, while the other holds a large apple which she eats. Her toenails are painted the colour of blood. Salomé fingers herself" (71). The Baptist's misogynistic curses in this scene ("Too vile for the grave, too vile for the grave. You are beyond redemption! Marked with devil blood, ruled by the moon! O hellish vixen! O cloven gender!" [71]) only serve as pleasurable fodder for Salomé's sexual imagination; she is neither intimidated nor contained by them. Sure of herself and defying the spiritual cleansing he offers, Salomé apes and mocks him with pretend upper-class pronunciation: "Cleanse me, Baptist. Take this yoke, the moon, under which ah slave, the terrible Emperess of mah body. Its climate, its seasons. I am woman. Cleanse me. Wash away all that's comely. Chasten me, Baptist, with your waters." Cave's Salomé strikes back at the Baptist not only because of his condemnations of her mother and herself but, more generally, because he condemns the whole female sex. At times sounding like a militant feminist and conscious of her power, Salomé seems to relish and enjoy their altercation. Knowing that she will prevail, she contemptuously insults him: "If I have my way, pompous turd, you won't have a brain much longer! (*She laughs.*) . . . Suit yourself, dick breath!" (71–72).

Like Wilde, Cave unites the themes of female sexuality and cruelty through the symbolism of the moon, the embodiment of the female principle, but he sexualizes them much more than Wilde does. In act 4, Salomé voyeurously witnesses John's execution, one "hand working diligently between her sugar thighs." She reaches her orgasm at the very moment of his decapitation, while "the moon blinks on and blood runs down the insides of SALOMÉ's dress," as if she experiences simultaneous sexual and menstrual release (74). The moon is Salomé's constant companion throughout the short play, appearing at times as a halo around her head or bearing silent witness to her perverse cruelty. The theme of female masturbation is the extreme physical counterpart to Wilde's philosophy of transgressive individualism, and the moon as the embodiment of the female principle becomes an overtly feminist symbol in Cave's play.

Salomé's final words indicate that she has seized John the Baptist's tongue—the physical enabler of the Word—"to teach her cunt to talk good" (75). In Cave's play, female sexuality thus symbolically consumes and usurps the most powerful patriarchal instrument, the power of the religious and the worldly Word, destroying it with orgiastic pleasure, obscenity, and violence that are worthy of a Georges Bataille. Cave's interpretation of Salomé's transgression as the embodiment of ultimate individualism and freedom continues and exacerbates the modernist Salome tradition begun by Wilde.

In Tom Robbins's 1990 best-selling popular novel *Skinny Legs and All,* the Salome theme appears as a less shocking, more popular mainstream feminist endorsement of female sexuality as a gateway to personal authenticity and self-fulfillment. Tom Robbins metaphorically utilizes and interweaves the figure of Salome and Salome's Dance of the Seven Veils (clearly based on Wilde's version but not mentioning it directly) with his main narrative about the sexual and aesthetic coming-of-age of his central female character, Ellen Cherry Charles. The novel employs two Salome figures, one in its main plot (a belly dancer named Salome who performs in an Arab-Jewish restaurant) and one in its allegorical, metanarrative frame, a symbolic Salome who dances in the primordial "room of the wolfmother wallpaper." As described in the novel's prelude as well as in interludes throughout, the symbolic Salome is an archetypal image of female sexual sublimity and organicity. She oversees the action from a hallucinatory, womblike room (said "room of the wolfmother wallpaper"), where she dances the "Dance of Ultimate Cognition, skinny legs and all" (Robbins 1–2), approaching a utopian state of intuitive knowledge and truth embodying ideal mental and physical balance. Robbins cleverly arranges the novel's narrative in seven chapters entitled "Veils" (The First Veil, The Second Veil, etc.) so that Ellen's character development becomes a symbolic reflection of this dance. As the novel paradoxically pretends to strip down while adding more and more layers, Salome's orgiastic dance in the room of the wolfmother wallpaper functions as a paradoxical focal point of primal origin and return, purporting to shed "the great illusions of mankind," among them the patriarchal denial of orgiastic sexuality and spiritual instinct, principles Robbins associates directly with liberated femininity. Robbins's popular New Age feminism proffers the idea that orgiastic sexuality is the key to women's spiritual fulfillment.

Salome's "Dance of Ultimate Cognition" eventually spills from the metanarrative into the main plot. Watching a young belly dancer by the name of Salome (a silent young girl of mysterious Arab-Jewish origin) perform the Dance of the Seven Veils at a restaurant, Ellen begins "to receive ideas" (402). After the dance, Ellen feels "as if she had reached an understanding in several significant areas, had reached it suddenly, effortlessly; had reached it—and this was the queerest part—during the hour and twenty minutes that she had spent watching Salome dance" (406). Connecting the religious and the erotic (faintly echoing the legacy of Flaubert's and Huysmans's renditions), the dance shocks as much as it fascinates. Inverting the usual order of unveiling, Robbins has Salome drop the most intimate veil first: "Everybody was shocked, even the unshockable. Yet nobody acted to stop the performance. Nobody. And Salome went on whirling and dipping and swooping and arching, and each time she arched, they found themselves looking into the prettiest and pinkest little slit that anyone could ever imagine, its folds delicate and mysterious, its tiny stinger aimed at them like the gun barrel of a felonious orchid" (402).

For Robbins, the female body and female sexuality embody the central connection to the earth. They signify the intrinsic intertwinement of the human body with the mysteries of the universe and with nature. In an interview, Robbins said, "I have always been a romantic—one of those people who believes that a woman in pink circus tights contains all the secrets of the universe" (Hoyser and Stookey 3). In the utopian Outside of time and space that Salome's dance signifies in *Skinny Legs and All,* past and future come together in the eternal, fulfilled present, which supplies profound ontological meaning: "A return to goddess worship becomes the solution to world religious strife and hate. . . . A return to the female will salve the wounds to the world that male dichotomous thinking has caused" (ibid. 37). Robbins seeks to "reconnect [humans] with the female principle of intuition, peaceful means, harmony with nature, and spirituality" (ibid.). Unfolding an ecstatic-physical fantasy of woman through the transgressive Salome, *Skinny Legs and All* argues that progress comes not by way of patriarchy, religion, or the rational mind but by way of ecstatic sex and women's physical and spiritual liberation—adapting Wilde's *Salomé,* rather awkwardly, to 1990s popular psychology and New Ageism.

The 1998 movie *The Governess* by Jewish-American director, producer, and screenwriter Sandra Goldbacher also centrally references the Salome theme—specifically the Dance of the Seven Veils—to unfold a feminist sexual and individual coming-of-age story. Set in the Jewish ghetto in London at the end of the nineteenth century, *The Governess* revolves around Rosina/Mary (played by Minnie Driver), a young Jewish woman with an overwhelming desire for physical, emotional, and intellectual independence. To escape her impending, poverty-imposed marriage to an older Jewish man, Rosina poses as a Christian governess to find work. In the gentrified country household in which she finds employment, she quickly becomes her employer's helpmeet for his scientific experiments, but she does not receive credit for her crucial intellectual contributions; Cavendish is too conventional a man, even after the two have become lovers. In one crucial scene, Rosina acts out Salome's Dance of the Seven Veils to sexually entice him and later takes the liberty of photographing his naked, sleeping body, symbolically taking the control of the voyeuristic camera eye from him. As Rosina establishes herself as his mental equal, Cavendish's ego cannot tolerate her independence, and he rejects her emotionally. The crisis gives Rosina the strength to leave Cavendish, establish her own photo studio back in London, and finally reject him when he repents to claim back her love. Rosina's experience inhabiting the role of Salome thus ushers in her irrevocable sexual and spiritual growth; it is a rite of passage toward becoming a strong, liberated, professional woman. The traditional misogynistic implications of the tropes of Salome and the Jewish temptress are thus turned around in this version, in favor of a feminist transformation of an initially weak, objectified female character trapped by circumstances. The film's feminist impulse is relatively tame when compared to the much larger transgressive potential of Wilde's original Salomé, however.

As we have seen many times throughout the history of the theme, the cultural fantasy of Salomé's sexual excess can carry multiple, sometimes contradictory moral values and meanings. In Robert Altman's film *Cookie's Fortune,* we find yet another, differently layered employment of the Salome figure as an icon of excessive-aggressive female sexuality. Here Salome's sexual individualism is a threat for a small-town, Southern social community, which unites against the female transgressor, the film's Salome, Camille Dixon (played by Glenn Close, an actress well known for her chilling cinematic femme fatale roles; overtones of Close's previous performances provide additional reading foils for the Salome scenes in the film). As in *A Man of No Importance,* humorous rehearsal scenes of Wilde's *Salomé* are connected with the main narrative in *Cookie's Fortune* and take on more serious allegorical significance as the story progresses. Camille, a hypocritical small-town diva who produces the play at the local parish hall, reveals her Salome qualities as she is prepared to sacrifice "the head of Willis Witley," an old family friend, to achieve her secret goals. To conceal the shameful suicide of her Aunt Cookie (played by Patricia Neal) and to annex Cookie's fortune, Camille knowingly puts the innocent Willis in jail for Cookie's supposed murder, dishing him up for a possible death sentence. As the plot progresses, Camille takes on more Salome qualities when her own secret sexual transgressions and various ruthless power ploys finally come to light. Ironically, through a series of coincidences, Camille herself is finally put in jail and blamed for Cookie's pseudomurder. In a powerful scene in which Camille slips into madness in her lonely prison cell, Glenn Close forcefully reenacts her Salome-themed Broadway role as Norma Desmond in Andrew Lloyd Webber's musical version of the Billy Wilder film classic *Sunset Boulevard.* Reciting some of Wilde's Salomé's lines and enacting a mad version of the Dance of the Seven Veils in her prison cell, Camille/Close wraps herself with rolls of toilet paper and dances herself into a mad rage. The nexus of the actress's star profile, both fictional and real—the profile of Gloria Swanson/Norma Desmond in *Sunset Boulevard* and that of Glenn Close/Camille Dixon in *Cookie's Fortune*—perpetuates the tropological use of Wilde's Salomé as the dangerous sexual and aesthetic transgressor.

Salome's/Close's role is not portrayed as pro-feminist—on the contrary, it harkens back to typical traits of the nineteenth-century femme fatale. But by comparing the regressive feminist versions of Cave and Robbins with *Cookie's Fortune's* Salome, crucial similarities come into view. Her strength, evil, and madness are anchored in Salome's excessive sexuality, just as Cave and Robbins had envisioned it. The only difference is that this Salome actually functions as a *negative* foil of excessive femininity, against which a community can rally. The expulsion and de facto elimination of the female transgressor is the precondition for the movie's happy ending, which tackles larger issues of racism and family values and establishes a utopian, integrated community of the new South. The ritual punishment of the criminal misfit Camille brings the satisfaction of justice and a new and better order, as the community emerges purified and stronger from the cathartic experience of Willis's redemption after the true culprit, Camille/Salome, has been jailed. Camille/Salome's scapegoating in *Cookie's Fortune* continues the tradition, begun in the gospels and continued in Flaubert, of condemning female political power play as perverse and dangerous.

In contrast, one perhaps more promising feminist interpretation of—in this case, Strauss's—*Salome* has been renowned filmmaker Atom Egoyan's production for Toronto's Canadian Opera Company, first offered in 1996 and revived in 2002 with a new cast. The latest revival "was greeted with more critical acclaim and public scorn than Egoyan's original production" (Armatage and Clark 308). Egoyan worked with giant video projection screens and complex superimposed images, split screens, and other sophisticated film techniques to create *Salome* as a multilayered tale of innocence, brutality, and revenge. The accompanying video multimedia images and movies showed symbolic scenes of Salome's childhood and youth, such as close-ups on a laughing girl's face, a blindfolded child in the woods, and a naked female body wrapped in mud and touched by disembodied hands. These images developed a complex web of associations of purity, filth, menace, and fear that interacted symbolically with the action on the opera stage and functioned as an entirely new commentary and explanation of Salome's character development. In one climactic series of images coinciding with the dance, Salome's childish face looked on in horror from the screen as the dancing Salome was gang-raped by her stepfather, Herod, and his helpers behind a real backlit screen on the stage below (for a detailed scene analysis, see Armatage and Clark 317–25).

Atom Egoyan effectively reinvented Wilde's text and Strauss's music as a provocative "feminist drama about the trauma of incest" (Kaye, "Salome's Lost Childhood" 128). In Egoyan's view, Herod and John the Baptist both victimize Salome: Herod by raping and objectifying her; John by refusing to look at and address her, despite the fact that he is a prophet—he does not even attempt to save her soul. Salome effectively saved herself in Egoyan's production: by following her transgressive desires to the end, she actually achieved a state of apotheosis very much in consonance with the postreligious ecstasy of Wilde's ending and the other fin de siècle Salomé texts described in chapters 1 and 2. According to Kaye, "[a] principal sequence in the [original] Canadian Opera Company production [of 1996] depicted the princess arising out of mud into clear, luminous water," so that the ending offered an unmistakable endorsement of Salome's transgression as a self-saving, cleansing, liberating act: "in Egoyan's hands, the opera speaks of Salome's liberation from the cesspool of an incest-racked household into the purifying sublimity of full consciousness" (129). This kind of psychological feminist interpretation—where Salome evolves from physical slavery and victimization to spiritual (if not rational) self-consciousness and full selfhood by literally slaying the psychological dragons that kept her down—reverses the terms of the regressive feminist equation in texts like *Skinny Legs and All* and Nick Cave's *Salome*. It also relegated the victim's role to Salome for most of the opera, hence toning down and revaluing the tempestuous transgressive force Wilde first gave her.

Similarly, another contemporary straight feminist-inflected interpretation of *Salomé*, Carlos Saura's stunningly beautiful flamenco film *Salome* (2002)—featuring Spanish flamenco icon Aida Gómez, Pere Arquillué, and an extensive dance ensemble cast—channels Salome's strong will, aggressive strength, and anger into a cathartic, ultimately harmonious ending. The film offers a rather faithful dance version of Wilde's *Salomé* but really emphasizes Salome's love for John the Baptist and the struggle between his sensuality and his spirituality. As Saura states in the documentary about the making of the film that accompanies the film's DVD version, the final scene suggested to him the tragic *Liebestod* of a Romeo and Juliet. Saura accordingly choreographed the final scenes of Wilde's play as a decadent love dance and wooing between Salome and John the Baptist's head. (The male dancer is ingeniously clad all in black, with a silver tray fastened on his shoulders and around his neck, so that it looks like his head is floating and swirling around Salome, as the two dancers reprise an earlier scene in which John the Baptist had almost given in to Salome's loving, gentle wooing before remembering his spiritual vows and turning away from her.) Saura's interpretation ends with Salome's dead body wrapped in a white shroud (symbolizing innocence and death) and peacefully united with Jokanaan's, as the soldiers deposit her on top of him and let the couple rest together for eternity. Again, Salomé's transgression and Wilde's shock ending are toned down in favor of a more familiar and comfortable interpretation of star-crossed lovers finally united.

This chapter has traced two dominant types of interpretations of *Salomé* in the twentieth century, male homoeroticism and organic-orgiastic female sexuality. While the need continues for separate scholarly inquiries into their respective genealogies and contexts in LGBTQ studies, queer theory, and feminist criticism,[18] they also share some cultural strategies, coalitions, and cultural contingencies that are worth comparing. They explain the sometimes astonishing, cross-pollinating cultural efficacy and naturalization of male and female images of transgression, such as the dandy and the New Woman or Wilde and Salomé.[19]

The supposedly progressive but ultimately problematic interpretations of Wilde's *Salomé* discussed in this chapter show the flip side of the modernist fantasy of transgression, as they paradoxically rely on and enact the very attitudes that undergird homophobia and antifeminism. Despite their well-meaning antihomophobic or pro-feminist impulses, these texts (empathetic narratives of sexual and social victimization and courageous individual overcoming) contain dangerous blind spots. They are essentially humanist projects arguing for inclusivity and tolerance, but they do so through problematic gestures of accommodation and normalization. Not only do they downsize and downplay the original transgressive force of Wilde's *Salomé,* but they ultimately fail their own antihomophobic and feminist projects, by proliferating some of the very oppressive structures they are ostensibly directed against.

Conclusion

Looking back at the adaptations and transformations discussed in the course of *Salome's Modernity,* one cannot help but notice their great formal range and ideological variety. Wilde and *Salomé* graduated from censored, perverse tempters of the innocent Victorians in the 1890s, to darlings of the European theatrical and operatic avant-garde in the 1900s (with Lugné-Poë, Reinhardt, and Strauss), to vehicles for fledgling feminist artistic innovation in modern female solo dance and the modernist art film in the 1920s (with Maud Allan and Alla Nazimova), to celebrated political icons for the gay rights struggle and certain forms of feminism. This astonishing rhetorical malleability of Wilde and Salomé in response to changing historical, cultural, moral, and political conditions and even to diametrically opposed cultural and social ends proves that the two tropes are floating, essentially empty signifiers that can take on different meanings in different contexts. It also shows the great attraction these icons have held for artists and other cultural agents, an attraction that continues on into our own day. It is both fitting and ironic that Wilde's *Salomé,* a text that derived some of its most important ideas from previous literary and artistic versions of the theme and employed them in new and fascinating ways to express the exhilarating and threatening spirit of modernity, has itself been adapted and radically transformed so many times.

Modern interpretations and investments in the Wildean *Salomé* may have differed widely with cultural context and circumstance over the last century, but throughout the trajectory that I have traced from symbolist poet Stéphane Mallarmé to Canadian filmmaker Atom Egoyan, several important constants have emerged. The red threads running through all of these versions are aesthetic and erotic transgression, as well as utopian modern individualism. *Salomé* first emerged from Wilde's immersion in Mallarmé, Flaubert, and Huysmans as a bridge text between symbolism, decadence, and modernism. While picking up crucial building blocks from his fin de siècle predecessors, Wilde also developed and unfolded a new, intrinsically modernist vision of aesthetic and erotic transgression and agency that radically reinterprets the old legend and, once and for all, switches its focus from religious dogma to secular, triumphant anthropocentrism. *Salomé* illustrates Wilde's anticipation of central modernist themes, such as the crisis of literary and linguistic agency, the rise of utopian modern individualism, and rebellion against established religious, aesthetic, moral, and social codes in response to the crucial literary, cultural, and religious crises of modernity.

Through its crucial changes to the literary and artistic theme of Salome, especially the final scene but also via the symbolist synesthetic style, Wilde's *Salomé* put an irreversibly secular emphasis on *physical* sensation and pleasure. As I have argued, the play develops a notion of secular sublimity that replaced existing metaphysical and moral discourses with an emphasis on physical, amoral, secular, utopian erotic and aesthetic agency through individual transgression. Especially in *Salomé's* outrageous finale, the sensual experience of the body's excess fills and overrides the emptiness of the soul, creating the illusion of ecstatic agency and freedom in the moment of transgression. *Salomé* puts forward a powerful and shocking vision of secular sublimity that replaces the search for the uplifted soul with the quest for the ecstatically fulfilled body.

These are the dramatic qualities Richard Strauss first recognized and creatively adapted in his operatic *Salome,* the first modernist music drama. Symbolist and decadent aesthetics emphasized corporal affect, synesthesia, sensation, and shock, and Strauss effectively translated Wilde's textual features into explosive modernist music that similarly stimulated, electrified, and intrigued audiences in the theater. In addition, Wilde and Strauss were not only conceptual modernists but also modern artist-marketeers, deliberately fusing provocative avant-garde innovation with strong appeals to popular taste. They employed styles and techniques meant to titillate, dazzle, and sell to a mainstream public, while also innovating the theatrical or operatic stage. Thus Wilde and Strauss proffered serious, experimental aesthetic ideas while still entertaining a crowd. Inevitably, in this decade after Wilde's scandalous 1895 trials, audiences also associated the operatic *Salome's* stylistic and thematic transgressions with sexual perversity and immorality, as the contemporary German and Austrian opera reviews that I have analyzed illustrate. This conflation between the work and the sexual proclivities and scandals of its author influenced or dominated not only the early reception of Strauss's opera but virtually all subsequent adaptations and appropriations analyzed in *Salome's Modernity.*

In the work of Maud Allan and Alla Nazimova, we encounter the first protofeminist and gender-transgressive versions of Wilde's *Salomé.* As the first female artist to adopt and adapt Wilde's Salomé with her own creative vision, Maud Allan was a sexual and aesthetic transgressor in her own right. Taking on the controversial role of Salomé, she bared large parts of her body at a time when such provocative exhibition of the female body on a public stage, even in the name of art, was seen as unladylike. As Salomé, she also inhabited a dangerously assertive and forceful femininity that could be and was easily associated with the suffragettes. Although she was no political rebel, others identified Allan as a feminist and as an artist whose *Vision of Salomé* encouraged ladies and ordinary women to break codes of modesty in clothes and behavior at a time when the suffragettes were marching in the streets. The Pemberton-Billing Trial demonstrates that on the back of Wilde, *Salomé,* and the unfortunate Maud Allan, a complex nexus of dominant attitudes, assumptions, and fears played itself out, illustrating the embattled relationships between sexuality, aesthetics, and ethics in early twentieth-century British culture and society. The trial catered to a hysterical national ideology demanding that art be brought back in line at a time of extreme national and political crisis. Allan's example shows that the perceived connection between challenging new art, nonconformist gender behavior, and suspected "perverse" sexuality provoked a strong impulse or need for cultural and legal censorship in the name of the state. Despite her tragic fall after a spectacular rise as an professional female artist, Allan's significant contribution to the history of modern dance and her equally significant contribution as a courageous woman who inspired other women to follow in her footsteps and realize their artistic ambitions remain her lasting legacy.

Alla Nazimova's pioneering filmic *Salome* also shows the personal and professional potential that some female modernists recognized in Wilde's aesthetics of transgression, as a platform for developing their own artistic and personal vision. As I highlight, it is important to realize that Nazimova came to the movies from strong, modern female lead roles in theater and modern drama, specifically Ibsen, when she decided to bring the art film to Hollywood via *Salomé.* Like Allan, she was interested in Salomé as a role that allowed her to pursue popular avant-gardist goals, feeding on and promoting her profile as a popular female star and fashion icon, while at the same time aligning herself with more avant-garde subject matter and transgressive gender roles. Both Allan and Nazimova walked a thin line between serious artistic aspiration, on the one hand, and a precarious association with Oscar Wilde's well-known sexual scandal, on the other, an association that both served and threatened their positions as independent female artists identified with artistic and sexual provocation. Excelling in their art meant exceeding common social and cultural standards of women's modesty in their lives, and both artists suffered serious consequences because of their own (real or perceived) transgressions: Allan's career was destroyed by the Pemberton-Billing Trial, and the box office flop of Nazimova's unusual art film ruined her financially and ended her brief artistic independence. In hindsight, Nazimova's movie stands out as the first daringly direct adaptation that incorporated and highlighted Wilde's and *Salomé's* homoeroticism. As such, it has remained influential for film and stage directors since (e.g., Ken Russell and Lindsey Kemp) who have creatively interpreted *Salomé* as Wilde's most intimate closet drama; for similar reasons, it is also still popular at gay film festivals today.

The past three decades have shown a broad and contradictory range of adaptations of Wilde's *Salomé,* most of which have directly grappled with Wilde's modernity, that is, the question of what his fate and his work, especially *Salomé,* may say to us today. In the final chapter of this book, I examined the ongoing impact of Wilde's sexual-aesthetic figurations on contemporary Western culture, where they remain culturally and politically active. Wilde and Salomé have remained powerful points of cultural and emotional identification because of the ways they ideally embody and symbolize still ongoing struggles in Western culture that pit the individual against a larger culture, from projects of liberation, such as feminism and LGBTQ civil rights, to individual sexual freedom, artistic agency, and legal or cultural censorship. Wilde's and *Salomé's* history has been one of struggle and tragedy, but it has also been one of historical triumph and inspiration.

Despite the respectability of the personal and social investment in Wilde and Salomé to which many of these versions testify, I identify two dominant trends within late twentieth-century representations of *Salomé,* which I provocatively call "homosexual humanism" and "regressive feminism" to set them apart from what I perceive as more efficacious and less fraught approaches to antihomophobic and feminist cultural criticism. Neither does justice to the complexity or enigma of the historical Wilde or *Salomé,* since they anachronistically enlist the author and the text in a project of their own as if it had always been theirs alone. More important, in my view, both of these trends, progressive and politically helpful as they may seem, paradoxically undermine the very antihomophobic and feminist projects they aim to support. In the large and vibrant area of innovative queer cultural production inspired by Wilde and *Salomé,* the shortcomings of such texts as *Salome's Last Dance* and *A Man of No Importance* become particularly clear when one compares them with those that I have marked as more truly innovative and interesting, such as Todd Haynes's *Velvet Goldmine,* Doric Wilson's *Now She Dances!* or Dorian Katz's *Kiss.* Stressing the inevitable artificiality, historical value, and emotional investment of genealogical queer readings through such symbolic ancestral figures as Wilde and Salomé, artists such as Haynes, Wilson, and Katz creatively lead the way toward new forms of queer representation that manage to avoid the political and social pitfalls of homosexual humanism.

As far as straight feminist readings of *Salomé* are concerned, I believe we have yet to see a convincing contemporary one that does not reduce Salomé to pure physicality. As we have seen, feminist-inflected texts since the 1980s now celebrate, instead of condemn, her aggressive, instinct-driven, excessive, orgiastic sexuality (Cave and Robbins), present her as the victim of sexual violence (Egoyan) or madness (Altman), or read her sentimentally through the romantic lens of star-crossed love (Saura). Perhaps, a progressive straight feminist reading of Salomé that goes beyond Wilde's play and adapts Salomé to our own times is actually impossible in light of the heavy misogynist cultural burden the Salome figure has carried for almost two thousand years. It remains to be seen what kind of a *Salomé* Al Pacino's much anticipated, forthcoming documentary *Salomaybe* will introduce.

The fact that we continue, at the beginning of this century, to be fascinated by Wilde and Salomé proves the ongoing cultural centrality of the aesthetics of transgression and the legacy of modernism in the twentieth and twenty-first centuries. The cultural associations between aesthetic and erotic transgression, between innovative art and representations of sexuality as a utopian source of self-transformation and self-transcendence, remain powerfully pervasive and persuasive elements even today. If there is one overarching historical lesson I have attempted to convey, it is that contemporary representations of gender and sexuality are still implicated in historical structures of modernist aesthetics and humanistic thinking and bring with them many inherited burdens, chances, and challenges.

My own approach to the topic and trajectory of *Salome's Modernity* has been motivated by my belief that genealogical, textual-contextual analyses of such representational stereotypes and structures can best enable a historically and politically informed critique of some of their most palpable effects on real people in the real world. Christopher Castiglia argues that the project of the present and the future is "to think critically about which stories [of queer histories, identity formations, and social and cultural alliances] are credited with access to the truth, to the social 'real'" (175). Gay studies, queer theory, and feminist criticism together have done crucial work to identify the complex gender politics and cultural, social, and political implications associated with representations of gay men, on the one hand, and women, on the other. In studying and teaching how such images as Wilde and Salomé have worked in the past and continued with variations over time, we may help deflate the still astonishing cultural efficacy, naturalization, and perpetuation of feigned innocence of such representations. By identifying and laying bare the strategies, goals, and functions of their modernist structures, I believe we gain access to one of the vast and, as of yet, still dimly lit basements of modernity: the powerful machinery of cultural images that continue to tell very limited stories of who and what "we" or "they" are, were, or may "mean," in the past, present, and future.

Notes

INTRODUCTION

1. Most recently, Robert Scholes, Paul Fortunato, and Ronald Bush have stressed Wilde's importance for modernist aesthetics.

2. To name just a few examples, Heather Marcovitch claims that *Salomé* extends Wilde's problematization of aestheticism that Wilde began in *The Picture of Dorian Gray;* Helen Tookey emphasizes the play's championing of the decadent femme fatale and her dangerous gaze, while Sarah Maier and Amanda Fernbach offer psychoanalytic approaches stressing the ambiguous fetishization of Salomé in symbolist and decadent literature. Charles Bernheimer, too, places *Salomé* firmly within decadent fin de siècle literature without commenting on its modernist elements. Previous scholarly studies also emphasized *Salomé's* alleged plagiarism or literary and cultural sampling, a critical tradition that had its first influential proponent in Mario Praz's *The Romantic Agony.* Norbert Kohl, by contrast, defends Wilde's grafting method as a serious artistic enterprise, arguing that it showed a high degree of sophistication and creativity.

3. According to Wilde's biographer Richard Ellmann, Wilde knew well the intriguing visual iconography of Salome from the Renaissance to his own present, which—except for Moreau's depictions—left him dissatisfied (*Oscar Wilde* 342–43).

4. The European fin de siècle literary and artistic movements called "symbolism" and "decadence" are notoriously difficult to delineate, since they share numerous literary and philosophical concerns with each other as well as with British aestheticism, as exemplified by Walter Pater, Wilde, and Arthur Symons. Rather than use *aestheticism* as an umbrella term to describe the style of Wilde's *Salomé,* which includes elements specific to symbolism and decadence, I employ *symbolism* to refer to the play's linguistic-poetic style and *decadence* to refer to particular content and themes. Symbolism emphasized synesthesia and evocation and participated in the reaction against the crisis of representation by stressing immaterial worlds over realistic description. Where I speak of *Salomé's decadent* content and themes, I mean to indicate the work's alignment with fin de siècle literature and art that thrive on a sense of cultural and

moral decay as well as with the post-Romantic indulgence in sensory stimulation, on the one hand, and deadening ennui, on the other, as celebrated in Joris-Karl Huysmans's *À rebours* (1884) and scathingly derided in Max Nordau's *Degeneration* (1892).

5. Ian Small, Melissa Knox, and Bruce Bashford give excellent overviews of recent Wilde scholarship trends.

6. The two principal etymological connotations of transgression, according to the *Oxford English Dictionary,* are "1. a. The action of transgressing or passing beyond the bounds of legality or right; a violation of law, duty, or command; disobedience, trespass, sin" and "1. b. The action of passing over or beyond. (Only as the etymological sense of the word)." See *Oxford English Dictionary Online,* s.v. "Transgression," http://dictionary.oed.com/ (accessed October 23, 2009).

7. Philosophical approaches to *Salomé* hold great promise, notes Philip Smith (163–64).

CHAPTER 1

1. Already in Flavius Josephus, the story of John the Baptist's beheading was presented as a political power struggle between John and Herod, although it did not involve Herodias. Josephus claimed that Herod was fearful of the Baptist's power to incite to rebellion the people of Galilee, a known seat of Jewish resistance to Rome. Neither Jew nor Roman, Herod found himself in a precarious position. John's open condemnation of Herod's unlawful marriage further endangered his grip on power. Herod had eloped with Herodias while she was still married to his brother Philippus. Mosaic law regards sexual contact with a brother's wife as incestuous (Leviticus 20:21, 18:16).

2. According to Anthony Pym, the number of treatments of the Salome theme in literature and the arts increased sharply between the middle of the nineteenth century and the 1880s–1890s.

3. Julie Townsend makes the same point in "Staking Salomé" (156–57).

4. Hugo Daffner, Helen Grace Zagona, Patricia R. Kellogg, Bram Dijkstra, Françoise Meltzer, and Linda Saladin provide useful analytical overviews of Wilde's major nineteenth-century predecessors. I am indebted to them in this chapter, even as I point to some of their shortcomings.

5. Three fragments of "Hérodiade" survive, of which only "Scène: La Nourrice—Hérodiade" was published during Mallarmé's lifetime, first in 1869 in the *Parnasse Contemporain* (1869), in edited form in *Le Scapin* (1886), and then again in the 1887 edition of Mallarmé's *Poésies.* Other fragments of the work were published postmortem: initially, "Cantique de Saint Jean" appeared in the 1913 revised and expanded edition of the *Poésies,* and the introductory monologue "Ouverture: La Nourrice (Incantation)" was published in *Nouvelle Revue Francaise* (1926). For an overview of the publishing history, see Szondi 36–40. Gardner Davies edited and published a few more surviving fragments, together with Mallarmé's notes and a chronology of the fragments.

6. Frank Kermode's *Romantic Image* analyzes Mallarmé's as well as Yeats's and Symons's reliance on the dancer as a central poetic metaphor and places the symbolist quest for perfect poiesis via dance in the context of Romanticism, a conclusion I

disagree with since it obscures these authors' modernist elements. For an excellent discussion of Mallarmé's dance metaphor, see Townsend's "Synaesthetics."

7. Mallarmé is notoriously difficult to translate, and translations vary widely; I quote from the French original and employ translations by Weinfield and Mills where appropriate.

8. "I wish my hair—which is no flower breathing / oblivion to human pains, but gold, / forever virgin of the aromatics—/ to keep in its cruel highlights and dull pallors / the sterile chill of metal, having reflected / from walls about my birth, jewels, bases / and armor, through my solitary childhood" (*Herodias,* trans. Clark Mills, 11, 13).

9. "I love the horror of virginity, / The dread my tresses give me when I lie / Retired at night, reptilian on my couch, / My useless flesh inviolate to the touch . . ." (trans. Weinfield, 34).

10. The published fragments of the story include the "Cantique de Saint Jean," the mystical lament of the severed head of Saint John the Baptist, but not Hérodiade's encounters, a dance, or the Baptist's beheading.

11. "O mirror! / Cold pool, frozen with ennui in the frame, / how often, for what hours, with dreams desolate / and seeking far under the lucid surface / like leaves below the ice, my recollections, in you I saw myself a distant shadow—/ but the nights, oh, when in your strict fount / I learned the nakedness of my poor dream!" (trans. Mills, 13).

12. See Paul de Man's unpublished dissertation, "Mallarmé, Yeats, and the Post-Romantic Predicament," and his "Impersonality in the Criticism of Maurice Blanchot" in *Blindness and Insight* (70).

13. Mallarmé repeatedly put "Hérodiade" off and took it up again, never considering it complete. In fact, even as he was holding court in Paris and experimenting with his new poetic aesthetics in such works as "Prose pour des Esseintes" (1884, a response to Huysmans' *À rebours*) and *Un coup de dés* (1897), Mallarmé remained obsessed with "Hérodiade." Constantly revising and perfecting the fragments, "Mallarmé conceived a text and an aesthetic [with them]. It is in relation to this first major work that the poet, in his *Correspondance,* discusses theory, evaluates progress or lack of it" (Wolf 1).

14. In English nineteenth-century visual culture, the type is observable in Pre-Raphaelite paintings. Maurice Maeterlinck, Hugo von Hofmannsthal, Rainer Maria Rilke, Heinrich Heine, Gerhart Hauptmann, and Peter Altenberg developed the literary type; Thomas Mann ironized the *femme fragile* cult in *Tristan* in 1903 (see Emonds 165–66). Ariane Thomalla writes that the *femme fragile* often symbolized a dying aristocratic family via pathological and morbid imagery; characteristic features are virginity or asexuality, symbolized by the colors white and silver, and ethereal delicacy.

15. In an earlier scene, Salammbô directly invokes this ambivalent aspect of Tanit as a fertilizer and destroyer: "all seeds, O Goddess, ferment in the dark depths of your moistness. When you appear, stillness sweeps over the earth, flowers close, the waves die down, and the world with its oceans and mountains sees itself in your face, as though in a mirror. You are white, gentle, luminous, immaculate, helping, purifying, serene! . . . But you are a terrible mistress! . . . It is through you that monsters are produced, fearsome specters, lying dreams" (52–53).

16. Flaubert may have taken a few hints from Mallarmé in his representation of

Salammbô as an isolated, tragic figure pining for change. Some scenes and language seem to follow "Hérodiade" closely (see especially "The Serpent" and "Ouverture"). For example, Flaubert describes Salammbô getting dressed assisted by her slave Taanach, and she also lives in a tower.

17. Wilde adopted the prophet's Hebraized name from Flaubert and slightly changed its spelling.

18. Flaubert takes care to point this out in his very first introduction of Salomé: "Under a bluish veil which concealed her head and breasts, one could just make out the arch of her eyes, the chalcedonies in her ears, and the whiteness of her skin. . . . Going up on to the dais, she removed her veil. It was Herodias as she used to be in her youth" (*Three Tales* 120).

19. In nineteenth-century medical, social, and political discourse, hysteria was commonly imagined as a mental disease in women, resulting from an excessive physical function of the uterus, which was supposed to produce undue assertiveness and "hysterical" behavior in women. (This pseudoscientific argument was often unfairly levied against the suffragettes.) Hysteria as well as syphilis was also often used as metaphor for imagined general spiritual and cultural decay; the decadents revalued them positively. For a feminist study of hysteria's cultural history, see Elaine Showalter's *Hystories*.

20. The popular fin de siècle association of the Jewish princess Salome with hysteria had anti-Semitic implications. According to Sander Gilman, pathological interpretations of the Salome figure impacted fin de siècle notions of Jewish character: non-Jewish authors often construed Salome as the embodiment of essential femininity and a sexual other, specifically conflating sexuality and race to represent the essential Jew ("Salome, Syphilis, Sarah Bernhardt" 197). On Salome and historical Jewish stigmatization, see Kuryluk 190–91.

21. Jean-Marie Charcot's and the Freudians' reinterpretations of the mystics' (especially Saint Teresa's) religious raptures as clinical examples of hysteria became popular scientific lore around this time (see Hanson 110–11).

22. This is illustrated by Des Esseintes's unabashed use of religious paraphernalia as decorations for Fontenay. For example, his window curtains have been "cut out of old ecclesiastical stoles," and two ancient and sacred "Byzantine monstrances of gilded copper which had originally come from the Abbaye-au-Bois at Bièvre" frame Des Esseintes's secular literary treasures (31). Similarly, Des Esseintes's love of obscure medieval Christian authors writing in Latin speaks of his superficial appreciation of their sensual aesthetic style and his disregard for the actual subjects of their religious poetry.

23. In chapter 2, the narrator describes the new locomotives on the Northern Railway by comparing one of the locomotives to "a smart golden blonde whose extraordinary grace can be quite terrifying when she stiffens her muscles of steel, sends the sweat pouring down her steaming flanks" and to "a strapping saturnine brunette given to uttering raucous, guttural cries" (37).

24. In Heine's poem, the mad Herodias kisses and caresses the Baptist's head, while laughingly tossing it up in the air like a child's plaything: "Rising nightly from the dead, she carries / the bloody head . . . / In her hand, on her wild chase— / But with female unpredictability // She tosses the head from time to time / Up in the air, laughing like a child, / And catches it again very adroitly / like a plaything" (caput XIX, lines 109–16, my translation). Jules Laforgue parodies Salomé even more ex-

tremely, as a bizarre, verbose scientist wearing jonquil chiffon dresses with black polka dots.

25. See Moog-Grünewald; Showalter, *Sexual Anarchy*; Dijkstra; and Menon. The association of femininity with *fatum* is also evident in prominent contemporary operas, such as Charles-Camille Saint-Saëns's *Samson et Dalila* (1877), Jules Massenet's *Hérodiade* (1881), and Georges Bizet's *Carmen* (1875).

26. André Gide, George Bernard Shaw, and Thomas Mann all commented on Wilde's affinity with Nietzsche (Julia Prewitt Brown xiii, 113n1).

27. In his translation of Nietzsche's *The Gay Science*, Walter Kaufmann translates *Übermensch* as *overman*, overriding the misleading earlier translation *superman* (by George Bernard Shaw and others). I think a better translation yet might be *beyondman*, which captures Nietzsche's idea of the figure's radical difference from ordinary humanity and adherence to an entirely different mode and concept of being. I quote Nietzsche's original word to preserve all of its German connotations.

28. For an interesting reading of *Madame Edwarda*'s religious aspects against Bataille's Hegelian-Kojèvian background, see Stoekl.

29. Throughout this essay, Foucault speaks of sexuality's limit in terms of an abstract linguistic and cultural figuration, not in any strict biological sense, even though Foucault personally experimented with sadomasochistic limit experiences.

CHAPTER 2

1. All unacknowledged translations in this chapter are my own.

2. Paul L. Fortunato does not discuss *Salomé* within the framework of Wilde's modernist aesthetics, although he states in a note that the play is indeed "in line with [Wilde's] consumer modernism" (150n2).

3. For Strauss's comments on his inspiration, see *Richard Strauss: Recollections and Reflections* (henceforth cited as *RR*) 150–51.

4. This is especially true of biographical readings of Salomé as Wilde's transvestite alter ego and as a mask for his closeted homoeroticism or of Wilde's play as a whole as an expression of dandyism and an experiment with social and literary masks. See Garber; Showalter, *Sexual Anarchy*; Finney; Donohue, "*Salome* and the Wildean Art of Symbolist Theatre."

5. The *Oxford English Dictionary*'s entry on *excess* lists "[an instance of] overstepping the limits of moderation" and "exuberance" among its synonyms. See *Oxford English Dictionary Online*, http://dictionary.oed.com (accessed October 23, 2010).

6. Remembering Wilde's visits at Ricketts's and Charles Shannon's Chelsea home in the early 1890s, C. J. Holmes corroborates this account, adding a few details. Wilde and Ricketts discussed extensive color schemes, presumably for their symbolic function within the play: "Wilde also stressed the absurdity of [Salome's promise] 'And I will give you a flower, Narraboth, a little *green* flower,' until Ricketts upset his complacency by saying that some flowers really were green. Then he talked of the appropriate stage-setting, rich, dim backgrounds with the Jews all in yellow, Iokanaan in white, Herod in deep blood-red, and Salome herself in pale green like a snake. . . . [Ricketts] certainly understood Wilde's intentions far better than Beardsley" (quoted in Wilde, *Oscar Wilde: Interviews and Recollections* 201).

7. Reinhardt's wildly popular production was attended by many notable progressive artists of the time, including the British avant-garde theater director J. T. Grein and the dancer Maud Allan (discussed in chapter 3). It launched an extraordinary *Salomé* vogue in Germany and Austria. During the 1903–4 theater season, 248 performances of the play took place in Germany alone, including 111 performances of Reinhardt's production. It helped reestablish Wilde's reputation as a progressive, brave avant-gardist who had been unjustly banned and prosecuted by British philistines. Despite *Salomé*'s British ban and Wilde's incarceration, the German public was extraordinarily receptive to his play.

8. This performance took place at the Deutsches Volkstheater on May 15, 1907. Because it was put on by an out-of-town company, the Vereinigte Theater in Breslau, at the popular Volkstheater rather than at the more official Wiener Hofoper (renamed *Wiener Staatsoper* in 1920) and had only a limited run, the censor's ban (which had led Mahler to resign as conductor in protest) could be circumvented. The Hofoper did not schedule *Salome* until 1918.

9. In his two earlier, unsuccessful operas *Guntram* and *Feuersnot,* Strauss had mimicked Wagner. *Salome* marked a spectacular turn of this relationship.

10. Strauss's application of the leitmotif technique differs from Wagner's in its progressivity: the motifs develop out of an initial statement, then change instrumental or thematic associations (see Puffett, *Richard Strauss: Salome* [henceforth cited as *RSS*] 75, 86–87).

11. To Adorno, Strauss's attitude also signified a certain admirable honesty about his work.

12. Herbert Lindenberger, e-mail to Petra Dierkes-Thrun, October 25, 2009.

13. Lindenberger himself examined Strauss's handwriting in Craft's original Salome score, looked through her costume closet, and wrote an unpublished, humorous opera play, "Miss Cramm," inspired by *Salome* and Craft, shortly after her death in 1960.

14. For Strauss's view of the affinities between Salome and Elektra, see *RR* 154.

15. Arthur Symons described Sarah Bernhardt's sensational impact on London audiences despite the fact that Bernhardt performed in French: "There was an excitement in going to the theatre; one's pulses beat feverishly before the curtain had risen; there was almost a kind of obscure sensation of peril, such as one feels when the lioness leaps into the cage, on the other side of the bars. And the acting was like a passionate declaration, offered to someone unknown; it was as if the whole nervous force of the audience were sucked out of it and flung back, intensified, upon itself, as if it encountered a single, insatiable, indomitable nervous force of the woman" (*Plays, Acting, and Music* 27–28).

16. The pamphlet held by the Clark Library is undated, but the date 1911 appears on the first page, in the dedication "Zu Barbara 1911."

17. Tydeman and Price give a good overview of the opera's censorship in Europe and the United States (125–29). There is some evidence that Strauss anticipated censorship and tried to circumvent it. He cut a line referring to Salomé's loss of virginity ("I was a virgin, and thou didst take my virginity from me" [*CCW* 605]) and an allusion to Herod's incestuous desire ("It is strange that the husband of my mother looks at me like that. I know not what it means. In truth, yes I know it" [*CCW* 586]). Strauss also altered the homoerotic subtext of the play by insisting that "the Page must be [sung by] a woman, not a tenor" (Strauss to Erich Engel, 1930, quoted in Wilhelm

102), thereby heterosexualizing the Page of Herodias's attraction for Narraboth. Perhaps Strauss knew of Lugné-Poë's similar decision, in the 1896 world premiere, to cast a female as the Page of Herodias.

18. Amy Koritz writes that the provocatively aggressive nature of Salome's advances and desires actually assumed dangerous political overtones in the London context. Just a few weeks earlier, on November 18, 1910, militant suffragettes had marched on the House of Commons. Against this background, the London *Times* critic's assertion that Salome's "hysterical confessions of fleshly desire" were "abnormal" and the *Spectator's* outraged criticism of Strauss's "glorification of [Salome's] erotomania" rung not only with the memory of Wilde's supposed perversity but also with cultural anxieties about reigning gender roles (Koritz, "Salomé: Exotic Woman" 259).

19. David Weir convincingly makes this point for the study of decadence in the preface and first chapter of *Decadence and the Making of Modernism;* see also Constable, Denisoff, and Potolsky. Matei Calinescu's seminal *Five Faces of Modernity: Modernism, Avant-garde, Decadence, Kitsch, Postmodernism* usefully bridges the temporal gap between decadence and modernism by including both on a spectrum of modern "faces" or aspects of modernity.

CHAPTER 3

1. In a 1908 *New York Times* interview, Isadora Duncan stated that she met Maud Allan, then an aspiring dancer, in Berlin and gave her tickets to her performance so Allan could study Duncan's technique. Duncan noted, "Some weeks afterward [Allan] gave imitations of some of my dances and announced herself as my pupil. Now in London she tells an interviewer that she has never heard of me before" (quoted in Kurth 228).

2. Since Rémy's score is no longer available today, it is unclear whether it was an entirely original piece written for *The Vision of Salomé,* as Maud Allan's biographer Felix Cherniavsky suggests (*Salome Dancer* 122), or if it was simply a reworking of Strauss's Dance of the Seven Veils, as Caddy writes (54).

3. Cherniavsky mentions a German cartoon entitled "Salome auf Reisen" that depicts "the figure of a scantily clad Maud Allan" standing right beside "a buxom operatic Salome," illustrating contemporary audiences' associations of Allan with Strauss's opera ("Maud Allan, Part III" 147).

4. Fuller excerpted some of her 1895 Salome dance pantomime in sensational appearances at the World's Fair in Paris in 1900 and later reprised the theme in a much revised and full-length evening program entitled *La Tragédie de Salomé* (1907, with a score by Florent Schmitt). For descriptions, see Bizot 72–73; Townsend, "Staking Salomé" 172–75; Garelick, *Electric Salome* 93–99.

5. Allan had briefly joined Fuller's dance troupe before striking out on her own, and it is even possible that Fuller directly assisted her in preparing *The Vision of Salomé* for London in 1908.

6. Allan also used this line of argument to explain her particular affinity for the role of the dancer Salomé: Salomé was probably "just as untaught" as Allan and "must frequently have stopped to look at the very self-same old Assyrian tablets" to find inspiration (Blathwayt 296).

7. Oscar Wilde possibly came in contact with the Delsarte school during his American lecture tour in 1882 (see Meyer).

8. Raymond Mander and Joe Mitchenson provide this history: "The Palace, Theatre of Varieties, Cambridge Circus, ... [was] built as the Royal English Opera House and opened in 1891. It changed its name and became a music hall the following year, first under Augustus Harris and then Charles Morton. On his death in 1904, it passed to Alfred Butt, who made it into one of the most famous variety houses in London. It ceased to be a music hall in 1914 with the revue craze and has remained a successful musical house ever since" (71, plate 73). Just four years after the king had endorsed Allan, in July 1912, the Crown ordered a Royal Command Performance of a complete music hall variety show, staged at the Palace Theatre. Mander and Mitchenson argue, "This performance . . . was an official recognition of the place of the music hall and variety stage in the entertainment world. Strangely enough, in retrospect this was the zenith of the halls and the decline appears to have set in from this moment." Interestingly enough, though, none of the famous Salome performers was part of this program, as a look at the program bill (plate 231) shows—probably reflecting the fact that the heyday of the "Salome craze" in London was over by 1912. Another variety Royal Command Performance followed at the London Coliseum in 1919; it was ordered by King George V "to show his appreciation of the generous manner in which the artistes of the variety stage have helped the numerous funds connected with the War." The year 1921 saw the inauguration of a series of Royal Variety Performances (plate 230).

9. Hoare speculates that Douglas knew of Theo's crime because Douglas's younger brother Sholto had been in California at the time of Theo's trial, and newspaper reports of Sholto's amorous exploits with an eighteen-year-old actress were published side by side with the news about Theo Durrant (78n).

10. Musicologist Larry Hamberlin's article is the exception, but he only studies a few selections from the extensive Salome-themed music hall sheet music. The British Library's collection of such songs is extensive and deserves further study.

11. Allan modeled repeatedly for Franz von Stuck (see Cherniavsky, *Maud Allan and Her Art* 41).

12. The phenomenon exceeds my purpose in this chapter, but Richard Bizot, Davinia Caddy, Alexandra Carter, David Krasner, Mary Simonson, Susan Glenn, Elizabeth Kendall, and Toni Bentley have provided excellent overviews of the Salome dance craze in Europe and the United States.

13. St. Denis had actually been asked by Max Reinhardt to perform in his 1907/8 season's revival of Salome, but the project fell apart because of St. Denis's excessive meddling and opposition to Wilde's original story line (see Tydeman and Price 139–40). St. Denis did not revisit the role of Salomé until 1931.

14. The Mud March was organized by the English suffragettes under the direction of Edith Pechey-Phipson (1845–1908), a leading chemist and one of the first female doctors and activists for women's health reform.

15. Allan lived in the west wing from 1910 through the early 1930s, and "[w]hen Allan was on tour in the USA in 1910, the newspapers reported that her friendship with Margot Asquith was greatly straining the marriage" (Bland 185).

16. Kendall writes that the bodies and costumes of "classical" dancers like Allan or Duncan "had a special appeal for women—because of their very [physical] unre-

straint . . . No wonder women filled the matinées to see the 'classic' dancers: the mere spectacle of graceful, musical, and uncorseted motion was an impelling sight, a prophecy" (80–81). See also Studlar 105–6.

17. For a discussion of this song, see Hamberlin 673–74.

18. Aimed at reducing the number of businesses trading or selling alcohol to the public by as much as a third, the Licensing Bill was meant to remedy the social ill of frequent and widespread alcohol abuse, which had been a sore topic for social reformers since the 1870s. The cartoon alludes to the fact that many such businesses had to close down abruptly, becoming sacrificial victims of the willful prime minister, just like John the Baptist fell victim to Salome (the Baptist's bloody mouth gag reads "Closure").

19. English libel law differentiates between civil (private) and criminal (public) libel. Obscene libel was a subcategory of criminal libel, offenses against the public order. Bland explains that "the Libel Act of 1843 decreed that for a criminal libel, the defendant needed to establish both the truth of the libel and its public benefit," which "allowed the libeler to assemble diverse witnesses and present much incriminating evidence," a legal strategy that only helped Billing in court (186).

20. The Labouchère Amendment, the clause in the Criminal Law Amendment Act in 1885 under which Oscar Wilde was also convicted, states, "Any male person who, in public or private, commits, or is a party to the commission of, or procures, or attempts to procure the commission by any male person of, any act of gross indecency shall be guilty of misdemeanour, and being convicted shall be liable at the discretion of the Court to be imprisoned for any term not exceeding two years, with or without hard labour." Anal intercourse, or "buggery," had been illegal since the so-called Buggery Act of 1533, but the Labouchère Amendment, which was only repealed in 1967, effectively extended the criminalization of homosexuality to any form of sex between men. Neither the 1533 Buggery Act nor the 1885 Labouchère Amendment mentioned same-sex acts between females; this was partly a symptom of cultural attitudes toward female sexuality, from which lesbians benefited, albeit at the price of manifest cultural invisibility. Jennifer Travis explains, "It was only *after* the trial brought by Maud Allan that a 1921 proposal to add a new clause to the Criminal Law Amendment Act was introduced in Parliament. The framers of the proposal sought to mimic the 1885 Labouchere Amendment with a clause that referred specifically to 'Acts of Gross Indecency by Females.' Because English legislators could not agree that sexual relations between women were possible, it was never ratified"; "Because there was no legislation with regard to women's 'acts of gross indecency' with other women, . . . Allan, unlike Wilde, did not suffer a criminal prosecution" (159–60, 147).

21. Jeffrey Weeks thinks that the Pemberton-Billing Trial paved the way for the 1921 Criminal Law Amendment Act, which added lesbianism as a punishable offense for the very first time (105–6).

22. Another historical context may have played some role for the association of homosexuality with treason and of sexual with patriotic "perversion," the case of Roger Casement (1864–1916), an Irish Protestant in the service of the British who was executed for his role in the Dublin Easter Rising of 1916. Notably, it was Justice Darling—the same judge who presided over the Pemberton-Billing Trial—who dismissed Casement's appeal of the death sentence in 1916.

23. Lord Alfred Douglas declared in the reactionary *Morning Post* that *Salomé* ap-

pealed to the Germans because of its sexual perversity and that the play's "perversions of sexual passions have no home in the healthy mind of England" (quoted in Bland 189).

24. Maud Allan was probably familiar with the term because, approximately in 1898, she had illustrated a two-volume sex manual for women with depictions of the female anatomy, the German *Illustriertes Konversations-Lexikon der Frau.* Had Billing known this fact, he might have further exploited it; it does not seem to have come up during the trial, however (Bentley 55).

CHAPTER 4

1. Later editors changed the 1922 title to *Salome: A Pantomime after the Play by Oscar Wilde.* The relationship between the original film and the versions available today has not been fully researched by scholars. Apparently three negative copies of the film were made, one for the United States (from which 250 positives were made), one for Europe, and one for South America (Morris 89). Patricia White reports, "The original release print of Salome was 5,595 feet with its running time put at sixty-five to seventy-nine minutes by Harrison's Reports (13 January 1923). In 1990 the George Eastman House restored a 35 mm print at 5,032 feet, which runs approximately sixty-seven minutes" (84n19). My own study of the film refers directly to the six-reel 35 mm version held at the Library of Congress in Washington, DC, which, at 5,122 feet in length, is the longest surviving version in existence; fortunately, it has recently been restored and made available to the public on DVD. For ease of reference, I include reel numbers of the Library of Congress print in my analysis of the film in this chapter. Besides the 35 mm print of the 1922 original, the Library of Congress also holds a 16 mm reedited, shorter version (ca. sixty-eight minutes), which silent-film collector Raymond Rohauer organized and showed in conjunction with an Aubrey Beardsley retrospective in New York in 1967. My own comparison of Rohauer's film with Nazimova's original (1922) 35 mm version revealed substantial differences in intertitles and editing. Another commercially available version is an extremely shortened thirty-eight-minute video distributed in the United States by Grapevine Video. A detailed analysis of the various prints' differences exceeds my topic and purpose in this chapter but would clearly be important for future scholarship on Nazimova's film.

2. Unidentified newspaper clippings, stamped January 1, 1906, and January 17, 1906, and newspaper clipping from the *New York Globe,* stamped January 17, 1906, Nazimova Collection, Library of Congress, Washington, DC.

3. Although Robins considered Ibsen a forerunner, she did not think he had gone far enough to support women's social and political progress (see Farfan).

4. The Nazimova Collection at the Library of Congress in Washington, DC, holds many reviews of Nazimova's 1907 *Hedda Gabler;* most are glowing. Some materials also relate to Nazimova's role as a fashion and advertising idol; in particular, her Hedda Gabler gowns garnered attention. Nazimova also appeared in advertisements for Lucky Strike and Fatima Turkish Blend cigarettes and for beauty products, such as Lux toilet soap.

5. The inscription, from December 29, 1914, is available in the Nazimova Collection at the Library of Congress in Washington, DC.

6. According to early film scholar Sumiko Higashi, "the attempt to ensure a degree of predictability in the movie industry settled upon formulated plots, such as the triangular love story with hero, heroine, and villain, which gave the viewers recurrent déjà vu" (iii–iv).

7. For overviews of Nazimova's films, see the articles in the bibliography by De-Witt Bodeen, Jack Spears, and Maeve Druesne.

8. According to Michael Morris, Theda Bara's 1918 *Salome* (discussed later in this chapter) had been banned in many parts of the country, and "[f]or this reason, Metro had rejected Nazimova's suggestion that she star in yet another film version" of the Salome story (84). Metro may have been afraid of censorship, but since they also turned down *A Doll's House,* it seems plausible that they wanted to rein in Nazimova's forays into the European art film.

9. It remains unclear whether Nazimova Productions was a project born of necessity after Metro decided to cancel her contract in 1921 or if she canceled her contract herself. Metro and Nazimova apparently did not split agreeably, and they offered divergent accounts.

10. The appendix to Lambert's biography includes an unpublished poem by Nazimova in which she describes her disappointment in her romantic relationship with Bryant and in Bryant himself as a habit-driven, emotionally unavailable "frigid man" interested in manly sports—perhaps a coded commentary on his possible homosexuality (397–400). In this poem, she also mentions that the next project after Ibsen and Wilde was to have been an adaptation of the Dostoevskian German-Jewish writer Jakob Wassermann's 1919 novel *Christian Wahnschaffe* (translated as *The World's Illusion*) (400).

11. Theda Bara starred in a steady series of popular melodramas, such as *A Fool There Was* (1914), *Sin* and *Carmen* (1915), *The Serpent* (1916), and *Camille* and *Cleopatra* (1917). Her career was effectively over by 1920: the public had become tired of her many variations of the same role. Bara made her last picture in 1926. As Sumiko Higashi points out, Bara's star personality and mysterious orientalist origins were wholly manufactured by the studio publicity departments to fit her vamp persona (55).

12. Hugo Münsterberg introduced the theatrical term *photoplay* for cinematic drama and argued that on account of its freedom from constraints of time, space, and causality, the cinema was in fact superior to theater: it possessed larger physical and mental possibilities of representation and effect and hence had greater potential for mimesis (361).

13. See Karl Beckson's authoritative article on the subject, "Oscar Wilde and the Green Carnation"; see also Donohue, "Distance, Death, and Desire in *Salome*" 127. The green carnation was the central literary symbol in two fictional accounts of Wilde's life and trials, the 1894 novel *The Green Carnation* by Robert Hichens and the 1960 film of the same title (see Stetz).

14. The two sequences dramatized Salomé's temptation by Herod's offers. In the first, Salomé imagines herself as a stylized moon in the midst of an art nouveau tableau of peacocks and clouds ("Salomé, thou knowest my white peacocks! In the midst of them thou wilt be like unto the moon in the midst of a great white cloud"). Adorned with peacock feathers and a peculiar flapperlike cap from which graceful antennae protrude to join the florid lines of the painted part of the scene, Nazimova's

photographed body literally merges with the dreamlike, Beardsleyesque tableau here ("'Salomé' Part 5," reel 5; see n. 1 in the present chapter). The second scene shows Salomé as a smiling flapper queen, kneeling on top of a very tall, glittering mountain of jewels, madly swinging her arms in ecstasy ("I have jewels hidden in this palace that thy mother even has never seen. Thou shalt be as fair as a queen when thou wearest them").

15. By contrast, the last title card of Grapevine Video's edited thirty-eight-minute version of the film, which differs from the original 35 mm Library of Congress print analyzed in this chapter, underscores this aspect. It explicitly condemns Salomé as a femme fatale, as if to give safe closure to this tale of excess: "And the moon was hid by a great cloud . . . And the stars disappeared. And nothing in the world was as black as the name of SALOME."

16. The Grapevine Video print includes Strauss's music, rendered on a Wurlitzer organ, and commentators of the film generally assumed that this was Nazimova's intended musical accompaniment for the film. Patricia White, however, thinks that the film's originally intended score was not Strauss's opera.

17. See also Kaplan.

18. At a private showing before the National Board of Review and journalists, apparently arranged by Nazimova to appease and favorably incline the censors prior to the movie's release in 1922, attendees were asked to respond to a questionnaire about the movie's artistic value, which included such questions as "Is Salome an exceptional picture?" and "Do you believe it realizes or forecasts the greater possibilities of the motion picture as a medium of art?" The overwhelming majority, 151 out of 182 reviewers, answered both questions in the affirmative (Morris 90–91). At another special preview showing before an audience of 1,300 at Rosemary Theatre in Ocean Park, California, in October 1922, viewers and reviewers were similarly enthralled, and several favorable reviews of the new "art" film followed.

CHAPTER 5

1. Daniel Brown shows that Norma Desmond's "identification with Wilde's character highlights the essential modernity that belongs to her idea of the star" and informs her killing of Joe Gillis, the film's Jokanaan figure (1226–28). On Swanson's biographical allegorization in the movie, see Fischer, "Sunset Boulevard."

2. With lavish sets, costume changes for Hayworth in every scene, and the luscious, saturated colors of the still relatively new Technicolor technique, the film unfolded a cinematic extravaganza of epic proportions around its sexy star, Rita Hayworth. The *Saturday Review* quipped, "this sanctimonious coupling of sex and Sunday School, of Rita and religion, is far more likely to please the Hayworth fan than the Bible student" (April 4, 1953, 43).

3. This film was withdrawn from the BBC after only one showing because of widespread protests and the Richard Strauss estate's threat of a lawsuit (Russell negatively portrayed Strauss as a vulgar, commercially minded, ruthless Nazi sympathizer). See Phillips 59–64.

4. There is historical precedence for the choice of an androgynous actress in Wilde's own insistence that the slender and petite Sarah Bernhardt play Salomé. Bern-

hardt had already had several cross-dressing roles in the 1890s and early 1900s, most notably as Shakespeare's Hamlet (captured in her first cinematic performance, *Le Duel d'Hamlet,* dir. Clément Maurice, 1900).

5. In another manipulation of historical events, the film indirectly blames Lord Alfred Douglas for Wilde's arrest. Shortly before the end, the jealous Bosie (who saw Wilde's betrayal with the Page of Herodias from the stage) tips the police off about Wilde's illegal activities, prompting Wilde's arrest. Russell's fictional condemnation of Bosie is not entirely far-fetched, as the historical Lord Alfred Douglas himself became one of the most vicious, homophobic attackers of Wilde after Wilde's death. See his hypocritical and self-serving smear campaign against Wilde in his autobiography, *Oscar Wilde and Myself,* and his subsequent participation in the Pemberton-Billing Trial.

6. In "Notes on Camp," Susan Sontag famously interpreted Wilde as a historical forerunner of camp. Wilde's ultimately tragic representation in *Salome's Last Dance,* however, does not fit Sontag's own definition, since she presents camp and tragedy as antithetical opposites.

7. Mr. Carson is fittingly named after Lord Queensberry's notoriously vicious defense lawyer, Edward Carson. Byrne's speech cites almost the entire second half of Wilde's trial statement on "the love that dare not speak its name," a phrase originally used by Lord Alfred Douglas in a poem he wrote at Oxford, where the two men first met. For a transcription of Wilde's original passage, see Hyde 201.

8. The musical *A Man of No Importance* (music by Stephen Flaherty, lyrics by Lynn Ahrens [Miami, FL: Warner Bros. Publications, 2003]) was offered as part of the Lincoln Center theatrical season and ran from September 12 to December 29, 2002. It won the Outer Critics Circle Award for "Best Off-Broadway Musical" and the 2003 GLAAD Media Award for "Outstanding New York Theater: Broadway and Off-Broadway."

9. According to Michel Foucault in volume 1 of *The History of Sexuality,* it is anachronistic to speak of Wilde's homosexual "identity," because Wilde's trials themselves were a fundamental trigger for the rise of the concept of the male homosexual. As Ed Cohen writes, they helped "crystalliz[e] the concept of 'male homosexuality' in the Victorian sexual imagination" and became "instrumental in disseminating new representations of sexual behavior between men that were no longer predicated upon the evocation of . . . sodomy"; hence Wilde became a privileged "figure around which new representations of male sexual behavior in England coalesced" (97, 99). Wilde's case also importantly influenced public and medical-scientific opinion on the subject. For example, Havelock Ellis's 1915 *Sexual Inversion* used the 1895 trials as a paradigmatic case for "inverts" in turn-of-the-century England. Exemplary scholarly studies of Wilde that take into account the historical imbroglio of Wilde's meaning for queer history and representation include Cohen's *Talk on the Wilde Side,* Alan Sinfield's *The Wilde Century,* and Jonathan Dollimore's *Sexual Dissidence.*

10. The critical trend to treat Wilde's homosexuality as a source for his work and to interpret his work as a mask for that source can be traced back to a 1956 essay by Edmund Bergler, which interpreted Wilde's work as direct evidence of the author's homosexuality ("Salome: The Turning Point in the Life of Wilde"), followed by Kate Millet's *Sexual Politics,* Gail Finney's *Women in Modern Drama,* and Elaine Showalter's *Sexual Anarchy.* Two more recent examples of psychological-biographical-homosexual treatments of Wilde's work are Gary Schmidgall's critical biography of Wilde, *The*

Stranger Wilde, and Melissa Knox's writings on Wilde, especially on *Salomé* (e.g., "Losing One's Head" and her biography *Oscar Wilde*). I concur with Ian Small's negative assessment of biographical work that seeks to recuperate the hidden gay Wilde (in Schmidgall's memorable pun, Wilde the "Ass-thete") but does so in a historically and theoretically sloppy manner. As Small points out (18–19), Schmidgall's greatest shortcoming is his failure to engage critically with the historical concept of "the homosexual" itself and with Wilde's important cultural role as a solidifier of that concept. A more carefully weighed example of biographical-literary speculation is Franz Meier's "Oscar Wilde and the Myth of the Femme Fatale," for example.

11. Two photographs from the Roger-Viollet archive in Paris had been mixed up, so that a 1906 picture of the Hungarian soprano Alice Guszalewicz in Strauss's opera was misidentified as a hitherto unpublished portrait of Wilde. The German Wilde scholar Horst Schröder first revealed Guszalewicz's identity in 1993, and Wilde's grandson Merlin Holland, who had tracked down the archival history of the picture and the origin of the confusion, reported the results of their respective findings ("Wilde as Salomé?"). A few months later, Elaine Showalter responded with an article that defended her reading of Wilde's play as a site of gender negotiation through Wilde's special investment in Salomé's queer desire: "From Wilde to Wilder to wildest, *Salomé* has always been the site for debates about sexuality, transgression, and sexual difference. We will miss the picture of Wilde as Salomé, but apart from footnotes, seeing Alice instead of Oscar isn't going to change a lot" ("It's Still Salome").

12. Julian Mitchell's screenplay renders some of Richard Ellmann's own speculations (e.g., about Wilde's first homoerotic seduction through Robert Ross) as supposed facts and centers the narrative around the contrast between Wilde's family life and his secret life in London's homosexual underground. In the film's dramatic voice-over, Oscar Wilde (portrayed by Stephen Fry) reads excerpts from "The Happy Prince" to his young sons, suggesting a clear alignment between the melancholy prince and Wilde.

13. Brett Farmer's *Spectacular Passions* and Paul Burston and Colin Richardson's *A Queer Romance* analyze queer spectatorship of the movies and television from a constructivist queer theory perspective rather than from an essentialist perspective.

14. Vito Russo's classic *The Celluloid Closet* describes the problematic history of homosexual representation in the movies.

15. Haynes's multiply layered *Poison,* a complex three-part parable about AIDS and queer desire, partly based on Jean Genet's seminal homoerotic film *Un Chant d'Amour* (1947), won the Grand Jury Prize at the Sundance Film Festival and was hailed by B. Ruby Rich (in "Homo Pomo") as an avatar of the New Queer Cinema. Haynes's *Far from Heaven* (2002, starring Julianne Moore) also thematizes male homosexuality and interracial love. Haynes's recent film *I'm Not There* (an innovative, fragmented, partly cross-dressing film biography of poet-musician Bob Dylan) is not overtly gay-themed, but it is clearly influenced by both queer and performance theory.

16. Wilson's awards include the first Robert Chesley Award for Lifetime Achievement in Gay and Lesbian Playwrighting (1994), a New York Innovative Theatre Award for significant contribution to Off-Off Broadway (2007), and numerous "Best Play" nominations or awards for his plays *Street Theater* (1982), *A Perfect Relationship* (1978), and *And He Made a Her* (1961).

17. To my knowledge, Cave's play has never been publicly performed.

18. I agree with Biddy Martin's caution (in "Sexualities without Genders and Other Queer Utopias") against competition and rivalry between queer theory and activism, on the one hand, and feminism, on the other, which sometimes entails misunderstandings and oversimplifications of the "other" side's projects.

19. Linda Dowling ("The Decadent and the New Woman in the 1890s") and Rhonda Garelick (*Rising Star*) discuss shared strategies and rhetorical intersections between the New Woman and the dandy or between the dandy and the star, but they do not examine their joined cultural and philosophical underpinnings or mechanisms and functions of these concepts in the context of modernist aesthetics.

Bibliography

Abrams, Brett L. "Latitude in Mass-Produced Culture's Capital: New Women and Other Players in Hollywood, 1920–1941." *Frontiers* 25 (2004): 65–95.

"Acting and English of Nazimova." *Harper's Weekly* 51 (February 16, 1907), 240.

Adorno, Theodor W. "Arnold Schoenberg, 1874–1951." In *The Adorno Reader,* ed. Brian O'Connor, 280–303. Oxford: Blackwell, 2000.

Adorno, Theodor W. "Richard Strauss: Part I." Trans. Samuel Weber and Shierry Weber. *Perspectives of New Music* 4 (1965): 14–32.

Allan, Maud. *My Life and Dancing.* London: Everett and Company, 1908.

Anger, Kenneth. *Hollywood Babylon.* San Francisco: Straight Arrow Books, 1975.

Armatage, Kay, and Caryl Clark. "Seeing and Hearing Atom Egoyan's *Salome*." In *Image and Territory: Essays on Atom Egoyan,* ed. Monique Tschofen and Jennifer Burwell, 307–28. Waterloo, Ontario: Wilfrid Laurier Univ. Press, 2007.

Arnold, LeRoy. "To Mme. Nazimova as Nora (After seeing the Actress' Portrayal of the Heroine in Ibsen's 'Doll's House')." *Theatre Magazine* 7 (August 1907): 218.

Aston, Elaine. *Sarah Bernhardt: A French Actress on the English Stage.* Oxford: Berg, 1989.

Bailey, Peter. *Music Hall: The Business of Pleasure.* Milton Keynes: Open Univ. Press, 1986.

Barnes, Djuna. "Alla Nazimova: One of the Greatest Living Actresses Talks of Her Art." In *Djuna Barnes, Interviews,* ed. Alyce Barry, 352–59. Washington, DC: Sun and Moon Press, 1985.

Bartlett, Neil. *In Extremis.* London: Oberon Books, 2000.

Bartlett, Neil. *Who Was That Man? A Present for Oscar Wilde.* London: Serpent's Tail, 1988.

Bartone, Richard C. "Todd Haynes." In *glbtq: an encyclopedia of gay, lesbian, bisexual, transgender, and queer culture.* http://www.glbtq.com/arts/haynes_t.html (accessed October 20, 2010).

Bashford, Bruce. "When Critics Disagree: Recent Approaches to Oscar Wilde." *Victorian Literature and Culture,* 2002, 613–25.

Bataille, Georges. *Madame Edwarda.* In *My Mother, Madame Edwarda, The Dead Man,* trans. Austryn Wainhouse, 135–59. London: Marion Boyars, 2000.

Bataille, Georges. "On Nietzsche: The Will to Chance." In *The Bataille Reader,* ed. Fred Botting and Scott Wilson, 330–42. Oxford: Blackwell, 1997.

Bataille, Georges. "The Pineal Eye." In *Visions of Excess: Selected Writings, 1927–1939,* ed. Allan Stoekl, trans. Allan Stoekl, Carl R. Lovitt, Donald M. Leslie, Jr., 79–90. Minneapolis: Univ. of Minnesota Press, 1985.

Becker-Leckrone, Megan. "Salome: The Fetishization of a Textual Corpus." *New Literary History* 26 (1995): 239–60.

Beckson, Karl. "Oscar Wilde and the Green Carnation." *ELT* 43 (2000): 387–97.

Beckson, Karl, ed. *Oscar Wilde: The Critical Heritage.* London: Routledge and Kegan Paul, 1970.

Beecham, Sir Thomas. *A Mingled Chime: An Autobiography.* Reprint, Westport, CT: Greenwood Press, 1976.

Beerbohm, Max. Review of Maud Allan's *The Vision of Salome. Saturday Review,* July 4, 1908, 138.

Benjamin, Walter. "The Work of Art in the Age of Its Reproducibility." Second version. In *Walter Benjamin, Selected Writings,* vol. 3, *1935–1938,* trans. Edmund Jephcott and Harry Zohn, 101–33. Cambridge, MA: Harvard Univ. Press, 2002.

Benkowitz, Miriam J. *Ronald Firbank: A Biography.* New York: Knopf, 1969.

Bentley, Toni. *Sisters of Salome.* New Haven: Yale Univ. Press, 2002.

Bergler, Edmund. "Salome: The Turning Point in the Life of Wilde." *Psychoanalytic Review* 43 (1956): 97–103.

Berman, Marshall. *All That Is Solid Melts into Air: The Experience of Modernity.* New York: Penguin, 1988.

Bernheimer, Charles. *Decadent Subjects: The Idea of Decadence in Art, Literature, Philosophy, and Culture of the Fin de Siècle in Europe.* Ed. T. Jefferson Kline and Naomi Schor. Baltimore: Johns Hopkins Univ. Press, 2002.

Bernheimer, Charles. "Huysmans: Writing Against (Female) Nature." In *The Female Body in Western Culture,* ed. Susan Rubin Suleiman, 373–86. Cambridge, MA: Harvard Univ. Press, 1985.

Bird, Alan. *The Plays of Oscar Wilde.* New York: Barnes and Noble, 1977.

Bizot, Richard. "The Turn-of-the-Century Salome Era: High- and Pop-Culture Variations on the Dance of the Seven Veils." *Choreography and Dance* 2, pt. 3 (1992): 71–87.

Bland, Lucy. "Trial by Sexology? Maud Allan, *Salome,* and the 'Cult of the Clitoris' Case." In *Sexology in Culture: Labeling Bodies and Desires,* ed. Lucy Bland and Laura Doan, 183–98. Chicago: Univ. of Chicago Press, 1998.

Blathwayt, Raymond. *Through Life and Round the World: Being the Story of My Life.* New York: E. P. Dutton, 1917.

Bockting, Margaret. "Performers and the Erotic in Four Interviews by Djuna Barnes." *Centennial Review* 41 (1997): 183–95.

Boden, DeWitt. "Alla Nazimova." In *More from Hollywood: The Careers of 15 Great American Stars,* 169–90. South Brunswick: A. S. Barnes, 1977.

Boeser, Knut, and Renata Vatková, eds. *Max Reinhardt in Berlin.* Berlin: Frölich und Kaufmann, 1984.

Böker, Uwe, Richard Corballis, and Julie A. Hibbard. *The Importance of Reinventing Oscar: Versions of Wilde in the Last 100 Years.* Amsterdam: Rodopi, 2002.

Bonte, C. H. "A Revolutionary Photoplay: Nazimova's 'Salome' Should Be the Beginning of a New Art Movement in American Studios." Newspaper clipping, Nazimova Collection, Library of Congress, Washington, DC.

Botstein, Leon. "The Enigmas of Richard Strauss: A Revisionist View." In *Richard Strauss and His World,* ed. Bryan Gilliam, 3–23. Princeton: Princeton Univ. Press, 1992.

Botstein, Leon, ed. "Richard Strauss and the Viennese Critics (1896–1924): Reviews by Gustav Schoenaich, Robert Hirschfeld, Guido Adler, Max Kalbeck, Julius Korngold, and Karl Kraus." Trans. Susan Gillespie. In *Richard Strauss and His World,* ed. Bryan Gilliam, 311–71. Princeton: Princeton Univ. Press, 1992.

Boyden, Matthew. *Richard Strauss.* Boston: Northeastern Univ. Press, 1999.

Bristow, Joseph, ed. *Oscar Wilde and Modern Culture: The Making of a Legend.* Athens: Ohio Univ. Press, 2008.

Bronski, Michael. "Positive Images and the Coming Out Film: The Art and Politics of Gay and Lesbian Cinema." *Cinéaste* 26 (2000): 20–26.

Brown, Daniel. "Wilde and Wilder." *PMLA* 119 (2004): 1216–30.

Brown, Julia Prewitt. *Cosmopolitan Criticism: Oscar Wilde's Philosophy of Art.* Charlottesville: Univ. Press of Virginia, 1997.

Burston, Paul, and Colin Richardson, eds. *A Queer Romance: Lesbians, Gay Men, and Popular Culture.* London: Routledge, 1995.

Bush, Ronald. "In Pursuit of Wilde Possum: Reflections on Eliot, Modernism, and the Nineties." *Modernism/modernity* 11 (2004): 469–85.

Butler, Judith. "Imitation and Gender Subordination." In *The Gay and Lesbian Studies Reader,* ed. Henry Abelove, Michele Aina Barala, and David M. Halperin, 307–20. New York: Routledge, 1993.

Butler, Judith. "Performative Acts and Gender Constitution: An Essay in Phenomenology and Feminist Theory." In *Performing Feminisms: Feminist Critical Theory and Theater,* ed. Sue-Ellen Case, 270–82. Baltimore: Johns Hopkins Univ. Press, 1990.

Caddy, Davinia. "Variations on the Dance of the Seven Veils." *Cambridge Opera Journal* 17 (2005): 37–58.

Cahun, Claude. "La 'Salomé' d'Oscar Wilde, Le procès Billing et les 47 000 pervertis du livre noir." In *Écrits,* ed. François Leperlier, 451–59. Paris: Jean Michel Place, 2002.

Cahun, Claude. *Heroines.* Trans. Shelley Rice. In *Inverted Odysseys: Claude Cahun, Maya Deren, Cindy Sherman,* ed. Shelley Rice, 43–94. Cambridge, MA: MIT Press, 1999.

Calinescu, Matei. *Five Faces of Modernity: Modernism, Avant-garde, Decadence, Kitsch, Postmodernism.* Durham, NC: Duke Univ. Press, 1987.

Carter, Alexandra. "London, 1908: A Synchronic View of Dance History." *Dance Research* 23 (2005): 36–50.

Castiglia, Christopher. "Sex Panics, Sex Publics, Sex Memories." *boundary 2* 27 (2000): 149–75.

Cave, Nick. "Salomé." In *King Ink,* 67–75. Los Angeles: Two Thirteen Sixty One Publications, 1993.

Cherniavsky, Felix. *Maud Allan and Her Art.* Toronto: Dance Collection Danse Press/es, 1998.

Cherniavsky, Felix. "Maud Allan, Part III: Two Years of Triumph, 1908–1909." *Dance Chronicle* 7 (1984): 119–58.

Cherniavsky, Felix. *The Salome Dancer: The Life and Times of Maud Allan.* Toronto: Mc-Clelland and Stewart, 1991.

Clarke, Eric. *Virtuous Vice: Homoeroticism and the Public Sphere.* Durham, NC: Duke Univ. Press, 2000.

Cohen, Ed. *Talk on the Wilde Side: Toward a Genealogy of a Discourse on Male Sexualities.* New York: Routledge, 1993.

Cohler, Deborah. "Sapphism and Sedition: Producing Female Homosexuality in Great War Britain." *Journal of the History of Sexuality* 16 (2007): 68–94.

Cohn, Robert Greer, and Gerald Gillespie, eds. *Mallarmé in the Twentieth Century.* Cranbury, NJ: Associated Univ. Presses, 1998.

Compton-Ricketts, Arthur. *I Look Back: Memories of Fifty Years.* London: Herbert Jenkins, 1933.

Constable, Liz, Dennis Denisoff, and Matthew Potolsky, eds. *Perennial Decay: On the Aesthetics and Politics of Decadence.* Philadelphia: Univ. of Pennsylvania Press, 1999.

Cookie's Fortune. Dir. Robert Altman. Perf. Glenn Close, Julianne Moore, Liv Tyler, Chris O'Donnell, Charles Dutton, and Patricia Neal. Sony Pictures Classic, 1999. Videocassette.

Cooper, Lady Diana. *The Rainbow Comes and Goes.* Boston: Houghton Mifflin, 1958.

Craig Wentworth, Marion. *War Brides.* In *War Plays by Women: An International Anthology,* ed. Claire M. Tylee with Elaine Turner and Agnès Cardinal, 15–26. London: Routledge, 1999.

Craven, Thomas. "Salome and the Cinema." *New Republic,* January 24, 1923, 225–26.

Daffner, Hugo. *Salome: Ihre Gestalt in Geschichte und Kunst; Dichtung—Bildende Kunst—Musik.* Munich: Hugo Schmidt Verlag, 1912.

Darnton, Charles. "While Mme. Nasimoff Trimmed a Hat." *The World,* [before 1906]. Newspaper clipping, Nazimova Collection, Library of Congress, Washington, DC.

Davies, Gardner. *Les Noces d'Hérodiade, Mystère.* Paris: Gallimard, 1959.

Davis, W. Eugene. "Oscar Wilde, *Salome,* and the German Press, 1902–1905." *ELT* 44 (2001): 149–80.

Dean, Carolyn J. "Claude Cahun's Double." *Yale French Studies* 90 (1996): 71–92.

Décaudin, Michel. "Un mythe de fin de siècle: Salomé." *Comparative Literature Studies* 4 (1967): 109–17.

De Foe, Louis V. "East Side, Like Russia, Goes to the Theatre to Be Taught." *The World,* February 4, 1906. Newspaper clipping, Nazimova Collection, Library of Congress, Washington, DC.

Dellamora, Richard. "Traversing the Feminine in Oscar Wilde's Salome." In *Victorian Sages and Cultural Discourse: Renegotiating Gender and Power,* ed. Thais E. Morgan, 246–64. New Brunswick, NJ: Rutgers Univ. Press, 1990.

de Man, Paul. "Impersonality in the Criticism of Maurice Blanchot." In *Blindness and Insight: Essays in the Rhetoric of Contemporary Criticism.* 2nd rev. ed., introd. Wlad Godzich. Minneapolis: Univ. of Minnesota Press, 1983.

de Man, Paul. "Mallarmé, Yeats, and the Post-Romantic Predicament." PhD diss., Harvard Univ., May 1960.

Derrida, Jacques. *Dissemination*. Trans. Barbara Johnson. Chicago: Univ. of Chicago Press, 1981.

Dickinson, Peter. "Oscar Wilde: Reading the Life after the Life." *Biography* 28 (2005): 414–32.

Dierkes-Thrun, Petra. "Arthur Symons' Decadent Aesthetics: Stéphane Mallarmé and the Dancer Revisited." In *Decadences: Morality and Aesthetics in British Literature,* ed. Paul Fox, 33–65. Stuttgart: Ibidem Verlag, 2006.

Dierkes-Thrun, Petra. "Salomé, C'est Moi? Wilde and Salome as Icons of Transgression." In *Approaches to Teaching the Works of Oscar Wilde,* ed. Philip E. Smith, 171–79. New York: Modern Language Association of America, 2008.

Dijkstra, Bram. *Idols of Perversity: Fantasies of Feminine Evil in Fin-de-Siècle Culture.* New York: Oxford Univ. Press, 1986.

Doan, Laura. *Fashioning Sapphism: The Origins of a Modern English Lesbian Culture.* New York: Columbia Univ. Press, 2001.

Doane, Mary Ann. *Femmes Fatales: Feminism, Film Theory, Psychoanalysis.* New York: Routledge, 1991.

Dollimore, Jonathan. *Sexual Dissidence: Augustine to Wilde, Freud to Foucault.* Oxford: Clarendon Press, 1991.

Donohue, Joseph. "Distance, Death, and Desire in *Salome*." In *The Cambridge Companion to Oscar Wilde,* ed. Peter Raby, 118–42. Cambridge: Cambridge Univ. Press, 1997.

Donohue, Joseph. "*Salome* and the Wildean Art of Symbolist Theatre." *Modern Drama* 37 (1994): 84–103.

Douglas, Lord Alfred Bruce. *Oscar Wilde and Myself.* 1914. Reprint, New York: AMS Press, 1977.

Dowling, Linda. "The Decadent and the New Woman in the 1890s." *Nineteenth-Century Fiction* 33 (1979): 434–53.

Druesne, Maeve. "Nazimova: Her Silent Films." Parts 1 and 2. *Films in Review* 36 (June–July 1985): 322–30; 36 (August–September 1985): 405–12.

Duchess of Sermoneta, Vittoria Colonna. *Things Past.* Foreword by Robert Hichens. New York: D. Appleton, 1929.

Dyer, Richard. *The Matter of Images: Essays on Representation.* 2nd ed. London: Routledge, 2002.

Dyer, Richard, and Julianne Pidduck. *Now You See It: Studies in Lesbian and Gay Film.* 2nd ed. London: Routledge, 2003.

Eagleton, Terry. *Saint Oscar.* Lawrence Hill, UK: Field Day, 1989.

Ellis, Sylvia. *The Plays of W. B. Yeats: Yeats and the Dancer.* New York: St. Martin's Press, 1995.

Ellmann, Richard. *Oscar Wilde.* New York: Knopf, 1988.

Ellmann, Richard. "Overtures to Salome." In *Oscar Wilde: A Collection of Critical Essays,* ed. Richard Ellmann, 73–91. Englewood Cliffs, NJ: Prentice Hall, 1969.

Eltis, Sos. *Revising Wilde: Society and Subversion in the Plays of Oscar Wilde.* Oxford: Clarendon Press, 1996.

Emonds, Friederike B. "Femme fragile." In *The Feminist Encyclopedia of German Liter-*

ature, ed. Friederike Eigler and Susanne Kord, 165–66. Westport, CT: Greenwood Press, 1997.

Evans, Caroline, and Lorraine Gamman. "The Gaze Revisited, or Reviewing Queer Viewing." In *A Queer Romance: Lesbians, Gay Men, and Popular Culture,* ed. Paul Burston and Colin Richardson, 13–56. London: Routledge, 1995.

Farfan, Penny. "From *Hedda Gabler* to *Votes for Women:* Elizabeth Robins's Early Feminist Critique of Ibsen." *Theatre Journal* 48 (1996): 59–78.

Farmer, Brett. *Spectacular Passions: Cinema, Fantasy, Gay Male Spectatorships.* Durham, NC: Duke Univ. Press, 2000.

Felski, Rita. *The Gender of Modernity.* Cambridge, MA: Harvard Univ. Press, 1995.

Fernbach, Amanda. "Wilde's Salomé and the Ambiguous Fetish." *Victorian Literature and Culture,* 2001, 195–218.

Finney, Gail. *Women in Modern Drama: Freud, Feminism, and European Theater at the Turn of the Century.* Ithaca, NY: Cornell Univ. Press, 1989.

Firbank, Ronald. *Five Novels: The Flower beneath the Foot; Prancing Nigger; Valmouth; The Artificial Princess; Concerning the Eccentricities of Cardinal Pirelli.* New York: New Directions, 1981.

Fischer, Lucy. *Shot/Countershot: Film Tradition and Women's Cinema.* Princeton: Princeton Univ. Press, 1989.

Fischer, Lucy. "Sunset Boulevard: Fading Stars." In *Women and Film,* ed. Janet Todd, 97–113. New York: Holmes, 1988.

Flaubert, Gustave. *Trois Contes, Oeuvres Complètes de Gustave Flaubert.* Paris: Louis Conard, 1910.

Flaubert, Gustave. *Three Tales.* Trans. Robert Baldick. Baltimore: Penguin, 1961.

Flaubert, Gustave. *Oeuvres Complètes de Gustave Flaubert.* Paris: Louis Conard, 1910.

Flaubert, Gustave. *Salammbô.* Trans. A. J. Krailshaimer. London: Penguin, 1977.

Fortunato, Paul L. *Modernist Aesthetics and Consumer Culture in the Writings of Oscar Wilde.* New York: Routledge, 2007.

Foucault, Michel. *The History of Sexuality.* Vol. 1, *An Introduction.* Trans. Robert Hurley. New York: Vintage, 1978.

Foucault, Michel. "A Preface to Transgression." In *Aesthetics, Method, and Epistemology,* ed. James D. Faubion, vol. 2, *Essential Works of Foucault, 1954–1984,* ed. Paul Rabinow, trans. Donald F. Bouchard and Sherry Simon, 69–87. New York: New Press, 1998.

Frank, Lee. "'Mentally Up to Date': Modern Ideas Are Just as Important as Stylish Costumes, Nazimova Finds." Newspaper clipping, Nazimova Collection, Library of Congress, Washington, DC.

Fuhrich, Edda, and Gisela Prossnitz, eds. *Max Reinhardt: "Ein Theater, das den Menschen wieder Freude gibt . . ."; Eine Dokumentation.* Munich: Albert Langen–Georg Müller Verlag, 1987.

Fuller, Loïe. *Fifteen Years of a Dancer's Life, with Some Account of Her Distinguished Friends.* Reprint, London: Herbert Jenkins, 1913.

Gagnier, Regenia. *Idylls of the Marketplace: Oscar Wilde and the Victorian Public.* Stanford: Stanford Univ. Press, 1986.

Gagnier, Regenia. "Wilde and the Victorians." In *The Cambridge Companion to Oscar Wilde,* ed. Peter Raby, 18–33. Cambridge: Cambridge Univ. Press, 1997.

Gagnier, Regenia, ed. *Critical Essays on Oscar Wilde*. New York: Hall and Maxwell Macmillan International; Toronto: Maxwell Macmillan Canada, 1991.

Garber, Marjorie. *Vested Interests: Cross-Dressing and Cultural Anxiety*. New York: Routledge, 1992.

Garelick, Rhonda K. *Electric Salome*. Princeton: Princeton Univ. Press, 2008.

Garelick, Rhonda K. "Electric Salome: Loie Fuller at the Exposition Universelle of 1900." In *Imperialism and Theatre: Essays on World Theatre, Drama, and Performance,* ed. J. Ellen Gainor, 85–103. London: Routledge, 1995.

Garelick, Rhonda K. *Rising Star: Dandyism, Gender, and Performance in the Fin de Siècle*. Princeton: Princeton Univ. Press, 1998.

Geng, Veronica. "Holly Woodlawn Meets Alla Nazimova." *Ms.* 2 (February 1974): 81.

Giffen, R. L. "Nazimova a Motion Picture Enthusiast." *Motion Picture Story Magazine* 3 (June 1912): 25, 166, 168.

Gilbert, Elliot L. "'Tumult of Images': Wilde, Beardsley, and 'Salome.'" *Victorian Studies* 26 (1983): 133–59.

Gilliam, Bryan, ed. *Richard Strauss and His World*. Princeton: Princeton Univ. Press, 1992.

Gilman, Lawrence. *Strauss' Salome: A Guide to the Opera with Musical Illustrations*. London: Lane, 1907.

Gilman, Sander L. "Salome, Syphilis, Sarah Bernhardt, and the 'Modern Jewess.'" *German Quarterly* 66.2 (Spring 1993): 195–211.

Gilman, Sander L. "Strauss and the Pervert." In *Reading Opera*, ed. Arthur Groos and Roger Parker, 306–27. Princeton: Princeton Univ. Press, 1988.

Girard, René, and Françoise Meltzer. "Scandal and the Dance: Salome in the Gospel of Mark." *New Literary History* 15 (1984): 311–32.

Glenn, Susan A. "The Americanization of Salome: Sexuality, Race, and the Careers of the Vulgar Princess." In *Female Spectacle: The Theatrical Roots of Modern Feminism,* 96–129. Cambridge, MA: Harvard Univ. Press, 2000.

Grasberger, Franz, ed. *Der Strom der Töne trug mich fort: Die Welt um Richard Strauss in Briefen*. Tutzing: Schneider, 1967.

Grasberger, Franz, and Franz Hadamowsky, eds. *Richard-Strauss-Ausstellung zum 100. Geburtstag*. Vienna: Österreichische Nationalbibliothek, 1964.

Guy, Josephine M., and Ian Small. *Oscar Wilde's Profession: Writing and the Culture Industry in the Late 19th Century*. Oxford: Oxford Univ. Press, 2000.

Hamberlin, Larry. "Visions of Salome: The Femme Fatale in American Popular Songs before 1920." *Journal of the American Musicological Society* 59 (2006): 631–96.

Hanson, Ellis. *Decadence and Catholicism*. Cambridge, MA: Harvard Univ. Press, 1997.

Hare, David. *The Judas Kiss*. New York: Grove Press, 1998.

Haynes, Todd. Interview with Nick James. *Sight and Sound* 13 (2003). http://www.bfi.org.uk/sightandsound/feature/297 (accessed October 20, 2010).

Haynes, Todd. *Velvet Goldmine*. Screenplay. New York: Hyperion, 1998.

Heine, Heinrich. "Atta Troll: Ein Sommernachtstraum." In *Heinrich Heine: Sämtliche Schriften,* ed. Klaus Briegleb, 4:491–570. Munich: Carl Hanser, 1978.

Higashi, Sumiko. *Virgins, Vamps, and Flappers: The American Silent Movie Heroine*. St. Albans, VT: Eden, 1978.

Hilmes, Carola. *Die Femme Fatale: Ein Weiblichkeitstypus in der nachromantischen Literatur*. Stuttgart: Metzler, 1990.

Hoare, Philip. *Oscar Wilde's Last Stand: Decadence, Conspiracy, and the Most Outrageous Trial of the Century.* New York: Arcade Publishing, 1997.

Holland, Merlin. "Biography and the Art of Lying." In *The Cambridge Companion to Oscar Wilde,* ed. Peter Raby, 3–17. Cambridge: Cambridge Univ. Press, 1997.

Holland, Merlin. "Wilde as Salomé?" *Times Literary Supplement* (London), July 22, 1994, 14.

Holloway, Robin. "*Salome*—Art or Kitsch?" In *Richard Strauss: Salome,* ed. Derrick Puffett, 145–60. Cambridge: Cambridge Univ. Press, 1989.

Horne, Peter. "Sodomy to Salome: Camp Revisions of Modernism, Modernity, and Masquerade." In *Modern Times: Reflections on a Century of English Modernity,* ed. Mica Nava and Alan O'Shea, 129–60. London: Routledge, 1996.

Hoyser, Catherine E., and Lorena Laura Stookey. *Tom Robbins: A Critical Companion.* Westport, CT: Greenwood Press, 1997.

Hutcheon, Linda, and Michael Hutcheon. "Staging the Female Body: Richard Strauss's *Salome.*" In *Siren Songs: Representations of Gender and Sexuality in Opera,* ed. Mary Ann Smart, 204–22. Princeton: Princeton Univ. Press, 2000.

Huysmans, J[oris]-K[arl]. *Against Nature.* Trans. Robert Baldick. London: Penguin, 1959.

Huysmans, J[oris]-K[arl]. *À rebours.* In *Oeuvres Complètes de J.-K. Huysmans,* vol. 7. Geneva: Slatkine Reprints, 1972.

Huyssen, Andreas. *After the Great Divide: Modernism, Mass Culture, Postmodernism.* Bloomington: Indiana Univ. Press, 1986.

Hyde, Montgomery H. *The Trials of Oscar Wilde.* 2nd ed. New York: Dover, 1973.

Hyman, Erin Williams. "Salomé as Bombshell, or How Oscar Wilde Became an Anarchist." In *Oscar Wilde and Modern Culture: The Making of a Legend,* ed. Joseph Bristow, 96–109. Athens: Ohio Univ. Press, 2008.

Ibsen, Henrik. *A Doll's House.* Ed. William-Alan Landes. Trans. William Archer. N.p.: Players Press, 1993.

Ibsen, Henrik. *Hedda Gabler and Other Plays.* Trans. Una Ellis-Fermor. Harmondsworth: Penguin, 1961.

Ibsen, Henrik. *Plays.* Vol. 1, *Ghosts; The Wild Duck; The Master Builder.* Trans. Michael Meyer. London: Methuen, 1994.

Jardine, Alice. *Gynesis: Configurations of Woman and Modernity.* Ithaca, NY: Cornell Univ. Press, 1985.

Jenks, Chris. *Transgression.* London: Routledge, 2003.

Joost, Nicholas, and Franklin E. Court. "*Salomé*, the Moon, and Oscar Wilde's Aesthetics: A Reading of the Play." *PLL* 8 Suppl. (1972): 96–111.

Kano, Ayako. *Acting Like A Woman in Modern Japan: Theater, Gender, and Nationalism.* New York: Palgrave, 2001.

Kaplan, E. Ann. "Is the Gaze Male?" In *Powers of Desire: The Politics of Sexuality,* ed. Ann Snitow, Christine Stansell, and Sharon Thompson, 309–27. New York: Monthly Review Press, 1983.

Katz, Dorian. *Kiss.* 2009. Illustration to Oscar Wilde's *Salomé.* Ink, acrylic, and blood on paper. Stanford Univ.

Katz, Dorian. "Our Sainte Thérèse of the Moon." Research paper, Stanford Univ., 2009.

Kaufman, Moisés. *Gross Indecency: The Three Trials of Oscar Wilde*. New York: Vintage, 1998.

Kaye, Richard A. "Gay Studies/Queer Theory and Oscar Wilde." In *Palgrave Advances in Oscar Wilde Studies*, ed. Frederick S. Roden, 189–223. London: Palgrave, 2004.

Kaye, Richard A. "Salome's Lost Childhood: Wilde's Daughter of Sodom, Jugendstil Culture, and the Queer Afterlife of a Decadent Myth." In *The Nineteenth-Century Child and Consumer Culture*, ed. Dennis Denisoff, 119–34. Burlington, VT: Ashgate, 2008.

Kellogg, Patricia R. "The Myth of Salome in Symbolist Literature and Art." PhD diss., New York Univ., 1975.

Kellogg-Dennis, Patricia. "Oscar Wilde's *Salome*: Symbolist Princess." In *Rediscovering Oscar Wilde*, ed. C. George Sandulescu, 224–31. Gerrards Cross: Colin Smythe, 1994.

Kendall, Elizabeth. *Where She Danced: American Dancing, 1880–1930*. New York: Knopf, 1979.

Kermode, Frank. "Poet and Dancer before Diaghilev." In *Puzzles and Epiphanies: Essays and Reviews, 1958–1961*, 1–28. London: Routledge and Kegan Paul, 1962.

Kermode, Frank. *Romantic Image*. 2nd ed. London: Routledge, 2002.

Kettle, Michael. *Salome's Last Veil: The Libel Case of the Century*. London: Hart-Davis, 1977.

Kift, Dagmar. *The Victorian Music Hall: Culture, Class, and Conflict*. Trans. Roy Kift. Cambridge: Cambridge Univ. Press, 1996.

Klein, Hermann. "'Salome' at the Metropolitan Opera House." *Theatre Magazine* 7 (March 1907): 70–71, vi.

Knapp, Bettina L. "Herodias/Salome: Mother/Daughter Identification." *Nineteenth-Century French Studies* 25 (1996–97): 179–202.

Knox, Melissa. "Losing One's Head: Wilde's Confession in *Salomé*." In *Rediscovering Oscar Wilde*, ed. C. George Sandulescu, 232–43. Gerrards Cross: Colin Smythe, 1994.

Knox, Melissa. *Oscar Wilde: A Long and Lovely Suicide*. New Haven: Yale Univ. Press, 1994.

Kohl, Norbert. *Oscar Wilde: The Works of a Conformist Rebel*. Trans. David Henry Wilson. Cambridge: Cambridge Univ. Press, 1989.

Kopelson, Kevin. *Love's Litany: The Writing of Modern Homoerotics*. Stanford: Stanford Univ. Press, 1994.

Koritz, Amy. "Dancing the Orient for England: Maud Allan's 'The Vision of Salome.'" *Theatre Journal* 46 (1994): 63–78.

Koritz, Amy. *Gendering Bodies/Performing Art: Dance and Literature in Early Twentieth-Century British Culture*. Ann Arbor: Univ. of Michigan Press, 1995.

Koritz, Amy. "Salomé: Exotic Woman and the Transcendent Dance." In *Gender and Discourse in Victorian Literature and Art*, ed. Antony H. Harrison and Beverly Taylor, 251–73. De Kalb: Northern Illinois Univ. Press, 1992.

Koritz, Amy. "Women Dancing: The Structure of Gender in Yeats's Early Plays for Dancers." *Modern Drama* 32 (1989): 387–400.

Korngold, Julius. "Richard Strauss's *Salome*: A Conversation." In *Richard Strauss and His World*, ed. Bryan Gilliam, 307–8. Princeton: Princeton Univ. Press, 1992.

Krasner, David. "Black Salome: Exoticism, Face, and Racial Myths." In *African American Performance and Theater History: A Critical Reader,* ed. Harry J. Elam, 192–211. Oxford: Oxford Univ. Press, 2001.

Kuhn, Annette. *Cinema, Censorship, and Sexuality, 1909–1925.* New York: Routledge, 1988.

Kurth, Peter. *Isadora: A Sensational Life.* Boston: Little, Brown and Company, 2001.

Kuryluk, Ewa. *Salome and Judas in the Cave of Sex: The Grotesque; Origins, Iconography, Techniques.* Evanston, IL: Northwestern Univ. Press, 1987.

Laforgue, Jules. "Salomé." In *Moralités Légendaires,* 137–73. Paris: Mercure de France, 1954.

Laforgue, Jules. "Salome." In *Moral Tales,* trans. William Jay Smith, 85–109. New York: New Directions, 1985.

Lambert, Gavin. *Nazimova: A Biography.* New York: Knopf, 1997.

Leisler, Edda, and Gisela Prossnitz, eds. *Max Reinhardt in Europe.* Salzburg: Otto Müller Verlag, 1973.

Levine, Lawrence W. *Highbrow/Lowbrow: The Emergence of Cultural Hierarchy in America.* Cambridge, MA: Harvard Univ. Press, 1988.

Lewis, Hanna B. "Salome and Elektra: Sisters or Strangers." *Orbis Litterarum* 31 (1976): 125–33.

Lewsadder, Matthew. "Removing the Veils: Censorship, Female Sexuality, and Oscar Wilde's *Salome.*" *Modern Drama* 45 (2002): 519–44.

Lindenberger, Herbert. "Miss Cramm." Unpublished play. Available at http://www.stanford.edu/~hslinden/plays/cramm.htm (accessed October 20, 2010).

Lindenberger, Herbert. *Opera in History: From Monteverdi to Cage.* Stanford: Stanford Univ. Press, 1998.

Maeterlinck, Maurice. *The Plays: Princess Maleine, The Intruder, The Blind, The Seven Princesses.* Trans. Richard Hovey. Chicago: Herbert S. Stone and Company, 1902.

Maier, Sarah E. "Symbolist Salomés and the Dance of Dionysus." *Nineteenth-Century Contexts* 28 (2006): 211–23.

Mallarmé, Stéphane. *Collected Poems and Other Verse.* Trans. E. H. and A. M. Blackmore. Oxford: Oxford Univ. Press, 2006.

Mallarmé, Stéphane. *Correspondance, 1862–71.* Ed. Henri Mondor. 2nd ed. Paris: Gallimard, 1959.

Mallarmé, Stéphane. "Hérodiade." In *Stéphane Mallarmé: Collected Poems,* trans. Henry Weinfield with commentary, 25–37. Berkeley: Univ. of California Press, 1994.

Mallarmé, Stéphane. *Herodias.* Trans. Clark Mills. New York: AMS Press, 1981.

Mallarmé, Stéphane. *Mallarmé in Prose.* Ed. Mary Ann Caws. New York: New Directions, 2001.

Mallarmé, Stéphane. *Oeuvres: Textes Établis Avec Chronologie, Introductions, Notes, Choix de Variantes et Bibliographie.* Ed. Yves-Palain Favre. Paris: Garnier, 1985.

Mallarmé, Stéphane. *Selected Letters of Stéphane Mallarmé.* Ed. and trans. Rosemary Lloyd. Chicago: Univ. of Chicago Press, 1988.

Mallarmé, Stéphane. *Selected Poetry and Prose.* Ed. Mary Ann Caws. New York: New Directions, 1982.

Mallarmé, Stéphane. *Selected Prose Poems, Essays, and Letters.* Trans. Bradford Cook. Baltimore: Johns Hopkins Univ. Press, 1956.

Maltby, Richard. "'To Prevent the Prevalent Type of Book': Censorship and Adaptation in Hollywood, 1924–1934." In *Film Adaptation,* ed. James Naremore, 79–105. New Brunswick, NJ: Rutgers Univ. Press, 2000.

Mander, Raymond, and Joe Mitchenson. *British Music Hall.* London: Gentry Books, 1974.

Man of No Importance, A. Film. Dir. Suri Krishnamma. Perf. Albert Finney, Brenda Fricker, and Tara Fitzgerald. Little Bird/BBC Films/Majestic Films, 1994. Videocassette.

Man of No Importance, A. Vocal score. Music by Stephen Flaherty. Lyrics by Lynn Ahrens. Miami, FL: Warner Bros. Publications, 2003. Print.

Mao, Douglas, and Rebecca L. Walkowitz, eds. *Bad Modernisms.* Durham, NC: Duke Univ. Press, 2006.

Marcovitch, Heather. "The Princess, Persona, and Subjective Desire: A Reading of Oscar Wilde's *Salome." PLL* 40 (2004): 88–101.

Marcus, Jane. "Salomé: The Jewish Princess Was a New Woman." In *Art and Anger: Reading Like a Woman,* 3–19. Columbus: Ohio State Univ. Press, 1988.

Martin, Biddy. "Sexualities without Genders and Other Queer Utopias." In *Coming Out of Feminism?* ed. Mandy Merck, Naomi Segal, and Elizabeth Wright, 11–35. Oxford: Blackwell, 1998.

Marvick, Louis Wirth. *Mallarmé and the Sublime.* Albany: State Univ. of New York Press, 1986.

Maudie: Revelations of Life in London Society. Ware, Hertfordshire: Wordsworth Editions Limited, 1996.

McCarren, Felicia. *Dance Pathologies: Performance, Poetics, Medicine.* Stanford: Stanford Univ. Press, 1998.

McDearmon, Lacy. "Maud Allan: The Public Record." *Dance Chronicle* 2 (1978): 85–105.

Medd, Jodie. "'The Cult of the Clitoris': Anatomy of a National Scandal." *Modernism/modernity* 9 (2002): 21–49.

Meier, Franz. "Oscar Wilde and the Myth of the Femme Fatale." In *The Importance of Reinventing Oscar: Versions of Wilde in the Last 100 Years,* ed. Uwe Böker, Richard Corballis, and Julie A. Hibbard, 117–34. Amsterdam: Rodopi, 2002.

Meltzer, Françoise. *Salome and the Dance of Writing: Portraits of Mimesis in Literature* Chicago: Univ. of Chicago Press, 1987.

Menon, Elizabeth. *Evil by Design: The Creation and Marketing of the Femme Fatale.* Urbana: Univ. of Illinois Press, 2006.

Merkel, Kerstin. *Salome: Ikonographie im Wandel.* Frankfurt am Main: Lang, 1990.

Messmer, Franzpeter, ed. *Kritiken zu den Uraufführungen der Bühnenwerke von Richard Strauss.* Pfaffenhofen: Ludwig, 1989.

Meyer, Moe. "Under the Sign of Wilde: An Archaeology of Posing." In *The Politics and Poetics of Camp,* ed. Moe Meyer, 65–93. London: Routledge, 1994.

Millet, Kate. *Sexual Politics.* New York: Doubleday, 1970.

Mitchell, Julian. *Wilde.* Screenplay. Introd. Stephen Fry. Afterword by Julian Mitchell. London: Orion Media, 1997.

"Mme. Alla Nazimova as Ibsen's Nora." *Theatre Magazine* 7 (March 1907): 72.

Moog-Grünewald, Maria. "Die Frau als Bild des Schicksals: Zur Ikonologie der Femme fatale." *Arcadia* 18 (1983): 239–57.

Morris, Michael. *Madam Valentino: The Many Lives of Natacha Rambova.* New York: Abbeville Press, 1991.

Mulvey, Laura. "Visual Pleasure and Narrative Cinema." In *Film Theory and Criticism: Introductory Readings,* ed. Gerald Mast, Marshall Cohen, and Leo Braudy, 746–57. 4th ed. New York: Oxford Univ. Press, 1992.

Münsterberg, Hugo. "The Means of the Photoplay." In *Film Theory and Criticism: Introductory Readings,* ed. Gerald Mast, Marshall Cohen, and Leo Braudy, 355–61. 4th ed. New York: Oxford Univ. Press, 1992.

Nassaar, Christopher S. "Vision of Evil: The Influence of Wilde's *Salome* on *Heart of Darkness* and *A Full Moon in March.*" *Victorian Newsletter* 53 (1978): 23–27.

Navarre, Joan. *The Publishing History of Aubrey Beardsley's Compositions for Oscar Wilde's Salomé.* N.p.: dissertation.com, 1999.

Nazimova, Alla. Letter to Nina Lewton. September 11, 1923. Nazimova Collection, Library of Congress, Washington, DC.

Nesbit, Edith. *Salome and the Head: A Modern Melodrama.* London: Alston Rivers, 1909.

Nietzsche, Friedrich. *The Complete Works of Friedrich Nietzsche.* Ed. Oscar Levy. Trans. M. A. Mugge. New York: Russell and Russell, 1964.

Nietzsche, Friedrich. *The Gay Science.* Trans. Walter Kaufmann. New York: Vintage, 1974.

Nietzsche, Friedrich. *Human, All Too Human: A Book for Free Spirits.* Trans. R. J. Hollingdale. 2nd ed. Cambridge: Cambridge Univ. Press, 1996.

Nordau, Max. *Degeneration.* Trans. George L. Mosse. Lincoln: Univ. of Nebraska Press, 1993.

Parish, James R. *Gays and Lesbians in Mainstream Cinema: Plots, Critiques, Casts, and Credits for 272 Theatrical and Made-for-Television Hollywood Releases.* Jefferson, NC: McFarland, 1993.

Pater, Walter. *The Renaissance: Studies in Art and Poetry.* Ed. Adam Phillips. Oxford: Oxford Univ. Press, 1986.

Peters, Julie Stone. "Performing Obscene Modernism: Theatrical Censorship and the Making of Modern Drama." In *Against Theatre: Creative Destructions on the Modernist Stage,* ed. Alan Ackerman and Martin Puchner, 206–30. Houndmills: Palgrave Macmillan, 2006.

Peterson, Ann. "An Interview with a Multiple Woman." *Theatre Magazine* 7 (August 1907): 219–21.

Phillips, Gene D. *Ken Russell.* Boston: Twayne, 1979.

Pidduck, Julianne. "After 1980: Margins and Mainstreams." In *Now You See It: Studies in Lesbian and Gay Film,* ed. Richard Dyer and Julianne Pidduck, 265–94. 2nd ed. London: Routledge, 2003.

Ponsonby, Sir Frederick. *Recollections of Three Reigns.* New York: E. P. Dutton, 1952.

Powell, Kerry. *Oscar Wilde and the Theatre of the 1890s.* Cambridge: Cambridge Univ. Press, 1990.

Powell, Kerry. "Wilde and Ibsen." *English Literature in Transition* 28 (1985): 224–42.

Pratt, George C. *Spellbound in Darkness: A History of the Silent Film.* 2nd ed. Greenwich: New York Graphic Society, 1973.

Praz, Mario. *The Romantic Agony.* Trans. Angus Davidson. 2nd ed. London: Oxford Univ. Press, 1970.

Price, Jody. *"A Map with Utopia": Oscar Wilde's Theory for Social Transformation.* New York: Lang, 1996.

Puffett, Derrick, ed. *Richard Strauss: Salome.* Cambridge: Cambridge Univ. Press, 1989.

Pym, Anthony. "The Importance of Salomé: Approaches to a Fin de Siècle Theme." *French Forum* 14 (1989): 311–22.

Raby, Peter. *Oscar Wilde.* Cambridge: Cambridge Univ. Press, 1988.

Raby, Peter, ed. *The Cambridge Companion to Oscar Wilde.* Cambridge: Cambridge Univ. Press, 1997.

Raymond, Jean Paul, and Charles Ricketts. *Oscar Wilde: Recollections by Jean Paul Raymond and Charles Ricketts.* London: Hamish Hamilton, 1932.

Review of *Salomé* by Oscar Wilde, performed by Max Reinhardt Company "Schall und Rauch," Kleines Theater, Berlin. *Bühne und Welt* 5 (1902): 215. Archive of Theatermuseum Köln-Wahn, Germany.

Review signed "Fred." "Salome." Review of Nazimova's film. *Variety,* January 5, 1923, 42.

Rich, B. Ruby. "Homo Pomo: The New Queer Cinema." In *Women and Film: A Sight and Sound Reader,* ed. Pam Cook and Philip Dodd, 164–74. Philadelphia: Temple Univ. Press, 1993.

Riquelme, Jean-Paul. "Shalom/Solomon/*Salomé:* Modernism and Wilde's Aesthetic Politics." *Centennial Review* 39 (1995): 575–610.

Robbins, Tom. *Skinny Legs and All.* New York: Bantam, 1990.

Robertson, W. Graham. *Time Was: The Reminiscences of W. Graham Robertson.* London: Hamish Hamilton, 1931.

Robins, Elizabeth. *Ibsen and the Actress.* London: Hogarth Press, 1928.

Röder, Adrian. *Salome.* Wiesbaden: Behrend Verlag, [c. 1912].

Rose, Marilyn Gaddis. "The Daughters of Herodias in 'Hérodiade,' 'Salomé,' and 'A Full Moon in March.'" *Comparative Drama* 1 (1967): 172–81.

Rose, Marilyn Gaddis. "The Synchronic Salome." In *The Languages of Theatre: Problems in the Translation and Transposition of Drama,* ed. Ortrun Zuber, 146–52. Oxford: Pergamon Press, 1980.

Ross, Robert. Preface. *Salomé—La Sainte Courtisane.* By Oscar Wilde. New York: G. P. Putnam's Sons, 1916.

Rubin, Gerry. "Sex, Lies, and the Home Office: The Pemberton Billing Trial (1918) and the Black Book." *Labour History Review* 60 (1995): 43–44.

Russell, P. Craig. *Salome.* Guerneville, CA: Eclipse Comics, 1986.

Russo, Vito. *The Celluloid Closet: Homosexuality in the Movies.* Rev. ed. New York: Harper and Row, 1987.

Saladin, Linda Ann. *Fetishism and Fatal Women: Gender, Power, and Reflexive Discourse.* New York: Lang, 1993.

"Salome." *Variety Movie Reviews,* January 1, 1922, 1.

Salome. Dir. Carlos Saura. Perf. Aida Gómez and Pere Arquillué. Homevision, 2002. DVD.

Salome. Dir. Wilhelm Dieterle. Perf. Rita Hayworth, Stewart Granger, Charles Laughton, and Judith Anderson. Columbia Pictures, 1953. Videocassette.

"Salome." Words by John P. Harrington. Music by Orlando Powell. New York: Jerome H. Remick and Company, 1909. British Library, London. Print.

Salome: An Historical Phantasy by Oscar Wilde. Perf. Alla Nazimova, Rose Dione, and Mitchell Lewis. Allied Artists and Distributors, 1923. Restored 35 mm print, Library of Congress, Washington, DC, Film Preservation Associates, 2001; Image Entertainment, 2003. DVD.

"Salome: Gorgeously Mounted Original Version of the Salome Tragedy—Majestic Pageantry and Marvellous Settings—Theda Bara's Striking Characterisation." *Bioscope* (April 3, 1919), 74.

Salome: Moralisch-musikalisch-hysterisch-altjüdisches Sittendrama frei nach Oskar Wilde. Augsburg: K. B. Hofbuchdruckerei Gebrüder Reichel, n.d.

Salome's Last Dance. Dir. Ken Russell. Perf. Glenda Jackson, Stratford Jones, Nickolas Grace, Douglas Hodge, and Imogen Millais-Scott. Jolly Russell Company/Vestron Pictures, 1989. Videocassette.

"Salome (The Sheep's Head and the Tin-Tack)." Written and composed by R. P. Weston, F. J. Barnes, and Harry Bedford. London: Star Music Publishing, 1908. British Library, London. Print.

Sammels, Neil. *Wilde Style: The Plays and Prose of Oscar Wilde.* Harlow, UK: Pearson Education, 2000.

Sayler, Oliver M., ed. *Max Reinhardt and His Theater.* New York: Benjamin Blom, 1968.

Schanke, Robert A. "Alla Nazimova: 'The Witch of Makeup.'" In *Passing Performances: Queer Readings of Leading Players in American Theater History,* ed. Robert A. Schanke and Kim Marra, 129–50. Ann Arbor: Univ. of Michigan Press, 1998.

Schmidgall, Gary. *Literature as Opera.* New York: Oxford Univ. Press, 1977.

Schmidgall, Gary. *The Stranger Wilde.* New York: E. P. Dutton, 1994.

Schuh, Willi. *Straussiana aus vier Jahrzehnten.* Tutzing: Schneider, 1981.

Scholes, Robert. *Paradoxy of Modernism.* New Haven: Yale Univ. Press, 2006.

Sedgwick, Eve Kosofsky. *Between Men: English Literature and Male Homosocial Desire.* New York: Columbia Univ. Press, 1985.

Sedgwick, Eve Kosofsky. *Epistemology of the Closet.* Berkeley: Univ. of California Press, 1990.

Sedgwick, Eve Kosofsky. "Tales of the Avunculate: Queer Tutelage in *The Importance of Being Earnest.*" In *Tendencies,* 52–72. Durham, NC: Duke Univ. Press, 1993.

Senelick, Laurence. "The American Tour of Orlenev and Nazimova, 1905–1906." In *Wandering Stars: Russian Emigré Theatre, 1905–1940,* ed. Laurence Senelick, 1–15. Iowa City: Univ. of Iowa Press, 1992.

Senelick, Laurence. *The Changing Room: Sex, Drag, and Theatre.* London: Routledge, 2000.

Seshadri, Anne Marie Lineback. "Richard Strauss, Salome, and the 'Jewish Question.'" PhD diss., Univ. of Maryland, College Park, 1998.

Shewan, Rodney. "The Artist and the Dancer in Three Symbolist Salomes." *Bucknell Review* 30 (1986): 102–30.

Shewan, Rodney. *Oscar Wilde: Art and Egotism.* London: Macmillan, 1977.

Showalter, Elaine. *Hystories: Hysterical Epidemics and Modern Media.* New York: Columbia Univ. Press, 1997.

Showalter, Elaine. "It's Still Salome." *Times Literary Supplement* (London), September 2, 1994, 13–14.

Showalter, Elaine. *Sexual Anarchy: Gender and Culture at the Fin de Siècle.* New York: Penguin, 1990.

Skaggs, Carmen Trammell. "Modernity's Revision of the Dancing Daughter: The Salome Narrative of Wilde and Strauss." *College Literature* 29 (2002): 124–39.

Siegel, Mark. "The Meaning of Meaning in the Novels of Tom Robbins." *Mosaic: A Journal for the Interdisciplinary Study of Literature* 14 (1981): 119–31.

Simonson, Mary. "'The Call of Salome': American Adaptations and Re-creations of the Female Body in the Early Twentieth Century." *Women and Music: A Journal of Gender and Culture* 11 (2007): 1–16.

Sinfield, Alan. *The Wilde Century.* London: Cassell, 1994.

Slide, Anthony. *The Silent Feminists: America's First Women Directors.* Lanham, MD: Scarecrow Press, 1996.

Small, Ian. *Oscar Wilde: Recent Research, a Supplement to Oscar Wilde Revalued.* Greensboro, NC: ELT Press, 2000.

Smith, Philip. "Philosophical Approaches to Interpretation of Oscar Wilde." In *Palgrave Advances to Oscar Wilde Studies,* ed. Frederick S. Roden, 143–66. Houndmills: Palgrave Macmillan, 2004.

Sontag, Susan. "Notes on Camp." In *Against Interpretation and Other Essays,* 275–92. New York: Farrar, Straus and Giroux, 2001.

Spears, Jack. "Nazimova." In *The Civil War on the Screen and Other Essays,* 117–63. South Brunswick: A. S. Barnes, 1977.

Spivak, Gayatri Chakravorty. "A Stylistic Contrast between Yeats and Mallarmé." *Language and Style: An International Journal* 5 (1972): 100–107.

Steinberg, Michael P. "Richard Strauss and the Question." In *Richard Strauss and His World,* ed. Bryan Gilliam, 164–89. Princeton: Princeton Univ. Press, 1992.

Stephens, John Russell. *The Censorship of English Drama, 1824–1901.* Cambridge: Cambridge Univ. Press, 1980.

Stetz, Margaret D. "Oscar Wilde at the Movies: British Sexual Politics and *The Green Carnation* (1960)." *Biography* 23 (2000): 90–107.

Stoekl, Alan. "Recognition in *Madame Edwarda.*" In *Bataille: Writing the Sacred,* ed. Carolyn Bailey Gill, 77–90. London: Routledge, 1995.

Stokes, John. *The French Actress and Her English Audience.* Cambridge: Cambridge Univ. Press, 2005.

Stoljar, Margaret. "Mirror and Self in 'Fin-de-Siècle' Poetry." *Modern Language Review* 85.2 (1990): 362–72.

Stoppard, Tom. *The Invention of Love.* New York: Grove Press, 1997.

Strauss, Richard. *Richard Strauss: Recollections and Reflections.* Ed. Willi Schuh. Trans. L. J. Lawrence. London: Boosey and Hawkes, 1953.

Strauss, Richard, and Romain Rolland. *Richard Strauss and Romain Rolland: Correspondence, Together with Fragments from the Diary of Romain Rolland and Other Essays,* ed. Rollo Myers. London: Calder and Boyars, 1968.

Strelow, Michael. "Dialogue with Tom Robbins." *Northwest Review* 20 (1982): 97–102.

Studlar, Gaylyn. "'Out-Salomeing Salome': Dance, the New Woman, and Fan Magazine Orientalism." In *Visions of the East: Orientalism in Film,* ed. Matthew Bernstein and Gaylyn Studlar, 99–129. New Brunswick, NJ: Rutgers Univ. Press, 1997.

Sunset Boulevard. Dir. Billy Wilder. Perf. Gloria Swanson, William Holden, Erich von Stroheim, and Nancy Olson. Paramount Pictures, 1950. Videocassette.

Symons, Arthur. *Plays, Acting, and Music: A Book of Theory.* New York: E. P. Dutton, 1909.

Symons, Arthur. *Studies in Seven Arts.* New York: E. P. Dutton, 1925.

Symons, Arthur. *The Symbolist Movement in Literature.* Reprinted, rev. and enlarged ed., New York: Haskell House, 1971.

Szondi, Peter. *Das lyrische Drama des Fin de siècle.* Vol. 4, *Studienausgabe der Vorlesungen.* Frankfurt am Main: Suhrkamp, 1975.

Templeton, Joan. *Ibsen's Women*. Cambridge: Cambridge Univ. Press, 1997.

Tenschert, Roland. "Strauss as Librettist." In *Richard Strauss: Salome,* ed. Derrick Puffett, 36–50. Cambridge: Cambridge Univ. Press, 1989.

Terada, Rei. "De Man and Mallarmé 'Between the Two Deaths.'" In *Meetings with Mallarmé in Contemporary French Culture,* ed. Michael Temple, 107–25. Exeter: Univ. of Exeter Press, 1998.

Theweleit, Klaus. *Male Fantasies: Women, Floods, Bodies, History.* Trans. Stephen Conway, Erica Carter, and Chris Turner. 2 vols. Minneapolis: Univ. of Minnesota Press, 1987.

Thomalla, Ariane. *Die "femme fragile": Ein literarischer Frauentypus der Jahrhundertwende.* Düsseldorf: Bertelsmann, 1972.

Thynne, Lizzie. "'Surely You Are Not Claiming to Be More Homosexual Than I?' Claude Cahun and Oscar Wilde." In *Oscar Wilde and Modern Culture: The Making of a Legend,* ed. Joseph Bristow, 180–208. Athens: Ohio Univ. Press, 2008.

Tookey, Helen. "'The Fiend That Smites with a Look': The Monstrous/Menstruous Woman and the Danger of the Gaze in Oscar Wilde's *Salomé.*" *Literature and Theology* 18 (2004): 23–37.

Townsend, Julie. "Staking Salomé: The Literary Forefathers and Choreographic Daughters of Oscar Wilde's 'Hysterical and Perverted Creature.'" In *Oscar Wilde and Modern Culture: The Making of a Legend,* ed. Joseph Bristow, 154–79. Athens: Ohio Univ. Press, 2008.

Townsend, Julie. "Synaesthetics: Symbolism, Dance, and the Failure of the Metaphor." *Yale Journal of Criticism* 18 (2005): 126–48.

Travis, Jennifer. "Clits in Court: *Salome,* Sodomy, and the Lesbian 'Sadist.'" In *Lesbian Erotics,* ed. Karla Jay, 147–63. New York: New York Univ. Press, 1995.

Tydeman, William, and Steven Price. *Wilde—Salome.* Cambridge: Cambridge Univ. Press, 1996.

Tylee, Claire M., Elaine Turner, and Agnès Cardinal. "Marion Craig Wentworth." In *War Brides,* by Marion Craig Wentworth, in *War Plays by Women: An International Anthology,* ed. Claire M. Tylee with Elaine Turner and Agnès Cardinal, 13–15. London: Routledge, 1999.

Untermeyer, Louis. "Nazimova as Hedda Gabler." *Theatre Magazine* 7 (August 1907): 219.

Velvet Goldmine. Dir. Todd Haynes. Perf. Ewan McGregor, Jonathan Rhys-Myers, Christian Bale, Toni Collette, and Eddie Izzard. Miramax, 1998. Videocassette.

Viereck, George Sylvester, and Paul Eldridge. *Salome, the Wandering Jewess: My First Two Thousand Years of Love.* New York: H. Liveright, 1930.

Wachman, Gay. *Lesbian Empire: Radical Crosswriting in the Twenties.* New Brunswick, NJ: Rutgers Univ. Press, 2001.

Walkowitz, Judith R. "The 'Vision of Salome': Cosmopolitanism and Erotic Dancing in Central London, 1908–1918." *American Historical Review,* April 2003. http://www.historycooperative.org/journals/ahr/108.2/walkowitz.html (accessed October 20, 2010).

Weeks, Jeffrey. *Coming Out: Homosexual Politics in Britain, from the Nineteenth Century to the Present.* London: Quartet Books, 1977.

Weigand, Elizabeth. "*The Rugmaker's Daughter:* Maud Allan's 1915 Silent Film." *Dance Chronicle* 9 (1986): 237–51.

Weir, David. *Decadence and the Making of Modernism.* Amherst: Univ. of Massachusetts Press, 1995.

White, Patricia. "Nazimova's Veils: Salome at the Intersection of Film Histories." In *A Feminist Reader in Early Cinema,* ed. Jennifer M. Bean and Diane Negra, 60–87. Durham, NC: Duke Univ. Press, 2002.

Whitworth, Michael H., ed. *Modernism.* Malden, MA: Blackwell, 2007.

Wilde. Dir. Brian Gilbert. Perf. Stephen Fry, Jude Law, Vanessa Redgrave, Jennifer Ehle, and Tom Wilkinson. Sony Pictures Classic, 1997. DVD.

Wilde, Oscar. *The Artist as Critic: Critical Writings of Oscar Wilde.* Ed. Richard Ellmann. Chicago: Univ. of Chicago Press, 1982.

Wilde, Oscar. *Collins Complete Works of Oscar Wilde: Centenary Edition.* Ed. Merlin Holland. Glasgow: Harper Collins, 1999.

Wilde, Oscar. *The Complete Letters of Oscar Wilde.* Ed. Merlin Holland and Rupert Hart-Davis. New York: Henry Holt and Company, 2000.

Wilde, Oscar. *The Letters of Oscar Wilde.* Ed. Rupert Hart-Davis. New York: Harcourt, 1962.

Wilde, Oscar. *More Letters of Oscar Wilde.* Ed. Rupert Hart-Davis. London: J. Murray, 1985.

Wilde, Oscar. *Oscar Wilde: Interviews and Recollections.* Ed. E. H. Mikhail. 2 vols. London: Macmillan, 1979.

Wilde, Oscar. *Oscar Wilde's Oxford Notebooks: A Portrait of Mind in the Making.* Ed. Philip E. Smith II and Michael S. Helfand. New York: Oxford Univ. Press, 1989.

Wilde, Oscar. *Salomé.* First autographed manuscript of 1891; First French edition of 1893; First English edition of 1894. Preface by Charles Méla. Introd. Sylviane Messerli. Paris: Presses Universitaires de France; Geneva: Fondation Martin Bodmer, 2008.

Wilde, Oscar. *Salomé: Drame en un Acte par Oscar Wilde.* Ed. Carl Fischer. Söcking, Germany: Bachmair, 1949.

Wilde, Oscar. *Salomé—La Sainte Courtisane.* Introd. Robert Ross. New York: G. P. Putnam's Sons, 1916.

Wilhelm, Kurt. *Richard Strauss: An Intimate Portrait.* Trans. Mary Whitall. New York: Thames and Hudson, 2000.

Williamson, George S. *The Longing for Myth in Germany: Religion and Aesthetic Culture from Romanticism to Nietzsche.* Chicago: Univ. of Chicago Press, 2004.

Williamson, John. "Critical Reception." In *Richard Strauss: Salome,* ed. Derrick Puffett, 131–44. Cambridge: Cambridge Univ. Press, 1989.

Wilson, Doric. *Now She Dances!* In *Return to the Caffe Cino,* ed. Steve Susoyev and George Birimisa, 405–62. San Francisco: Moving Finger Press, 2007.

Wilson, Doric. Personal Web site. http://www.doricwilson.com (accessed October 20, 2010).

Wolf, Mary Ellen. *Eros under Glass: Psychoanalysis and Mallarmé's "Hérodiade."* Columbus: Ohio State Univ. Press, 1987.

Wolfreys, Julian. *Transgression: Identity, Space, Time.* Houndmills: Palgrave Macmillan, 2008.

Wong, Linda Pui-ling. "The Initial Reception of Oscar Wilde in Modern China: With Special Reference to *Salome.*" *Comparative Literature and Culture* 3 (1998): 52–73.

Wong, Linda Pui-ling. "Salomé in Chinese Dress: Guo Moruo's 'Three Rebellious Women.'" *Journal of Irish Studies* 17 (2002): 118–25.

Wright, Louise E. "D. H. Lawrence's Allusions to Maud Allan." *Notes and Queries* 51 (2004): 169–71.

Yeats, William Butler. *The Collected Poems of William Butler Yeats*. Ed. Richard J. Finneran. New York: Collier Books–Macmillan, 1989.

Yezierska, Anzia. *Salome of the Tenements*. Introd. Gay Wilentz. Urbana and Chicago: Univ. of Illinois Press, 1995.

Zagona, Helen Grace. *The Legend of Salome and the Principle of Art for Art's Sake*. Geneva: Librairie E. Droz, 1960.

Zhou, Xiaoyi. "Salomé in China: The Aesthetic Art of Dying." In *Wilde Writings: Contextual Conditions*, ed. Joseph Bristow, 295–318. Toronto: Univ. of Toronto Press, 2003.

Index

Page numbers in italic denote figures.

Acosta, Mercedes de, 140
Adorno, Theodor, 8, 69, 73, 77, 208n11
aestheticism, 30, 44–45, 73, 82, 160, 170, 203n2; defined, 203n4
Allan, Maud, 83–124 (chap. 3); autobiography of, 97–100, 106–7; and the Ballets Russes, 97; brother a murderer, 84, 97, 120, 210n9; and Claude Cahun, 100–111, 115–16, 123–24; "The Cult of the Clitoris," 112, 119, 212n24; feminist aspects of her work, 12, 54; and homosexuality or "perversity," 91, 110–24, 143, 159, 160; in music hall and popular culture, 88, 89–94, 102; and the Pemberton-Billing Trial, 12, 83, 109–24, 154, 199, 200, 211n19; in *The Rugmaker's Daughter* (film), 94; and the suffragettes, 83–84, 100–109, 110, 199, 122, 159, 209n19, 210n14; *The Vision of Salomé*, 12, 83, 84–109, 122, 125. *See also* music hall; Salome dance craze; Salome dancers
alter ego, 3, 12, 78, 167, 171, 207n4
Anger, Kenneth, 146
anti-semitism, 32, 57, 63, 66, 72, 74–75, 111, 142, 192, 206n20

Archer, William, 134
Aristotle, 9
Armatage, Kay, 193
Arnold, Matthew, 9, 45
Arzner, Dorothy, 140
Asquith, Herbert (prime minister), 100, 103, 211n18. *See also* Salome cartoon
Asquith, Margot, 100, 120, 210n15
Aston, Elaine, 74

Bakst, Léon, 96
Ballets Russes, 94, 96, 97, 141
Bantock, Granville, 109
Bara, Theda, 141–42, 158, 213n8, 213n11
Barnes, Djuna, 132–33
Barthes, Roland, 176
Bartlett, Neil, 178
Bartone, Richard, 181
Bashford, Bruce, 204n5
Bataille, Georges, 2, 3, 176, 190; excess and ecstasy in, 9, 49–50; horror in, 49–50, 99; *Madame Edwarda*, 49–55; and Nietzsche's death of God, 51–52
Beardsley, Aubrey, 5, 91, 144, 162, 170
Becker-Leckrone, Megan, 15
Beckson, Karl, 213n13

Beecham, Sir Thomas, 80
Beerbohm, Max, 63, 91
Benjamin, Walter, 77
Benkowitz, Miriam, 94
Bentley, Toni, 85, 92, 94, 102, 108,
    210n12, 212n24
Berg, Alban, 66, 70
Bergler, Edmund, 215n10
Berman, Marshall, 8
Bernhardt, Sarah, 3, 4, 5, 28, 73–74, 88,
    126, 186, 208n15, 214n4
Bernheimer, Charles, 203n2
Bizet, Georges, 207n25
Bizot, Richard, 77, 83, 90, 94, 95, 97,
    141, 209n4, 210n12
Bland, Lucy, 112, 114, 118, 119–20
Blathwayt, Raymond, 86, 209n6
Blunt, Wilfrid, 4
Bock, Artur, 94
Bockting, Margaret, 133
Bodeen, DeWitt, 213n7
Bodley Head (John Lane and Elkin
    Mathews), 5
Böker, Uwe, 6
Botstein, Leon, 58
Boyden, Matthew, 75
Brandes, Friedrich, 67, 74
Brenon, Herbert, 137
Bristow, Joseph, 7
Broken Goddess (dir. Peter Dallas, star-
    ring Holly Woodlawn), 147
Bronski, Michael, 179
Brown, Daniel, 161, 214n1
Brown, Julia Prewitt, 73, 207n26
Bryant, Charles, 139–40, 213n10
Burke, Edmund, 72
Bush, Ronald, 203n1
Busoni, Ferruccio, 66, 84
Butler, Judith, 175, 181
Butt, Alfred, 90

Caddy, Davinia, 100, 209n2, 210n12
Cahill, Marie, 102
Cahun, Claude, 110–11, 115–16,
    123–24. *See also under* Allan, Maud
Calinescu, Mateo, 209n19
Caravaggio, Michelangelo Merisi da, 186

Carter, Alexandra, 89, 92, 210n12
Casement, Roger, 211n22
Castiglia, Christopher, 201–2
Cave, Nick, 188–90, 193, 195, 201,
    216n17
Cazalis, Henri, 60
Charcot, Jean-Martin, 37, 206n21
Cherniavsky, Felix, 90–109 passim,
    209nn2–3, 210n11
Clark, Caryl, 193
Clarke, Eric, 180
Cléopâtre (by Victorien Sardou), 29. *See
    also* Bernhardt, Sarah
Cohen, Ed, 215n9
Cohler, Deborah, 110
Colonna, Vittoria (Duchess of Sermon-
    eta), 88
Communist Manifesto, 33
Compton-Ricketts, Arthur, 88, 97
Constable, Liz, 209n19
consumerism, 35, 40, 54, 69, 73, 81,
    82, 126, 141, 147, 148, 157, 207n2
Cooke, Serrell. *See* Allan, Maud: and the
    Pemberton-Billing Trial
Cookie's Fortune (dir. Robert Altman),
    188, 192–94
Cooper, Lady Diana, 100
Corballis, Richard, 6
Corelli, Marie, 112
Corinth, Lovis, 64
corporalization of affect, 17, 59–65, 198
Craft, Marcella, 72, 208n13
Craven, Thomas, 145
crisis of the modern subject, 2–3, 8, 17,
    25, 40, 42–43, 55, 57, 58, 188, 198
"Cult of the Clitoris, The." *See under* Al-
    lan, Maud

Daffner, Hugo, 204n4
Dance of the Seven Veils: Maud Allan's
    interpretation of, 86, 87, 88, 89–91,
    97–100, 209n2; in Cave, 189; in
    Cookie's Fortune, 193; in Flaubert,
    30–31; in *The Governess,* 192; in
    Huysmans, 36–39; in *Maudie* (anony-
    mous novel), 104; in Nazimova, 145,
    147, 156–57; in *Pall Mall Gazette* car-

ions and techniques, 140–41, 145,
147–48; and homoeroticism, 12,
125–26, 143–47, 159, 200; and
money, 140, 158; and *Salome's Last
Dance* (dir. Ken Russell), 165–66
Nesbit, Edith, 103–5
Newbolt, Rev. William Charles Edmund
(canon of St. Paul's Cathedral), 102
new modernist studies, 7–8
New Queer Cinema, 181, 216n15
New Stage Players, 6, 106
New Woman, 12, 103, 104, 105, 134,
195, 217n19. *See also* suffrage, suf-
fragettes
Nietzsche, Friedrich, 2, 3, 17, 25; in
Bataille and Foucault, 51–52; death of
God, 3, 33, 47–48; forgetfulness,
39–40, 42, 43; free spirits, 47–48,
136; *Übermensch*, 47, 207nn26–27
Nordau, Max, 203–4n4
Now She Dances!. See Wilson, Doric

O'Neill, Eugene, 129
orientalism, 13, 32, 43, 70, 75–77, 94,
95, 96, 98, 116, 120, 134, 141, 142,
144, 156, 160, 177, 213n11
Orlenev, Paul, 127, 128, 134. *See also*
Nazimova, Alla: and St. Petersburg
Players

Palace Theatre, 88, 89, 90, 92, 94, 101,
102, 103, 210n8. *See also* Allan,
Maud: in music hall and popular cul-
ture; music hall
Parish, James, 157
Pater, Walter, 3, 9, 40, 44–45, 48–49,
203n4
Patience (Gilbert and Sullivan), 5
Pavlova, Anna, 97
Pemberton-Billing, Noel, 109–22 passim
Pemberton-Billing Trial. *See under* Allan,
Maud
Peterson, Ann, 129, 139
Pfitzner, Paul, 66
Pickford, Mary, 138
Pierné, Gabriel, 85
Pigott, Edward F. Smyth, 4–5

Ponsonby, Sir Frederick, 88
popular avant-gardism, 10, 73–78, 82,
158–59, 160, 198, 199
positive image activism, 178–79, 186
Potolsky, Matthew, 209n19
Powell, Kerry, 73–74, 134
Praz, Mario, 203n2
Price, Steven, 6, 13, 28, 63, 80, 208n17
Profumo affair, 170
Prossnitz, Gisela, 64
Puffett, Derrick, 67, 69, 70, 208n10
Punch, 5
Pym, Anthony, 204n2

Queer as Folk (TV series), 180
queer criticism and theory, 7, 21, 161,
175–87, 195, 201, 202, 215n9,
216n13, 216n15, 217n18. *See also*
Bland, Lucy; Butler, Judith; Castiglia,
Christopher; Clarke, Eric; Dollimore,
Jonathan; Dyer, Richard; Kaye,
Richard; Kopelson, Kevin; Sedgwick,
Eve Kosofsky; Travis, Jennifer

Raby, Peter, 63
Rambova, Natacha, 125, 138, 144, 145,
146
Ravel, Maurice, 66
Raymond, Jean Paul, 63
Regnault, Henri, 15
regressive feminism, 187–97, 200–
201
Reinhardt, Max, 6, 63–65, 74, 75, 83,
85, 108, 208n7, 210n13
religious mysticism, 26, 50, 52, 206n21
Relph, George, 109
Rémy, Marcel, 85, 209n2
Retté, Adolphe, 4
Ricketts, Charles, 6, 62–63, 207n6
Riquelme, Jean-Paul, 2, 40
Robbins, Tom, 188, 193, 195, 201
Robertson, W. Graham, 63
Robins, Elizabeth, 130, 131, 134, 212n3
Röder, Adam, 79–80
Rolland, Romain, 79
Rose, Marilyn Gaddis, 16, 18
Ross, Robert, 65, 115